Canadian Writers and Their Works

CANADIAN WRITERS AND THEIR WORKS

FICTION SERIES · VOLUME FIVE

 EDITED BY

ROBERT LECKER, JACK DAVID, ELLEN QUIGLEY

INTRODUCED BY GEORGE WOODCOCK

ECW PRESS, 1990

CANADIAN CATALOGUING IN PUBLICATION DATA

Main entry under title:

Canadian writers and their works: essays on form,
context, and development : fiction

Includes bibliographies and indexes.
ISBN 0-920802-43-5 (set). — ISBN 1-55022-027-6 (v. 5)

1. Canadian fiction (English) — History and criticism.*
2. Authors, Canadian (English) — Biography.* I. Lecker,
Robert, 1951– . II. David, Jack, 1946– .
III. Quigley, Ellen, 1955– .

PS8187.C36 1982   C813'.009   C82-094801-2
PR9192.2.C36. 1982

The publication of this series has been assisted by grants from the Ontario Arts
Council and The Canada Council.

This volume was typeset in Sabon by ECW Type & Art, Oakville, Ontario. Printed
and bound by University of Toronto Press, North York, Ontario.

Published by ECW PRESS, 307 Coxwell Avenue, Toronto, Ontario M4L 3B5.

The illustrations are by Isaac Bickerstaff.

CONTENTS

PREFACE

Canadian Writers and Their Works (CWTW) is a unique, twenty-volume collection of critical essays covering the development of Canadian fiction and poetry over the past two centuries. Ten volumes are devoted to fiction, and ten to poetry. Each volume contains a unifying Introduction by George Woodcock and four or five discrete critical essays on specific writers. Moreover, each critical essay includes a brief biography of the author, a discussion of the tradition and milieu influencing his/her work, a critical overview section which reviews published criticism on the author, a long section analyzing the author's works, and a selected bibliography listing primary and secondary material. The essays in each volume are arranged alphabetically according to last names of the writers under study.

This is Volume Five of the Fiction Series of *Canadian Writers and Their Works*. Other volumes in the series will be published as research is completed. The projected completion date for the entire series is 1991.

The editors wish to acknowledge the contributions of many people who have played an important part in creating this series. First, we wish to thank the critics who prepared the essays for this volume: Gary Boire, Helen Hoy, John Orange, George Woodcock, and Alan Young. We are also indebted to the production and design teams at both The Porcupine's Quill and ECW Type & Art, and to Pat Kenny and Stephanie Termeer, who keyboarded the manuscript in its initial typesetting phase. Our sincere thanks also go to Ken Lewis, and his associate Scott Mitchell, for their excellent technical editing.

RL/JD/EQ

Introduction

GEORGE WOODCOCK

Poetry is on the whole more quickly responsive to the shifts in general consciousness than fiction, perhaps because the lyric and the elegiac modes are largely dependent on the crystallization of the immediate impression, whether it is an emotion or an image. Fiction, from the mere fact that it takes longer to gestate, tends to relate itself to deeper and slower changes in collective sensibilities and attitudes. It is rather like the relation between the *plein air* sketch and the studio painting, or the snapshot and the daguerrotype. And so it is not surprising that the development of a poetry sensitive to a specific Canadian environment and polity began in the 1880s, while a parallel development in fiction did not really begin much before the 1930s. In a similar way, genuinely experimental poetry was being written in the late 1920s by poets like W.W.E. Ross and Dorothy Livesay and A.J.M. Smith, while — with the exception of Howard O'Hagan's disregarded *Tay John* in 1939 — it is hard to think of a genuinely experimental Canadian novel before Sheila Watson's *The Double Hook* in 1959.

However, the cases of poetry and fiction are parallel in the sense that, for both, there was a transition between the recognition of the need for a literature that springs from local or national experience and which is new in the sense of its changed objectives and material, and the development of the experimental forms that bespeak a new voice as well as a new perception. In this sense the writers which this volume includes — Hugh MacLennan, Morley Callaghan, Thomas Raddall, and Ernest Buckler — resemble the so-called Confederation Poets who started to work roughly half a century before. With their Western contemporaries like F.P. Grove, Martha Ostenso, and the slightly earlier Robert J.C. Stead, they represent a transitional generation that is important at least as much for its intent as for its achievement. It is arguable that there are earlier Canadian novelists as capable as any of those discussed here, such as James De Mille and Sara Jeannette Duncan, but those writers, lacking an adequate local readership and the kind of literary world that might support them, looked outward for publishers and readers and even, like Duncan, sought most of their material in what in those days seemed more interesting settings than the Canadian homeland.

The generation represented here was the first among novelists that turned deliberately to Canada for its material, that found a responsive readership at home and at least the beginnings of an adequate literary infrastructure, and in the process, with varying degrees of deliberation, added a cultural dimension to the transition from a colonial to a national outlook that developed so strongly among Canadians during and between the two world wars.

The four writers are close contemporaries, born within five years of each other: Callaghan and Raddall in 1903, MacLennan in 1907, and Buckler in 1908. They were all boys during the Great War; they grew into manhood in the roller coaster interbellum years when the false boom of the 1920s gave way to the Depression and World War II, a time of rapidly changing social mores and of political radicalization. Three out of the four are Maritimers, with Torontonian Morley Callaghan the sole exception; MacLennan and Raddall shared the Halifax explosion of 1917 as a cataclysmic event of childhood, while MacLennan and Buckler were studying during the same years at Dalhousie University. Finally, all four have adapted to current uses the traditions of romance and realism that had developed by the time they began writing. Formally, in fact, they have been adapters more than they have been imitators.

In the past, I have written extensively on Hugh MacLennan and fairly extensively on Morley Callaghan and I should say at the outset that I appreciate the fairness with which Helen Hoy and Gary Boire respectively have treated my views in their essays on the two novelists, even when they partially or wholly disagreed with them. On Raddall I have written comparatively little and on Buckler almost nothing, and perhaps for this reason alone it may be appropriate to address my specific remarks first to these two writers.

It has been Raddall's fortune and misfortune to succeed as a popular writer. He himself has claimed, as Alan R. Young notes in his essay on him, that "My deep preference . . . would be the writing of history," and there is no doubt that he has been a fine regional historian, presenting well-researched material more vividly and readably than most of his academic rivals. This consideration is not really peripheral to our view of him as a novelist, for his books have been best when he has been guided by his concern for the exactitude of historical background and the plausibility of action, and least good when he departs, as Young rightly notes he does in *The Governor's Lady*, in the direction of "costume romance."

Many critics in the past have treated Raddall as a writer marginal to the mainstream of Canadian literature. Desmond Pacey talks disparagingly of his novels about "fancy-dress personages,"[1] and I myself, as Young recalls, have written negatively about his short stories. If I granted the excellence of the story-telling in his novels about the Nova Scotian past, I also claimed that this kind of excellence in fact placed them "far nearer to writers like Conrad and Robert Louis Stevenson than to Canadian writers of the present generation."[2]

Essentially the disagreements between the apologists for Raddall and those who consider him a minor writer in terms of the Canadian novelistic tradition rest on the question of the contemporary relevance of well-crafted writing in an obsolete genre, and while Young grants that his "critical assessment . . . largely sides" with the apologists, I find myself among those who are less than convinced about Raddall's lasting importance, at least as a historical novelist.

Young himself brings forward the evidence that establishes Raddall's formal conservatism. The list of fiction writers for whom the novelist expressed admiration and who seem to have influenced him notably — Cooper, Kipling, Stevenson, Conan Doyle, and Conrad — includes, except for Conrad, none of the real writing masters of the age, and modernism of any kind appears to have left him untouched. Young himself also remarks that "frequently Raddall's fiction follows the classic model first established by Scott," and he notes the essential conservatism of the social and political values that the historical novels project.

Young lays the claim that Raddall has been "the most distinguished present-day exponent of the historical romance in Canada," and this may indeed be true. One might even go farther and grant that Raddall, because of his documentary accuracy and his fine story-telling, is in fact among the best of all Canadian historical romancers, certainly far better than Sir Gilbert Parker and his ilk. But the fact seems to remain that, except in popular fiction where it survives in a degenerated form, the historical novel of the kind Raddall has done so well belongs, like its subject matter, to the past, and that, while

7

there has indeed been a revival of historical fiction as a serious genre in the hands of writers like Anthony Burgess and — in Canada — Timothy Findley, it has taken ironical and metafictional directions far removed from Raddall's practice or intent.

But Raddall has not been merely concerned with history in its factual and fictional forms. He has also written three novels of contemporary life, and one of these, *The Nymph and the Lamp*, will probably outlast in interest even the best of his historical novels. Here Raddall calls on experience rather than on research as he creates a memorable image of a Nova Scotian offshore island as a setting for his love triangle, an image so memorable that the island as much as Isabel Jardine, the "nymph," stays intensely in one's memory. As John Moss puts it, "Image and symbol merge in this novel quite brilliantly, as do characters and place. The effect is romance, realistically conveyed."[3]

This is hardly the place to go at length into regional differences between fictional approaches, but one cannot help noting that the Nova Scotian novelists tended to be influenced by the traditions of romance while their Prairie contemporaries were more closely dominated by realistic and even — in the case of Grove — by naturalistic inclinations. Both Ernest Buckler and Hugh MacLennan show this romantic tendency, and the difference between them and their Western counterparts may well be due to the fact that in the Prairies during the interbellum, white society was still at the pioneer stage, with not much in the way of a past, whereas Nova Scotians lived with a long history that has played an important role in their literature, for Raddall has been only one among a number of local historical novelists.

Ernest Buckler is not a historical novelist, but a strong sense of the past, and of a settled rural society with its special ways of living and its oral traditions, is never absent from his writings. Douglas Spettigue, in an essay first published in *Canadian Literature* entitled "The Way It Was: Ernest Buckler," points out how recurrent this phrase is in Buckler's writings, how powerful a role reminiscence plays in all his fiction, and how this links his work with one of the constant strains in Canadian writing — that which unites the popular and sentimental rural idyll of the turn of the century with more clearly novelistic forms and often takes the shape of recollections of "childhood scenes set on the farm or in the village and attempting to capture the flavour of a way of life that can no longer be the way it was."[4]

8

In Buckler's case the simple nostalgia that characterizes many idylls of this kind is complicated by the pull of urban civilization, of the sophisticated culture that has its setting outside the rural community. His own life was largely controlled by this polarity, for, like Paul Creed, the Prospero in his second novel, *The Cruelest Month*, he went away from his rural Nova Scotia to study and to work in Toronto, found that he did not like the life of the city though he was attracted to its culture, and in 1936 returned to the family farm in the Annapolis Valley, where he remained until his death in 1984, living a life of semi-reclusion and devoting himself painstakingly to his writing.

Perhaps it was the reclusion, or perhaps it was the slow elaboration of his books, that served to mark off Buckler's writing so clearly from that of his contemporaries. He was not really interested, though he excelled in evocative description, in the realism to which both MacLennan and Callaghan veered, and he was in no sense a social novelist. Though the actual verses he wrote can only be classed as bad, his stress on symbolism and multiple imagery gave his writing a kind of elegiac poeticism, so that something near to the atmosphere of an idyll was created in which the action tended to be parabolic rather than plausible. A distinct cleavage of approach as a writer mirrored the division in his own mind between the countryman and the sophisticate. He was a regional novelist in the sense of calling up nostalgically a dead or dying rural way of life in a particular locality, yet at the same time he aspired to an early twentieth-century cosmopolitan tradition by making his two novels very near to *Künstlerroman*, books concerned with the emotional wounds that create the artist's peculiar sensibility and in the process detach him from the currents of a "real" life. Thus, the artist manqué, David Canaan, must incur death to obtain his mountaintop moment of transcendental enlightenment, while his grandmother Ellen, secure in the inarticulate traditions of the land, completes her own creation, the many coloured rug made out of the garments of the dead and the living and symbolizing the continuities in human life that proceed outside the artist's vision.

Self-consciousness and its inadequacies are perhaps the main themes of Buckler's second novel, *The Cruelest Month*, whose resemblance to Thomas Love Peacock's conversational novels of manners critics have been slow to observe. In this novel, as Douglas Spettigue remarks, Buckler "examines city people whose complexities are word-shaped, whose pastime is finding the words for their

9

own emotions."[5] In the end, emotions and external events — notably a forest fire started inadvertantly by one of the city guests — take precedence over the play of words and ideas, and the guests depart, sadder if not wiser, while Paul Creed, the intellectual whose retreat to the country parallels Buckler's own, finds fulfilment with his illiterate housekeeper, Letty, a simple, shrewd, untalkative country-woman who resembles the archetypal earth mother.

The taking of pains is evident both in the slow construction of Buckler's novels and in the unusual elaboration of the prose. In a very interesting essay, "The Genesis of Ernest Buckler's *The Mountain and the Valley*,"[6] Alan R. Young demonstrates the way in which Buckler worked over the same material in various ways, eventually constructing *The Mountain and the Valley* largely by adapting previously written stories and fitting them into the larger framework of a novel. Reading this article, one is impressed by the relative narrowness of Buckler's inventiveness in plotting, the comparatively few basic situations that he developed, writing and rewriting and changing from one form to another, over what was after all a long literary career of forty years since his first stories began to appear in the 1940s.

To some Buckler's prose is satisfying because of its richness; to others, as W.J. Keith has remarked, "this way of writing is too cloying."[7] In his essay on Buckler in the present volume, John Orange defines and defends the novelist's prose:

In his short stories, then, Buckler perceptibly struggles for the exact symbol, word, or figure of speech that will contain both intensity and accuracy of emotion and at the same time focus the story's theme. His prose is influenced by poetry, and like poetry it depends on rhythm, association, and ornamentation of language in order to be both concrete and connotative. Hence we find a proliferation of metaphors, similes, images, conceits, and sound effects (alliteration and assonance) in the prose sentences. The effect of poetic devices inserted into prose is that they slow down the speed of the writing and give it a meditative quality. Its primary appeal is to the emotions and to the synthesizing function of the imagination, but it encourages a secondary effect of contemplation, so that it has a metaphysical thrust like that of imagist poetry. Taken too far it becomes euphuism — which is often sentimental, discontinuous, a parody of itself.

> However, Buckler learned to control his prose by experimenting in his short stories. In his first novel he brought it to maturity.

I agree with this description of Buckler's early prose in the short stories. But, except for a little tightening and tidying, I see no great difference in *The Mountain and the Valley*. It is written in an over-decorated and over-elaborate manner, lush rather than mature, and Buckler still follows that *ignis fatuus*, a poetic prose, declining to recognize that prose has its values and virtues and does not need to borrow others. As Keith remarks, "the style sets the book apart in a somewhat ambiguous way, rather like David's scar within the narrative itself."[8] Some readers, at least, prefer *The Cruelest Month*, where the very Peacockian structure of conversation and argument assures that here at least we have prose that aspires to be nothing more.

Between the two of them, Hugh MacLennan and a Morley Callaghan emerging from more than a decade of virtual silence tended to dominate the 1950s in Canadian fiction, and of the two, MacLennan, with his clear extra-literary message of Canadian self-realization, was undoubtedly the more widely read and the more influential, so that literary historians have been inclined to refer to the period as the MacLennan decade.

In many ways MacLennan and Callaghan are greatly dissimilar writers. Their conceptions of the writer's role have differed widely, and so have their styles, both personal and literary. But they have shared throughout their careers a desire to shake free of the domination of the Old World, and this in spite of the fact that MacLennan spent several of his formative years in Oxford and Callaghan did the same in Paris, and also in spite of the profound influence of classical Greek epic and drama on the archetypal structures of MacLennan's fiction.

Callaghan went to the extent of declaring himself in his one autobiographical work, *That Summer in Paris*, to be "intensely North American" and "intellectually, spiritually, . . . but splendidly and happily, alien" to the "very British city" of Toronto.[9] Though he has not been so explicit, MacLennan's constant preoccupation with the development of a Canadian consciousness and with Canada's relationship to the elephantine power that shares a subcontinent with it, implies that he also developed early a North American, as distinct from a narrowly American, consciousness. It would be hard, though the effort has sometimes been made in the case of Callaghan, to slot either of them into a history of American literature, so locally Canadian have been the social and topographical landscapes within which they have mostly developed their fictional visions, while the moral preoccupation of their books carry them beyond the narrow bounds of a continental setting. Both could, I think, be regarded as mental citizens of Canada, which is North American, and of the world, but with no imperial loyalties — to either London or New York — between the local and the global.

Yet both were affected by the literary movements that took place after the Great War in the United States. Like many earlier Canadian writers — James De Mille, John Richardson, etc. — they had found New York a nearer and more receptive market for their books than London, and this was the kind of accident that helped to turn their attention towards the young American writers who seemed to be developing a new literary language that was appropriate to their time and place. And it was perhaps more than coincidence that attracted both of them in their early writing years towards Ernest Hemingway, with his radical stylistic simplification, his power of rendering action in telling prose, and his willingness to face up, without Jamesian circumlocution, to the hard choices of life and death.

Callaghan's involvement with Hemingway was close and personal; he knew him at the *Toronto Star* and later in Paris, and Hemingway not only gave him direct literary advice but also arranged for the first publication of his writings in expatriate periodicals run by American editors. Advice and assistance were accompanied by influence; both the style and the characterization in some of Callaghan's early stories and in an apprentice novel like *Strange Fugitive* are largely derivative from Hemingway, though by the early 1930s Callaghan had shaken off his dependence and was writing his own kind of prose in his own kind of moralist récits.

With MacLennan the influence was much less direct; there are no early passages that can be easily matched with similar passages in Hemingway, as is the case with Callaghan. But he went through an early phase of admiration for Hemingway which was followed during the 1950s by a sharp reaction against the nihilism into which by this time the American writer seemed to him to have descended. Elspeth Cameron, in an essay "Of Cabbages and Kings: The Concept of Hero in *The Watch That Ends the Night*," has very convincingly traced the kind of dialectic by which MacLennan resolved in his largest novel the tension between his admiration and his revulsion for Hemingway, and how he used that resolution "as a springboard to launch a hero he thought reflected the new age"; the hero was not, as might be expected, the obviously Hemingwayesque Jerome Martell, but the almost banal narrator, George Stewart:

> Although the splendid Jerome might seem remote from the lives of average readers because his particular "human condition" was unusually dramatic and his "human spirit" remarkably strong, George Stewart was a man with whom any reader could imaginatively trade places in order to see the importance, the depth and even the beauty of the age-old pattern.[10]

But while it is true that the universality of the age-old pattern is a theme of MacLennan's writings, and that he is constantly warning us about the worldwide collapse of a stable order ("patristic," in his phraseology, as compared with the "matristic" permissiveness he fears and condemns), we still see MacLennan, both in his works themselves and in the remarkably thorough analysis of them Helen Hoy has given us in her essay, as primarily a social novelist. I have remarked elsewhere that if there is any writer in whose works we can find a Canadian equivalent of Balzac's *La Comédie Humaine*, it is Hugh MacLennan.

Indeed, a cultural historian of Canada dealing with the fifty-odd years between, say, 1910 and 1965, could do no better than start with the corpus of MacLennan's works — the seven novels, supplemented by the four hundred essays, slight and serious, dealing with a vast range of the aspects of life and letters in our age. The major areas of Canadian preoccupation over that period are all there: the emergence of a sense of nationhood in *Barometer Rising*; the tension between two cultures in a single land in *Two Solitudes*; the uneasy relationship between Canada and the United States in *The Precipice*; the destructive heritage of ancient religious prejudices in *Each Man's Son*; the bitter awakening from the idealistic dreams of the 1930s in *The Watch That Ends the Night*; the generational conflicts that during the 1960s took negative political forms in Canada as much as any other western country in *The Return of the Sphinx*; the dismal record of political dishonesty and blindness that may doom our civilization in *Voices in Time*; and all supplemented by the multitude of notations on morals and manners and tastes and fashions in the essays.

MacLennan has always been unashamedly didactic; he has always believed that the writer must teach the lessons that are appropriate to his time, and he has always considered the artifice of his novels secondary to the themes. But in the process, rather like his historian counterpart, Donald Creighton, who was also determined to teach lessons about Canadian nationality, he has managed to give a powerful mythical quality to much that he creates. As I and other critics have shown, he has always been ready to appropriate and adapt for his own uses the classical myths he learnt in his youth, of wandering Odysseus and doomed Oedipus, but he can also create his own myths out of contemporary events. His recreation of the Halifax explosion in *Barometer Rising* and his thrilling account of Jerome's flight from his mother's murderer in *The Watch That Ends the Night*, loom over the early decades of the Canadian novel as great examples of powerful writing and high imaginative intensity, and at the same time, as striking symbolic statements.

In a very felicitous comparison, Helen Hoy remarks:

> . . . he is the E.J. Pratt of Canadian fiction, a lone Canadian mythmaker, innovative in his choice of national and "non-literary" subject matter, distinctive in his documentary and social focus, conventional, even old-fashioned, in his choice of form. Too individual to be a model for subsequent writers, MacLennan's work is a turning point in the development of a distinctly national literature.

MacLennan always laid the claim to be mentally slow on the uptake, to be intuitive rather than intellectual, to take a long time to realize the implications of what he was writing, but readers who admire the elaborate didactic structure of his books and the sharp brightness of many of his essays are inclined to be sceptical. On the other hand, it is clear that fictional creation does not come readily to MacLennan. His books take him a long time to produce, since he writes and rewrites, relegating hundreds of thousands of words to the waste-basket or the archives, and reaches the final form only with great effort. He is one of those writers who are made — even self-made — rather than born, and this may perhaps explain the lack of formal originality in his writings. As Hoy points out, his plots tend to be formulaic and melodramatic; he regularly uses the devices of popular romance; his style — particularly when he is dealing with male-female encounters — is, as Hoy remarks, "frequently mawkish and evasive." Younger writers have been inspired by his devotion to solving the problems of Canadian nationality, but nobody has really learnt much from him about the arts of writing and he has had virtually no imitators, even though his novels were sufficiently powerful in their own way to dominate a generation in Canadian fiction, as Pratt's conservative epics did in Canadian poetry.

Morley Callaghan has never figured as a Canadian nationalist, even a literary one, yet, at the time when the temptation to follow a career in the United States must have been great, he elected for Toronto, despite all the features of its life that he disliked. It was a natural instinct that led him, of the same kind that eventually led Mordecai Richler back to Montreal; Toronto was the place where he had grown up and which provided that bank of images a writer accumulates in the first twenty years of his life and afterwards expands only slowly, if at all. The life of the twin cities of central Canada, Toronto and Montreal (for Callaghan always an oddly anglophone place), provided him the kind of setting sufficiently metropolitan to enable him to endue his fictional visions with locality without descending into provincialism. Callaghan, like Raymond Souster in poetry, became in fact a member of that very rare species, the truly regional Toronto writer.

It was also, perhaps, a self-preserving instinct that kept Callaghan in Toronto. In his earlier years he had the kind of encouragement that might have made a rasher young man pull up his roots and head for the deceptively green fields of New York. Not only did Hemingway place his stories in avant garde magazines, but Scott Fitzgerald brought them to the notice of Scribners, the New York house that published his first books. American writers complimented him extravagantly, and he tells with naïve satisfaction in *That Summer in Paris* how Sinclair Lewis said to him, "Flaubert would have loved your work," and how Hemingway told him that "Tolstoy couldn't have done my 'Wedding Dress' story any better."[11] But Callaghan wisely ignored such siren voices and chose, instead of the probability of remaining a minor New York writer, patronized by celebrities, to make his own way in the Canada where in the fullness of time he became a living classic.

If MacLennan was never tempted to experimental writing at any time, Callaghan did for a while take his modest place in the mainstream of North American modernism, writing his early stories and at least his first novel in the laconic style which Hemingway and others had developed; a realist intent found expression in a prose whose sharp and stony clarity seemed to be the counterpart of imagism in verse. But once Callaghan had made his choice to remain in Canada, he developed his own novelistic form and his own approach to language and imagery. His condensed moralist récits of the 1930s are in their own small way genuinely experimental works of fiction. In *Such Is My Beloved, More Joy in Heaven*, and *They Shall Inherit the Earth*, he used tight structure and an admirably controlled prose to produce parables that were well suited to his special purpose. Callaghan was as much aware as MacLennan of the problems of his time, but instead of seeing them from a socio-political standpoint, he viewed them as moral problems that challenged accepted religious practices and attitudes rather than fundamental beliefs. He was probably closer in his perceptions at this period to French-Catholic radical writers like François Mauriac and Georges Bernanos than he was to the American writers with whom he had associated in his youth. In spite of his proclaimed rejection of metaphorical prose, Callaghan developed in these simple novellas ways of handling both image and symbol that proclaimed him a born writer in a way that MacLennan never was. He started off with a natural feeling for words and the power of sharp visualization that goes with imagist kinds of writing.

But such gifts are not necessarily durable, and the promise Callaghan showed in the 1930s was only partially sustained. Only two of his later books show the degree of artistry and the sureness of tone he developed in the works of the 1930s; these were his memoir, *That Summer in Paris* (1963) and his late novella, *Close to the Sun Again* (1977). The long interval between these books and the works of the 1930s began with a period of virtual silence lasting from 1937 when *More Joy in Heaven* appeared, to 1951 when he published *The Loved and the Lost*. During that long unproductive interlude, whose cause can only be conjectured, the only book of any significance he wrote was the juvenile novel, *Luke Baldwin's Vow* (1948), which until recently has been neglected by the critics.

When Callaghan took up novel writing again at the beginning of the 1950s, his experimental period was clearly at an end. He abandoned the tense, concise form of the 1930s and attempted to write large complex novels that drew to a great extent on the conventions of romance; he failed in that field largely because of the laconism of his dialogue, which was well-suited for short stories or moralist novellas, but seemed gauche and jejune in a more elaborately structured kind of fiction. *The Many Colored Coat* was partly redeemed by its strong ironic element, but both *The Loved and the Lost* and *A Passion in Rome* had more ambition than authenticity, and it was not until Callaghan returned to formal modesty that he was really successful again.

Gary Boire has approached Callaghan selectively rather than comprehensively, and the advantage of this approach is that it saves both the critic and the reader from considering Callaghan's less successful books, though whether picking out the plums is the best critical approach is obviously a matter of debate. Perhaps one cannot object greatly to the fact that Boire gave close attention to only one of Callaghan's early novels, *Strange Fugitive*, and virtually ignored *It's Never Over* and *A Broken Journey*, since these are all apprentice works in which we see Callaghan struggling out from under his early American influences and becoming the real literary self that emerges in the short novels of the 1930s. At this point, however, though *Such Is My Beloved* and *More Joy in Heaven* make a neat pair for purposes of comparison, as Boire has used them, it seems unfortunate that the central piece of the 1930s triptych, *They Shall Inherit the Earth*, is left out, since it is the most complex of the three novels and has a special interest because it shows how closely aware Callaghan was of the social situation in the 1930s, even though he was not one of those who found in political action a viable approach.

Coming to the period of Callaghan's longer novels in the 1950s and 1960s, there is no doubt that in picking *The Many Colored Coat* Boire has chosen the most successful of the three, but one still asks why he did not examine more closely the real failures of the period, *The Loved and the Lost* and *A Passion in Rome*, since it is surely of interest that a writer so sure of his way in the shorter fictional forms, the story and the récit, should have been so much at sea when he embarked on large and intricately planned novels in the conventional manner.

To give attention to *Luke Baldwin's Vow* is enterprising, because the book has up to now received so little attention and is, after all, the only link between the shorter novels of the 1930s and the later longer novels. But one wonders at the elaborate defence Boire presents of *A Fine and Private Place*, which even writers friendly to Callaghan greeted with embarrassment on the author's behalf. In this work of mingled resentment and vanity, Callaghan projects himself in the character of an unappreciated novelist and, none too indirectly, praises himself and damns his critics. Twenty years ago Edmund Wilson set a strange hare running when he called Callaghan "the most unjustly neglected novelist in the English-speaking world."[12] That was patently untrue in 1965, and even less true in 1975 when Callaghan published *A Fine and Private Place*, for by then he had received both the Molson Prize and the Royal Bank Award, as near to the Nobel as a Canadian can achieve on his or her own soil.

The case of Callaghan really brings us back to the kind of claims we can make for Canadian writers. Callaghan's flatterers compared him with Tolstoy and Flaubert and sometimes even today one hears these comparisons echoed. But there is no work of his that has the sheer scale of *War and Peace* or *Anna Karenina*, nor did he share Tolstoy's command of the elements of time and place in fiction; and he was never an innovator as original as Flaubert nor did he share his fine and accurate sense of the word. It is like comparing rye whisky with vodka and Armagnac; they are different drinks entirely. And the real question arises: why do we have to make comparisons with writers in other times and places? Every artist's achievement relates first to his or her own time and place, and can be seen best within the setting of his or her own tradition. Sometimes there are foreign influences that are interesting, indeed. Sometimes it is valuable to compare the way in which, say, a Russian writer has rendered the life of the steppes and a Canadian writer the life of the prairie. But these are very specific matters. They are not comparisons of total oeuvres. In terms of final achievement every writer stands on his or her own and must be judged alone. Nobody thinks of comparing Tolstoy with Callaghan. And surely it only belittles Callaghan's special achievement to feel it necessary to compare him with Tolstoy. We are all, in the night of creation as in the night of death, alone.

NOTES

[1] Desmond Pacey, rev. of *At the Tide's Turn and Other Stories*, by Thomas H. Raddall, *Arcadian Adventures with the Idle Rich*, by Stephen Leacock, *Habitant Poems*, by W.H. Drummond, and *Poets of the Confederation*, ed. Malcolm Ross, *Queen's Quarterly*, 68 (1961), 180.

[2] George Woodcock, "Raddall: The Making of the Story-teller," *Saturday Night*, Nov. 1976, p. 69.

[3] John Moss, *A Reader's Guide to the Canadian Novel* (Toronto: McClelland and Stewart, 1981), p. 230.

[4] D.O. Spettigue, "The Way It Was: Ernest Buckler," in *The Canadian Novel in the Twentieth Century: Essays from* Canadian Literature, New Canadian Library, No. 115, ed. George Woodcock (Toronto: McClelland and Stewart, 1975), p. 147.

[5] Spettigue, p. 155.

[6] Alan R. Young, "The Genesis of Ernest Buckler's *The Mountain and the Valley*," in *Modern Times*, Vol. III of *The Canadian Novel: A Critical Anthology*, ed. John Moss (Toronto: NC, 1982), pp. 195–205.

[7] W.J. Keith, *Canadian Literature in English*, Longman Literature in English (London: Longman, 1985), p. 148.

[8] Keith, p. 148.

[9] Morley Callaghan, *That Summer in Paris: Memories of Tangled Friendships with Hemingway, Fitzgerald, and Some Others* (Toronto: Macmillan, 1963), p. 22.

[10] Elspeth Cameron, "Of Cabbages and Kings: The Concept of Hero in *The Watch That Ends the Night*," in *Modern Times*, Vol. IIII of *The Canadian Novel: A Critical Anthology*, ed. John Moss (Toronto: NC, 1982), pp. 126–27.

[11] Callaghan, pp. 69, 38.

[12] Edmund Wilson, "Morley Callaghan of Toronto," in *O Canada: An American's Notes on Canadian Culture* (New York: Farrar, Straus and Giroux, 1965), p. 9.

*Ernest Buckler
and His Works*

Ernest Buckler (1908–84)

JOHN ORANGE

Biography

ERNEST REDMOND BUCKLER was born on 19 July 1908 in Dalhousie West, Nova Scotia, the third of five children and the only son of Appleton and Mary (Swift) Buckler. Buckler's ancestors settled in the Annapolis Valley in Nova Scotia and can be traced back to a 1784 muster roll of Loyalists containing the name of Ernest's great-grandfather, John. Ernest's grandfather, Joseph, established a farm in the Annapolis Valley, so the family roots are deep into the soil of that region. Ancestors on his mother's side apparently go back to such illustrious figures as Jonathan Swift.

Accounts of Buckler's early family life in the country and his boyhood education can be found throughout his writing, notably in the early chapters of *Ox Bells and Fireflies: A Memoir*[1] and in such articles as "Last Stop before Paradise," "School and Me," and "A Little Flag for Mother."[2] He has described his childhood as uneventful, "except for those terrific events of the spirit that come from living in the country, in a family where the tea canister had to be tipped from one end to the other to sort out every last penny when it was time to go to the store."[3] The landscape of the region around Dalhousie West, Annapolis Royal, and Bridgetown serves as the backdrop for most of Buckler's short stories and novels. The idyllic tone of a child's harmony with this natural surrounding is intense in Buckler's work.

Buckler completed his high school training just before he turned thirteen. He spent the next five years working both at home and, during the summer, at a rather posh lodge in Greenwich, Connecticut, in order to earn money so that he could attend university. From 1925 to 1929 Buckler studied philosophy under Dr. Herbert L. Stewart and mathematics with Professor Murray Macneill at Dalhousie University in Halifax. He developed an interest in literature during these years. Hugh MacLennan attended in the same years; and the

ERNEST BUCKLER

most influential literary figure there at the time was Archibald MacMechan. Visitors to the university included such notables as Bliss Carman, Wilson MacDonald, and Charles G.D. Roberts. In his final year, Buckler published an article and six poems in the student newspaper.[4]

In 1930 Buckler began studies at the University of Toronto for his M.A. in Philosophy. He was required to write seven long essays and four shorter ones for his degree, and those essays, now in the manuscript collection at the Thomas Fisher Rare Book Library, indicate an interest in the works of Aristotle, Spinoza, Kant, and Croce. Some possibly significant titles from these essays are "Aristotle's Theory of Conduct," "Relation of Leibnitz to Locke," "Relative Merits of the Schools of Association and Apperception," "Spinoza's Conception of Experience and Its Evolution," and "Progress of Idealism from Kant to Lötze."[5] Buckler lived in Trinity House and recalls happy, stimulating days at university (despite initial loneliness) under the tutelage of Professor George Brett.[6] After he graduated, he accepted a job as an actuary with the Manufacturers' Life Insurance Company in Toronto, where he worked for the next five years. He lived alone and usually he ate out. He never fully adapted to big city living. At Trinity House he had made the acquaintance of J.K. Thomas, then editor of *The Trinity Review*, and in 1933–34 he had two short stories published in that little journal.[7] He also tried writing poems in these years and spent some time reading current stories, especially those of such contemporaries as Ernest Hemingway, F. Scott Fitzgerald, John Dos Passos, and Morley Callaghan.

Buckler's father had died in 1932. Partly because he was needed at home, partly because of his aversion to city living, and also because his own health was chronically delicate, Buckler decided to return to the Annapolis Valley in 1936 to live on the farm with his mother, his sister Nellie, and her husband. His interest in literature continued to grow and, noticing an advertisement in *Coronet* magazine for a writing contest, he decided to try for the one-hundred dollar prize. He won first prize, the article was published, and in the same year, 1937, he began to write to the "Sound and Fury" column of *Esquire* magazine, commenting mostly on the quality of the fiction that the editors were publishing. Many readers wrote the magazine praising Buckler's letters, and eventually the editor, Arnold Gingrich, invited Buckler to submit articles of his own. Gingrich rejected these articles as "stiff and terribly self-conscious,"[8] but Buckler was obviously thinking about various kinds of stories, prose styles, and structures in fiction. Buckler's columns, articles, and reviews suggest that he developed as a theorist of literature at the same time that he was trying to write poems and stories. In fact he published a review in *The New York Herald Tribune Book Review* in April 1939 — the first article for which he was paid.[9]

That same year Buckler moved (with his mother) to Centrelea, about three miles south-west of Bridgetown, in order to help out an ailing aunt and uncle. He continued to work the family's 140-acre farm until 1980, supplementing his farm income with income earned from his writing. He began publishing articles in the "Back Page" section of *Saturday Night* in 1941 and continued to write for that magazine until 1948. His short story "One Quiet Afternoon" was published in *Esquire* in April, 1940, and for the next three decades he published stories in a variety of magazines, including *Maclean's*, *Chatelaine*, *The Atlantic Advocate*, *Weekend*, and *Reader's Digest*.[10] He also sold radio plays to the CBC.[11] In 1948 he won a *Maclean's* fiction contest for his story "The Quarrel,"[12] and in 1957 and 1958 his short stories won the President's Medal from the University of Western Ontario.[13]

His first novel, *The Mountain and the Valley* (1952), was published in New York and sold 7,000 copies in hardcover. It was well received and attracted a good deal of attention. CBC radio adapted it a number of times, and the book has since gone through a number of paperback editions.[14] The next novel, *The Cruelest Month*, was not very successful when it was published in Canada in 1963, but *Ox Bells and Fireflies: A Memoir* (1968) was an immediate success. All three novels have been reproduced in McClelland and Stewart's New Canadian Library series.

Buckler continued to publish articles and book reviews (the latter in New York and Los Angeles) throughout the 1960s, but his writing slowed down somewhat in the next decade. However, he did collaborate with the photographer Hans Weber to produce a descriptive study called *Nova Scotia: Window on the Sea* (1973), and a retrospective collection of his short stories, *The Rebellion of Young David and Other Stories*, was published in 1975. Readers were surprised in 1977 by *Whirligig*, a selection of witty articles and verse, though Buckler had been writing that sort of thing for the "Mermaid Inn" column in *The Globe and Mail*. *Whirligig* won the Stephen Leacock

Medal for humour in 1978. In the same year he also won the Hudson's Bay Company Award.

Buckler's quiet dedication to writing has also been honoured by a Canada Council Scholarship (1960–61) and Fellowships (1964–65, 1966–67); a Centennial Medal (1967); honourary degrees from the University of New Brunswick (1969), Dalhousie University (1971), and Acadia University (1978); and an Order of Canada award (1974). He attempted to carry on two professions at once. He wrote painstakingly slowly; consequently, his total canon is not large. He became a spokesman for a community and a region, and though he lived in relative isolation, he felt this was good for his writing. In his lifetime, he was very much aware of what the rest of the world has to offer, but he chose to stay close to his traditions and to be faithful to his regional roots. His writing is a testament to the wisdom of that decision.

In the fall of 1982, a tribute to Buckler was organized by Claude Bissell. About one hundred friends gathered at Mountain Lea Lodge, a retirement home in Bridgetown where the author had been forced to move in 1981 because of failing health. Letters from admirers, such as Margaret Laurence and Margaret Atwood, were read, and Dr. Bissell read passages from Buckler's novels. Buckler's eyesight had deteriorated so that he could not write, but he had the company of two of his three sisters, Nellie and Olive, who lived in Bridgetown. Buckler died on Sunday, 4 March 1984, at the age of 75, and is buried in All Saints Parish Cemetery, Gibson's Lake, Nova Scotia.

Tradition and Milieu

Buckler's fiction encompasses at least three trends in late nineteenth- and early twentieth-century Canadian fiction. By the time Buckler began writing in the 1940s, *regionalism* was a firmly established tradition in Canadian prose. Buckler's fiction is not only regional but also psychological and autoreferential in focus. These two trends — the psychological and the autoreferential — were international imports slowly gaining the attention of Canadian novelists when Buckler began writing.

Buckler's fiction is traditional in its regional flavour, with its predominantly rural and village setting. Other Canadian writers, such as Charles G.D. Roberts and Lucy Maud Montgomery, had written very popular novels about life in the Maritimes, and in the first half of this century, such storytellers as Frank Day Parker, Will R. Bird, Thomas Raddall, and Charles Bruce continued the tradition of using East Coast settings, history, and details of daily life in fiction. One impulse behind this kind of regional writing seemed to be an interest in defining and mythologizing the writer's own community — its history, values, manners, folklore, and sensory textures. Elsewhere in Canada, such writers as Robert Stead, Raymond Knister, Martha Ostenso, Frederick Philip Grove, W.O. Mitchell, Gabrielle Roy, and Sinclair Ross have written about rural communities, but the last three in particular select details from their immediate environments and experiences to express their visions of what is universal in the human condition. Although an intensely regional writer, Buckler is also always at pains to evoke the general out of the particular without in the least falsifying his own sense of time and place. In this respect, he can be seen as a mid-century regional writer who very successfully integrates his philosophical and artistic vision with his own memories and rural experiences. His influence on later writers is difficult to pin down, but such writers as Margaret Laurence, Alice Munro, Matt Cohen, and Alden Nowlan have expressed admiration for Buckler's work.[15] To some extent their themes and their fidelity to their sense of place, and the kind of people who can be found there, are extensions of the same tradition.

Although the *psychological novel* can be traced back to the middle of the nineteenth century in Europe, fiction writers in Canada did not show an interest in detailed psychological studies of character until the 1940s. Flashes of psychological portraiture can be found in the novels of Grove, Callaghan, and MacLennan, but it is fair to say that their main interests were socio-political, moral, and historical (respectively), rather than psychological. It isn't until Gabrielle Roy and Sinclair Ross (Raymond Knister is an exceptional case) began publishing in the 1940s that we find writers in Canada whose primary focus is the psychological layering of a character's responses to his or her environment, complete with symbols appropriate to those responses. Ernest Buckler's short stories indicate his interest in this kind of fiction from the very beginning of his career. How he developed this interest is not certain, but his letters to *Esquire* magazine indicate that he had read many American writers, including Hemingway, Dos Passos, John Steinbeck, Fitzgerald, Sherwood Anderson, and William Faulkner.[16] The American writer he most strongly resembles is James Agee, particularly because in his prose style Buckler developed a richness of texture and emotional resonance that one does not find in the earlier American novelists. Though Agee's *A Death in the Family* (1957) is a later novel than Buckler's *The Mountain and the Valley* (1952), the two writers are contemporaries, and their prose styles are in many ways similar. Psychological fiction became the predominant kind of Canadian fiction in the late 1950s. Margaret Laurence, Margaret Atwood, Mordecai Richler, Robertson Davies, and a host of others concentrate on the psychological development of character, often expressed in symbols, in their novels. None of these writers, however, uses Buckler's prose style, and even Alice Munro, whose psychological insights are at least as penetrating as Buckler's, does not allow herself the lyrical intensity that he does.

The most experimental element in Buckler's fiction is his tendency to write stories about writers — often writers who struggle and fall short of their goals as artists. Because of the breakdown of a public background of traditional beliefs and values in the nineteenth century, writers were increasingly forced inward in their search for a coherent vision of reality. Art gradually became not only more subjective and personal, but it was expected to be a means of self-discovery as well. As Dorothy Van Ghent suggests, the modern artist began to use his autobiographical art in order to discover "a new conceptual and aesthetic form which [would] give him an imaginative grasp of his world."[7] It did not take long for some writers to realize, however, that they could simply trap themselves in a solipsism which ran counter to a culture dominated by empirical views of reality. The only way out of the resulting dilemma was for the writer to adopt an ironic attitude or tone as a form of self-defence without excluding the possibility of self-discovery. In English literature, James Joyce's *A Portrait of the Artist as a Young Man* (1914–15) can be viewed as a seminal work incorporating all of these issues at once.

There are few examples of this kind of literature in Canada before the mid-1940s when Ross, Roy, and particularly Buckler became interested in it. In fact, *The Mountain and the Valley* can be viewed as a watershed in the *Künstlerroman* form. A number of Buckler's short stories and all of his novels deal, at least partially, with writers struggling with their work. By implication, the stories have a strong autobiographical tendency, but at the same time Buckler maintains an ironic detachment from his main characters and their aesthetic theories. Buckler's stories, then, are among the first in Canadian fiction to deal with a set of themes and forms already well established on the other side of the Atlantic.

Since the late 1950s a great many Canadian writers have developed this kind of self-conscious fiction which examines the artist and his art. Sinclair Ross's *As for Me and My House* (1941), P.K. Page's *The Sun and the Moon* (1944), and Gabrielle Roy's *Street of Riches* (1957) were among the first. Since then, Margaret Laurence, Leonard Cohen, Hugh Hood, Alice Munro, Clark Blaise, Margaret Atwood, Robertson Davies, Morley Callaghan, and a number of other writers have produced at least one novel dealing with the artist's role and the nature of art. Ever since Cervantes' *Don Quixote*, this kind of fiction has been of course a common way for novelists to investigate the novel's major focus — the relationship of illusion and reality, art and life. It would be inaccurate to say that Buckler's work influenced all of those who wrote about the themes which interested him, but he was one of a few writers at mid-century who introduced these issues into Canadian fiction. In sum, Buckler's work is Canadian and international in the best sense, and he has been, in his modest way, an innovator in Canadian fiction.

Critical Overview and Context

Because Buckler began as a short story and features writer for magazines, he did not attract critical attention until the publication of his first novel in 1952. Since then, criticism of his work has been sporadic (partially because of the author's publishing schedule) and uneven. The direction of Buckler criticism has shifted gradually from a tendency to evaluate him as a lyrical, regional apologist to a tendency to read his work ironically as well.

The Mountain and the Valley was initially published in New York and it attracted considerable attention in the United States.[18] The novel was also reviewed in the major Canadian newspapers, and it is fair to say that most of the reviews were very favourable. Many of the reviewers concentrated on the richness of Buckler's style, citing his gift for finding correlatives for human emotions in the details of rural settings.[19] A few reviewers felt that the prose was too elaborate or that too often it strained for effect, but at the same time even those reservations were offset by admiration for Buckler's perspicuous description of psychological responses and family interactions.[20] The ending of the novel, when it was mentioned at all, was assessed as ambiguous,[21] though a handful of reviewers made a half-hearted attempt to place David's death in a metaphysical or transcendental context.[22]

Warren Tallman first drew attention to *The Mountain and the Valley* as a significant work of Canadian fiction in his article "Wolf in the Snow."[23] Tallman described the main character, David Canaan, as a typical isolated protagonist in Canadian fiction. According to Tallman, David represents a need for community identity, but he is paralyzed and cannot move either towards positive action or towards real self-discovery. He sustains childlike romantic illusions and fails to emerge from his isolation. The only other preliminary remarks on Buckler's work were made six years earlier in 1955 when R.E. Watters in a public lecture complained that this fine novel was unjustly ignored by Canadian critics; however, this lecture was not published until 1972.[24]

Buckler's second novel, *The Cruelest Month* (1963), was not widely reviewed by Canadian newspapers but did receive some attention in academic journals. Reviewers complained about the lengthy dialogue in the novel, the relative lack of action, the "self-consuming" style of the prose, and the stiff and contrived structure.[25] Claude Bissell, R.G. Baldwin, and Dave Godfrey admired many aspects of the work, but most critics found it dissatisfying, and none recognized any ironic treatment of the characters at the end of the story, except Godfrey, who mentions that they all seem to be self-deluded throughout.[26]

In 1967 interest in Buckler picked up again with Douglas Spettigue's article on the recurring symbolic patterns in the novels,[27] and with Gregory Cook's lengthy M.A. thesis "Ernest Buckler: His Creed and Craft." Both studies were thoughtful, serving to bring Buckler's writing to the forefront in the study of Canadian fiction. Each critic describes the universal concerns in the stories and novels and relates Buckler's various stylistic techniques to his themes. Spettigue emphasizes the structure of the novels, and Cook adds a good deal of background information about Buckler's roots and sense of place.

The next year *Ox Bells and Fireflies: A Memoir* (1968) was enthusiastically reviewed by critics who had by now become very familiar with Buckler's works, those who could see how this fictional

PS 8191 S6 M92 1974

John Moss   Patterns of Isolation

PS 8061 A56
          Volumes

Robert Lecker The Annot. Bib.
          of Canada's Major

          Authors

PS 8077 I16 1978

Paul Cappon   In Our Own House

PS 8187 D6 1979

Moral Vision in the Canadian Novel
          D.J. Dooley

ith slaughter of infected herds have the beef and dairy
close to purging the nation's cattle herds of

ation with Strain 19 has been used in the past in
al and public bison herds in state and national parks,
m found that few records are available to help judge
ffectiveness of such efforts. The worry with Strain
at it will persist into sexual maturity and cause
lle says, although data on this question are fairly
results have been published yet from the handful of
under way on the biosafety and efficacy of RB51 in
adults.

Cullough suggested that answers could be obtained
gencies contracted to collect and analyze data from
herds that are already being vaccinated with
gencies expanded current experimental research or
ine trial on a public bison herd outside the national
ild also be required to find effective ways to
vithout rounding up animals in the national park or
ntrating them on feed grounds. Injecting vaccine
or scattering it in foods or baits all present
stical problems.

urdles are overcome, the NRC team pointed out

memoir fit into the whole canon, and how it expressed a philosophical, metaphysical, and even mystical vision, even though at first
glance it seemed to be a pastoral idyll.[28] Claude Bissell hailed the
book as "a Canadian masterpiece."[29]

With the burgeoning of Canadian literary criticism in the next
decade, Buckler's work attracted the kind of analysis that it warrants.
His manuscript collection was acquired by the University of Toronto
in 1969, and nine theses were completed on his work by 1974. Most
of the theses concentrated on Buckler's use of symbolism to pattern
his first two novels and on his treatment of the artist figure as isolated
and alienated from his community. Ian Atkinson's thesis (1969)
discusses the artist figure in the context of modal structures.[30] Bernita
H. Harris (1969) examines the overlay of imagery from T.S. Eliot's
"The Waste Land" in *The Cruelest Month*, stressing the ironic effect
of Buckler's symbols and images and the theme of the search for
renewal.[31] My own thesis (1970) examines the stories and novels as
"poetic" visions of the human condition and also, for the first time,
includes an analysis based on quotations from Buckler's letters
indicating he intended the endings of his first two novels to contain
a good deal of irony — a point that other critics have subsequently
developed.[32] Other theses by Richard Reichert (1971), Einhard F.H.
Kluge (1972), William Ronald Walker (1972), Jean Huntley Willmott
(1974), and Ronda Hustler (1985) deal with communication, time, the
function of the artist, and intentional irony in Buckler's fiction.[33]

In 1972 Gregory Cook edited *Ernest Buckler*, an anthology of
reviews, sections from theses, and articles. This book seemed to
spark William French in *The Globe and Mail* as well as other
reviewers in periodicals to wonder why there wasn't more Buckler
criticism.[34] In the meantime, *Nova Scotia: Window on the Sea* was
greeted with tepid reviews, where it was reviewed at all. Most of the
reviewers praised Buckler's prose style when it pleased them, and
complained when it seemed too complex or obscure or "poetic."[35]
Since 1972, at least one article or book on Buckler's fiction has been
published each year, and some controversies gradually have surfaced
about the best interpretation of *The Mountain and the Valley*.

Alan R. Young, for example, in an analysis of the novel's form,
points out that Buckler departs from the conventional formula of
the pastoral in the paradoxical triumph of David's death.[36] In the
same vein, Clara Thomas compares David's "mystical experience"
at the peak of South Mountain to that of Henry David Thoreau on

the summit of Mount Ktaadn, as described in his *Maine Woods*.[37] A number of other critics evaluate David's death in more ironic and tragic terms. Eileen Sarkan argues that David uses his imagination to withdraw from his outer world; his romantic imagination denies him a social identity and ironically this causes his death.[38] Eleven further critical studies have been published which debate (among other related issues) whether or not Buckler's treatment of David Canaan's death is to be interpreted ironically or tragically or as a mystical and transcendental release. J.M. Kertzer, for example, argues that David is trapped ironically by time and eventually by memory.[39] Douglas Barbour cites David's wilful and selfish nature as the source of his misuse of his artistic powers of communication.[40] Alan R. Young supports the direction of Barbour's interpretation in two articles and a monograph by quoting sections from Buckler's letters which suggest his intention to treat David ironically as self-deluded and tragically isolated.[41] However, Bruce F. MacDonald, Robert D. Chambers, Andrew Thompson Seaman, and Sister A.M. Westwater emphasize universal themes which go beyond psychological or sociological analysis and point to a philosophy of transcendence as the novelist's response to the alienation implicit in the human condition.[42] They read the ending as ambivalent, in that it is ironic and tragic yet triumphant because David discovers the powers of his inner life.

Recent criticism of Buckler's work attempts to resolve this debate by discussing the relevance of Buckler's prose style. Gerald Noonan and D.J. Dooley closely examine the two styles in *The Mountain and the Valley*, one for David and one for the other characters. They argue that this counterpointing of styles enhances the pattern of irony in the novel.[43] Laurence Ricou assesses the use of figurative language in the novel, concluding that it helps to underline the childlike quality of David's imagination, thus emphasizing his arrested development.[44] Sarah Dyck compares David to Boris Pasternak's Zhivago in *Dr. Zhivago* and sees the end of both novels as final transfigurations.[45] Marilyn Chapman, Robert J. Stewart, and L.M. Doerksen tend to accept David's death as some sort of release into perfect unity, though in each case the interpretation of the novel seems rather vague.[46]

My own short overview of *The Mountain and the Valley* in the *Profiles of Canadian Writers* series stresses the poetic and tragic dimensions in Buckler's writing.[47] Andrew Thompson Seaman extends the discussion of Buckler's tragic vision and attempts to attribute it to "Buckler's own worst fears about himself"; he also contrasts Buckler's tragic preoccupation with himself with the "humanitarian vision of Charles Bruce as reflected in *The Channel Shore*."[48] And in a dissenting article, Lawrence Mathews argues that *The Mountain and the Valley* "has no significant merit" and that critics have falsely elevated the novel to the status of a Canadian classic without demonstrating why it should be accepted as such.[49] Mathews cites the weakness of "language" in the novel and challenges traditional critical valorizing of tragic, ironic, and symbolic complexity in the novel. Mathews' essay, despite its occasional unfairness to Buckler, invites more rigorous scrutiny of the novel and may stimulate a fresh look at the process by which critics compile the list of Canadian classics.

Buckler's other work has not received extensive treatment. The publication of his selected short stories in *The Rebellion of Young David and Other Stories* in 1975 was welcomed by all its reviewers, and the stories were praised for their pastoral moods, their psychological realism, and their craftsmanship; at the same time, some of the stories were described as too sentimental, old-fashioned, or conventional in design.[50] *The Cruelest Month* was issued in paperback in 1977 with an introduction by Alan R. Young; Young's comments are extended in his monograph *Ernest Buckler*.[51] Robert D. Chambers' monograph *Sinclair Ross and Ernest Buckler* is the only other sustained discussion of *The Cruelest Month*.[52] Whereas Chambers reads the novel as outlining a movement from a wasteland through purgation towards regeneration and redemption, Young wonders whether or not the characters at the end are still self-deceived. *Ox Bells and Fireflies* gained an introduction by Young when it was published in paperback in 1974, but it too has not received any very extensive analysis outside of discussions by Young, Chambers, and myself.[53] All three studies treat the structure of the volume as a sign of Buckler's ideas on time, progress, death, nature, and transcendence. *Whirligig* was a surprise to most reviewers; on balance, it was received favourably, although most of the notices contained reservations about the kind of humour Buckler writes.[54]

The Mountain and the Valley clearly has a lasting place in Canadian fiction. The novel has a richness of texture and meanings which continue to reward close study. *Ox Bells and Fireflies* and the stories in *Nova Scotia: Window on the Sea* have yet to be analyzed fully, and *The Cruelest Month* is only beginning to draw academic interest. As Canadian literary studies grow, the body of critical material on Buckler's writings will be a significant part of that growth.

Buckler's Works

As a fledgling writer, Buckler wrote philosophy essays, poems, articles, letters, and reviews. He published only two short stories between 1928 and 1940; however, an early essay published in *Coronet* and most of the letters to *Esquire* magazine indicate that Buckler was thinking about his own tastes in fiction.[55] At times he sounds very confident in his judgements, and at other times he is clearly searching for a path for himself — testing opinions, deriding the latest fashions, even hiding behind an ironic or satiric persona. In another essay called "How to Write an Artistic Novel," he writes that he discovered this guide to writing artistically in a bottle which "smelled faintly of bitter almonds and Vat 69,"[56] and that sums up the combination of tones one finds in most of his early articles and poems about writing. In some ways, Buckler has never lost his ambivalent attitude towards the power of the word; in much of his later work, the artists are usually both smug and humble, triumphant and failing, hopeful and despairing, often at the same time. The early poems are packed with metaphors and symbols and they are often humourous and earthy. Taken together, his essays and poems can be seen as faint precursors of a later synthesis of styles and themes in the fiction. By 1940 Buckler was writing:

> There's a book, they say, in every male or
>   female as the case may be;
> Including, I suppose me.
> . . . .
> To tell the truth, I fear that, come my time to bring
>   forth what's inside me,
>   — I shall probably abort,
> And give birth, prematurely, to a story short.[57]

That year he published his short story "One Quiet Afternoon" in *Esquire*, and he continued to publish at least one short story each year (six in 1957 and four in 1958) until 1965.

His short stories have attracted only slight critical attention, with critics treating the stories as preludes to Buckler's first novel.[58] Most of the themes, characters, and even some episodes from the stories are repeated in the later novels. There are stories, for example, about men who are forced to return to the country (often for health reasons) after a brief stay in the city, and the central characters usually conclude that the honesty of the former way of life is preferable to the sophistication of the latter way. Many of the stories describe the intricate and delicate network of emotions which links members of rural families, and a number of them deal with the isolation of characters with special sensibilities from their communities.

These isolated characters are often artists who are misunderstood or who lack confidence in their own powers. Curiously enough, an early but undated poem by Buckler contains a perspective and an image cluster which recur in the short stories and are associated with the artist figure:

BLEEDING IN THE DARK

The still remembering sun of Indian
   Summer touches the poet's face
   in the afternoon
Through the pane. Everything always
   through a pane.
   It's getting late, the time for other
   things is gone
And who can say in a lifetime
   what happens in a second?
Who can say anything as perfect
   in a lifetime as the filigree
   of frost crystal on an outhouse
   window?
The soft moon silvers through
   the laughter of children,
   lacing their swift skates
   like arrows over the frozen
   brook.

In another version, the last line is:

Sharper than skates is the memory of
the watcher.[59]

The title refers to a wounded deer, and that same image is associated with artists in some later stories and with David Canaan in the Prologue to *The Mountain and the Valley*. The artist is an observer, separated from childhood joy and from nature's perfect beauty by a pane (the word is a homonym for pain). His separation seems to be a condition of his being an artist in the first place. The autumn season, late afternoon light, and the final image of skating children all suggest a preoccupation with lost time and the importance of memory. The two central rhetorical questions also anticipate major concerns in the rest of Buckler's work — concerns about time and art, with the imperfections and transience of artistic creations compared to the perfection and permanence of nature's creations.

The most satisfying short stories investigate these themes and are successful because Buckler employs a style and a narrative structure which together capture exactly the emotional quality of his experience of rural life, the passing of time, the nature of the artistic sensibility, and the artist's romantic aspirations and frustrations. There are a number of short stories which are flat and dull precisely because Buckler departs from his central preoccupations. Sometimes he writes contrived and conventional stories for a magazine audience or an editor demanding more traditional forms and themes. He cannot be blamed for this kind of diversion, of course, but it is clear, in hindsight, that his best stories are directly related to his attempts to express his closest concerns in an appropriate style and form.

Buckler's desire to write serious, original fiction is clear in his story "Another Christmas," where he recounts a young writer's inner reflections on the experience of writing fiction:

You don't know what it is like in the ghost-world of words. . . .
And the first day you tried to tell a thing that had happened,
truly, and the right-feeling words would not come, and the ones
that had a move and a speaking in them, the ones that brought
the thing outside you, clearer and shapelier than you had ever
thought you knew it . . . the first day those would not come at
all but only the springless bones-of-words, and you sat there
feeling the white-tight silence of the very doors and everyone
else seemed to be busy with something alive, the real thing . . .

they could not even *guess* what that sort of emptiness was like. And the other times when you did get something truly, then your mind was feverish and swarming with everything there was, to tell. . . . There was more in any *one* of these little things than you could ever tell in your whole lifetime . . . you couldn't tell that because there were a million things in it to tell, and a million ways to tell every one of them, and only one way for each of them was right. And you tried desperately to find a single light that would come suddenly so that everything would fall into place as if you were looking at a picture that was only broken lines at first but as you looked at it, steadily, suddenly all the broken lines flowed into a single image, and the separate lines were gone and everything was part of the same thing.

But you never found that single light . . . that single plan. No one ever did. So how could the little separate part you had told matter at all?[60]

It is this quest for artistic expression which characterizes Buckler's best work.

The stories collected in *The Rebellion of Young David and Other Stories* contain many of Buckler's best early writing, including "The Quarrel," "Penny in the Dust," "The Wild Goose," "The First Born Son," "The Clumsy One," and the title story. To that list could be added "The Snowman," "The Darkest Time," and "The Trains Go By." Typically, in these stories, what Buckler admires most in his rural characters is their consanguinity with nature and with each other. They do not *need* to articulate their feelings of closeness, possibly because they know words are inadequate to the task. City people and artists who shape those feelings into thoughts and words do so only because they no longer take part in the rhythm of their surroundings. However, as narrators of the stories, these articulate characters have gained a clarity of vision and memory which enables them to find significance in their personal histories. Consequently, there is always a bifocal perspective in these stories — one of sympathy and another of irony — which helps to underline the tensions between youth and age, loss and gain, country and city, heart and mind, art and life. In this way, Buckler can elicit the universal elements in the human condition out of very local events.

Time functions as a hidden character in each of the stories. Ecstatic moments of wholeness are reserved for the young; as characters grow older those moments occur less frequently. The background rural characters seem resigned to this process; as the narrator remarks in "The Dream and the Triumph": "Somehow in the country men never seemed to skate after life stopped its circling just above their shoulders and settled on them" (*RYD*, p. 68). The artist-narrator reacts to time's passing differently. Instead of resigning himself to the present, he searches the past as a way of recapturing the intensity of childhood experience. He concentrates on a moment of wholeness in his youth in order to discover what it was, what hidden imperfection at its centre, caused it to shatter. In "The Quarrel," for example, the narrator remembers both his excited anticipation of a day at the carnival and the exploding of those expectations one by one.

> I should have had warning of the quarrel. The moments before it had been so perfect.
>
> . . . .
>
> I ran around outdoors, the whole day burst and trembling about me. They had broken it, like glass, and no matter how perfectly you fitted the pieces together again, you'd know that the mending was there. I was such a foolish child that when a thing which was to have been perfect was spoiled the least bit, it was spoiled entirely. (*RYD*, pp. 44–45)

This ironical view of innocence can be understood only from the narrator's new position of experience. The tension between the two views of life runs through every phrase of the story. At the carnival (a version of the city) nothing matches the child's expectations. The fortune teller turns out to be an obvious fraud. His father cannot ring the bell in the strength machine, and his mother's tablecloth does not win the contest. On the way home, however, his father awkwardly breaks the spell of the quarrel between him and his wife by telling her that her tablecloth is still the best one. At home the boy realizes that the tablecloth is beautiful — it belongs there, and the narrator longs for "the light of some single penetrating phrase" to tell "how it was" (*RYD*, p. 51). The narrator then remarks, "I think I saw then how it was with all of us. Not by understanding of course, but, as a child does sometimes, with the lustrous information of feeling" (*RYD*, p. 52). And that night, in bed, the retrospective narrator tells us:

I had never been so consciously happy in my whole life.

But I didn't take any chances this time. I repeated the words from my prayer, quickly, intensely, "If I should die before I wake. . . . If I should die before I wake . . . ." (*RYD*, p. 53)

The boy wanted to hold onto the precious moment through the night to the next day. The bemused tone of the narrator simply hints at the foolish romanticism of youth. The irony of the story is that in waking the boy (now narrator) became a victim of time. Only by dying could the boy have made the moment permanent. The implicit irony is attributable more to Buckler's hand than to his narrator's. This is one example of the balance between Buckler and his artist characters which enables him to develop subtle ironic and rich effects, while at the same time exploring universal human emotions (his own included, obviously) and the human condition. "The Quarrel" brings together most of the themes of the early short stories.

Another story, "Penny in the Dust," is useful for exploring related aspects of Buckler's style. This story, like the others listed above, contains a central object around which a number of associated meanings cluster. The narrator, when he was a boy, loses a new penny in the dust when he is daydreaming, and he then runs to hide in his room, too ashamed to tell his parents that he was burying it and pretending it was treasure. His father later finds the penny for him and explains that he did not have to hide because he would not have been beaten. In order to assure the father that he was not hiding from *him*, the boy confesses that he was pretending that the penny was treasure he could share with the family. The father, with tears in his eyes, embraces the boy — "The only time in my seven years I had ever seen tears in his eyes" (*RYD*, p. 7) — and kept the penny. In a short prologue and epilogue, we learn that the father has now died and that the narrator has found the penny in the pocket of the suit in which the old man will be buried. He leaves it there. The penny, then, holds a good deal of symbolic significance. It served as the currency of love between father and son when neither could articulate their love. It remains a hidden, yet real, presence in the father's coat and thus is a message to the son across time. It was buried in dust — a romantic dream covered by death — symbolizing the imperfection at the core of a moment of wholeness. By burying the penny, the narrator paradoxically puts it beyond the reach of time and death. The symbol of their family bond, buried forever, acts as a gesture against death, the way art, too, in its attempt to crystallize the perfect moment, is a gesture against both time and death (*cf.* the function of the buried spinner in "David Comes Home," the globe of sea-water in "Yes Joseph, There Was a Woman," the ring in "Cleft Rock with Spring.") The object is used to catch all the variegations of feeling and to fuse them with literary associations for poetic effect.

In his short stories, then, Buckler perceptibly struggles for the exact symbol, word, or figure of speech that will contain both intensity and accuracy of emotion and at the same time focus the story's theme. His prose is influenced by poetry, and like poetry it depends on rhythm, association, and ornamentation of language in order to be both concrete and connotative. Hence we find a proliferation of metaphors, similes, images, conceits, and sound effects (alliteration and assonance) in the prose sentences. The effect of poetic devices inserted into prose is that they slow down the speed of the writing and give it a meditative quality. Its primary appeal is to the emotions and to the synthesizing function of the imagination, but it encourages a secondary effect of contemplation, so that it has a metaphysical thrust like that of imagist poetry. Taken too far it becomes euphuism — which is often sentimental, discontinuous, a parody of itself. However, Buckler learned to control his prose by experimenting in his short stories. In his first novel he brought it to maturity.

The Mountain and the Valley is still the most studied work by Buckler. The prose is dense with imagery, sensuous detail, and modifiers which add emotional intensity. The structure of the novel is held together by recurring symbols and by a narrative point of view, which, though it shifts among many characters, is nevertheless focused so intimately on the emotional and psychological responses of the protagonist, David Canaan, that the reader is drawn into the very centre of his painful dilemma. Buckler must have realized how completely his prose would arouse sympathy for David, because he decided to intrude here and there in the story in his own voice in order to generate ironic distance in the reader's response. The fact that the novel is also an examination of a potential writer who fails gives it a self-reflective dimension which further deepens and complicates its design.

When Buckler submitted the manuscript of *The Mountain and the*

Valley to the Atlantic Monthly Press for publication in 1950, he received a rejection notice and some editors' reports which provoked him to defend his work. His letter of response sets down his intentions for the novel and some information about its construction:

I hope its several intentions are clear enough. Among them, this village's *representation of the universal situation in microcosm*; the subtlety of its people's joys and sorrows despite their helplessness to express them, (Here, I think I may be excused if sometimes I paraphrase these feelings in somewhat more recondite language than would be natural to the people themselves. A little elucidatory aside seems to me far less intrusive than to let undue illumination creep into the dialogue; which in these people I'm describing is never informative of anything, unless you twist and manipulate it a hundred miles from anything they'd actually say.), the gradual dispersal of family-oneness both in the leading characters and (in parallel) in the village itself, as progress (?) laps closer and closer; how the day is an extra character in every situation (much as in Hardy's novels) . . . .

David's precocity and temperament may at first make him seem like a eugenic sport. Chris, of course, with his uninhibited sensuality (as contrasted with David's, inhibited always, as is everything else of his, by reflection), etc., is the more average country boy. But I think that as circumstances develop, the recurrent dichotomy in David's nature (country or city boy? Naive or sophisticate? Harsh or tender? Over-child or over-adult? Serious or comic? Homebody or alien?) will be seen to be traceable, inevitably, to Ellen's perceptiveness and romanticism, his mother's alternate open-heartedness and melancholy, his father's dogged will . . . . Incidentally, their lives are all sort of decrescendo (the idyllic part of them, coming at first, may make for an apparently slow, conflictless, beginning; yet the "cloud no bigger than a man's hand" is supposed to be implicit almost immediately); but if you consider their peaks of peculiarly vivid happiness, I figure their balance of satisfaction is actually positive. . . .

And speaking of accuracy, there's quite a bit of symbolism in the thing, but the intention is never artificial or pretentious. And if the language comes out sometimes a little poetic, that's *not* because I'm striving to be picturesque; it's the very opposite. It's because I'm struggling for the accurate expression. (Aren't the deliberate approximations of prose sometimes the subtler affectation, anyway?)[61]

In the same letter, he answers a charge that the novel's pace is too slow because there is very little plot development. In another letter, Buckler emphasizes the psychologically inevitable conclusion of the novel and its ironic aspects:

> I agree with you that the novel is more a picture than a development . . . but I stubborn[ly] dispute Miss Beck's "its individual events have no relation of cause and effect." I still believe they are integral to the whole and psychologically inevitable. The cause and effect are not always spelled out, I concede. But surely, especially in a novel of this sort, something may be left to implication. . . .
> As for the idea that David's death was an arbitrary device to end the story, *it actually happens to be the very first thing I wrote; the foundation of the whole thesis.* (Later I split the opening chapter and shifted that part to the epilogue.) It was to be the crowning point of the whole dramatic irony, (and, of course, the most overt piece of symbolism in the book) that he should finally exhaust himself climbing the mountain, and, beset by the ultimate clamour of impressions created by his physical condition and his whole history of divided sensitivities, come, at the moment of his death (prepared for, not only by long accounts of the results of his fall, but by the medical officer's advice to him at the time of his enlistment examination; and, more immediately, by the excitement, the panic, the climbing), achieve *one final transport of self-deception*; that he would be the greatest writer in the whole world.[62]

Although critical readers should be wary of what authors say of their own works, a writer has to be appreciated and understood according to what he set out to do, and Buckler's comments in these letters are helpful in establishing a context for interpretation.

In the Prologue to the novel, David Canaan is standing at a window looking out at a highway which leads out of the valley where he has spent his life; he is thinking about a log road which leads up the mountain he has always intended to climb. The imagery in this section (bare window, frozen fields, "white washed houses," "gaunt limbs of maples," David's "smile-scar," wounded deer, "milk-ice," and "withered aftergrass" underlines his isolation, loneliness, and fall towards death.[63] Although the reader cannot yet appreciate the importance of these images, the rest of the novel is, as J.A. Wainwright notes, "held in a perspective that would not otherwise exist; as a result, the reader will not only pay closer attention to the flaws inherent in the seemingly perfect life of the Canaan family, but he will also be prepared from the outset for the inevitable changes in and decline of David's life."[64] The reader is also introduced to characters who reappear and symbols which recur later in the novel at crucial times. The effect of this Prologue is to create a sense of impending tragedy. For example, David sees a man go by named Herb Hennessey: "He'd never gone into another house, as far back as when David was a child. He'd been the strangest creature in the world to the children" (p. 16). Hennessey later appears at each of David's real disappointments; he comes to represent a figure of David's fate — a *Döppelganger* figure representing a loss of childhood wholeness. A hair ribbon, a sailor, a blood-stained tablecloth, the kitchen — all are examples from the first few pages of images which help to establish a context for irony because of the way they are used in the body of the novel.

In the Prologue, the figure of the grandmother, Ellen, is extremely important. Ellen is seen hooking a circular rug with rags torn from "whole" garments: "She selected each rag carefully for texture and colour" (p. 15). Her creation symbolizes the way the novel itself is being written. Each strip of cloth stimulates the remembrance of a character who will be developed or an incident which will be expanded in the novel proper. Each colour signifies something about the wearer, and in this way the prologue contains the whole novel within itself. David's father Joseph's cloth is grey and was worn "the day he went back to cut the keel" (p. 15); later we learn this was the day he died. His cloth encompasses the interior rings (p. 15) and in turn is encompassed by a border made from a coat which we later learn belonged to Ellen's husband Richard (p. 17). The red tablecloth is bloodstained from David's accident; this accident becomes the central episode of "Part Five: The Scar." "No washing could ever get the stain out" (p. 17), Ellen remembers, and this permanent stain is symbolic of David's condition. Ellen is making a "target pattern of circles" from carefully selected memories (p. 15). Her "creation" is linked significantly with David the potential artist; he had marked the circles for her, and he had, incidentally, inherited the "fine graining" of her face (p. 15). Ellen's memories find their way into her creation, whereas David's creations are "word-shaped."

In the Epilogue, Ellen chooses the last two concentric circles for the rug: the scarlet cloak David had worn while acting in a school play (which represents his first abortive attempt to be inside of an artistic creation) and a piece of her own white lace for the very centre of the artifact. The rags in the rug are arranged in circles of chronological time (Richard, Joseph, Martha, Chris, Anna, David), except for Ellen's, which is at the centre of the pattern. If the rug is a symbol of the novel in process, Ellen represents the true controlling centre and functions as the surrogate for Buckler. In the novel *proper*, though, David is at the centre but is thrown into ironic contrast as an artist with Ellen, who *does* complete her work whereas David cannot. Because the Prologue and Epilogue deal with the same moments in time, the novel itself is structured in a circular fashion — in the Epilogue David recalls the very first incident in the book. David's final climb and transfiguration also completes a circle. The Prologue, then, establishes the central concerns in the novel and sheds a soft light of irony over all of the incidents in David's story. The Epilogue strengthens this light.

The novel is divided into six sections and each section contains a series of crucial episodes in David's life. At the end of each section, David experiences a trauma which is potentially liberating for his growth, but in each case, his response is to retreat. At the end of "Part One: The Play," for example, David feels humiliated when his moment of romantic drama is rudely shattered by a crude comment from the audience, and he runs home to hide in his room. At the end of "Part Two: The Letter," he makes love for the first time with his girlfriend Effie, but then turns away from her towards his peers and towards an outsider, Toby, for friendship. In the next section, Effie dies, and David blames himself for her death. In "Part Four: The Rock," he falls, scars himself, and wilfully cuts himself off from his brother Chris in the process. Finally, in "Part Six: The Train," he is alienated from Toby and from his twin sister Anna (p. 279), who was closest to him as a child (p. 6).[65] In James Joyce's *A Portrait of the Artist as a Young Man*, a novel with which *The Mountain and the Valley* has sometimes been compared, Stephen Dedalus uses these moments of trauma to escape the various nets which trap him.

David's response is just the reverse:

> You could build a wall about yourself, for safety's sake, but whenever you chose you could level it. That wasn't true, he saw now. After a while you could beat against the wall all you liked, but it was indestructible. (p. 275)

The wall is made of circumstances, time, and, to a great extent, David's own romanticism.

Instead of dealing with any of his difficulties in a realistic and growth-enhancing way, David escapes by projecting a romantic image of himself onto some distant future. For example, when his first attempt to climb the mountain is postponed because of the death of a war hero, David decides he will be "the greatest general in the whole world" (p. 41). When he cannot buy Anna all she wants for Christmas, he decides he will someday be the richest man in the world (p. 61). He sees himself later as "the best skater" (p. 73), the greatest actor (p. 82), the most potent lover (p. 101), the best fiddle player (p. 290), the most famous mathematician (p. 290), the best dancer, and the most experienced traveller (p. 291). Reality always falls short of his expectations. After his first act of sexual intercourse with Effie, he feels guilt, responsibility, and

> a kind of loss. She was like a part of himself that had slipped away where he could never again be able to watch it all the time. . . . He thought how he'd been going to marry the loveliest or richest or most famous woman in the world. That seemed like a different time. (p. 113)

These episodes prepare us for what Buckler in his letter calls "one final transport of self-deception" when, in the Epilogue, David believes his true calling is to be a writer. Once again he sees himself as "the greatest writer in the whole world" (p. 299).

His romanticism, moreover, is part of his inheritance from his grandmother Ellen, from whom he received the "fine graining" on his face. There is, in fact, an intricate network of symbols connecting David to Ellen through Anna. Ellen had a sailor lover who told her about the world beyond the valley, and she tells Anna her story. Anna marries a sailor, Toby, who also disappears at sea. When David cannot leave home (Anna does), Ellen gives him her locket with the sailor's picture in it, and later David gives the locket to Anna, who thinks she sees Toby's picture in it. All along David thought that he himself had been pictured there (p. 172). More irony is added to this motif of romantic dreams of escape in another part of the novel when Joseph, David's father, is killed when he goes up the mountain to cut down the only tree in the area suitable for a ship's keel (p. 173).

The novel is structured by a number of these interlocking networks of symbols and images. David's first trip up the mountain, for example, is aborted because of the deaths of Pete Delahunt and Spurge Gorman. The incident prefigures David's death as a result of his climb up the same mountain and also establishes a complicated set of relationships and incidents. Pete Delahunt is Effie's father, and his wife, Bess, has a bad reputation among the women in the community. David has a dream of being seduced by Bess just before he goes up the mountain on that same day. He later loses his virginity with Effie, and when she dies of leukemia, he blames himself and seeks out Bess for a sexual act of consolation, atonement, and guilt. Martha, David's mother, is jealous of Bess, and after a quarrel about her, Joseph retreats from his wife by going up the mountain to cut the keel tree. Spurge Gorman's wife, Rachel, is the source of Martha's jealousy, and her daughter, Charlotte, eventually seduces David's brother, Chris, causing further fragmentation of the family unit. Consequently, the deaths of the fathers in the opening chapter prefigure the deaths of a number of characters (Joseph, Effie, David); they also lead to the break-up of families and the fragmentation of the community. In this way, the deaths sound a knell for the collapse of a whole way of life — the end of an era.

The network of relationships just described (and there are a number of such networks) serves not only to structure the novel but also to provide links between the psychological and the sociological elements in it. Viewed from one angle, the novel is a study of the intense emotional ties among inarticulate family members. Viewed from a slightly different angle, it concerns the gradual fragmentation of a rural family, and by extension, the decline of an enclosed community, just at the time when Canada itself is being pulled into an international and cosmopolitan world. David Canaan's loss of innocence is dramatized by his divided loyalties. On the one hand, he desires the security of his parents' way of living, the warmth of his mother's kitchen, the routine of farm work. This world is associated with the *valley* of the novel's title. On the other hand, he desires adventure, fame, sophistication, and satisfactions of the intellect — all of which are represented by the *mountain*. His inevitable loss of innocence, a quality associated in the novel with cohesiveness, wonder, and unity with nature, is anticipated in all of the episodes of his youth. On Christmas Eve, for example, when David feels the family's solidarity most, each of its members, except (significantly) Ellen, has a dream which symbolizes fear, disappointment, and death (p. 66). In the new year, the family is pictured together in the house while a storm rages outside. David cannot yet know the significance of that storm:

> The afternoon was totally safe, because the storm kept them all in the house together. Nothing could get at them from outside. Nothing could leave. (p. 74)

On another occasion, when David is thirteen, the family seems to be united on a day of perfect weather. The irony is that David feels their indivisibility in the family cemetery: "The day they fixed the graves was the one day when the family was indivisible" (p. 87). At the centre of every perfect moment lurks its destruction. From this point in the novel to the end, Buckler's "microcosm" suffers its "decrescendo." David contacts an outsider, Toby, who eventually takes Anna to the city. The family moves into a new house, and David occupies the attic. He also betrays Effie three times, quarrels with his father, and runs away from home, only to return and sob on a bridge which symbolically spans the gap between his home and the outside world: "He sobbed because he could neither leave nor stay. He sobbed because he was neither one thing nor the other" (p. 171).

David's bifurcated personality is caused not only by his romantic predispositions but also by a related activity in his hyperactive imagination. His thoughts become "word-shaped," and he uses the words to heighten moments of joy or wholeness. For David, these moments become epiphanies which take him outside of time and place. Once he realizes how powerful words can be, he (characteristically) relies on them to perfect his every experience. The words equate the subjective self and the objective world in ecstatic moments, but they also serve to separate David from others:

> Sometimes when all three worked together, David would try to imitate their sober speech. He'd wish his thoughts could just

move along with the pace of the day, as theirs did. But this morning he wouldn't part with his secret extra senses for anything. (p. 28)

The difficulty here is that David does not know how to integrate his artistic abilities into his life in the valley. From the beginning, he relies on the power of the word for absolute release or escape, never considering that it could be put to use to knit together all the people and things around him into a regional mythology. Instead, he uses words as weapons against his father, brother, neighbours, and friends.

An early instance of David's exaggerated belief in the power of words is the description of his reactions while he is playing the male lead in a school play. Words have the power to make him the centre of community attention, and he feels he can take them into his perfect world of make-believe. His response is both romantic and egocentric:

Oh, this was perfect. There was a bated wonder coming from their faces: to know that this was David, but a David with the shine on him (they'd never suspected!) of understanding and showing them how everything was. (p. 81)

When he decides to kiss Effie, the female lead, even though the gesture is not in the script, a coarse comment from the audience (which, incidentally, includes Herb Hennessey) shatters David's illusory world and his fragile self-esteem. Typically, he over-reacts:

Once he had been trying to imitate the smile of a Zane Grey hero in the mirror and he'd turned and Chris was standing in the door. He felt the shame of having spoken the foolish words in this goddam foolish play as he'd felt shame then. (p. 82)

He retreats to his room at home. Buckler adds images of a broken mirror, a scar, and a boot covered with snow. In his anger, David decides that he hates everyone in the community. One can expect such a reaction from a child, but David never seems to outgrow completely his feeling of shame and anger at not being appreciated by his rural community. He fails to recognize that his vocation should be to use his "secret extra senses" *for* them rather than to expect something *from* them.

Consequently he uses his powers of imaginative articulation as weapons and gradually seals himself into his own chrysalis.[63] While they are trying to move a huge rock, he goads his father into striking him so that he will have an excuse to run away. He uses unusual words, such as "immaterial," to show his peers that he is superior to them (p. 144). He excludes Chris from a trip up the mountain with Toby and Anna — a trip which would have succeeded in reaching the top if Chris had gone along. His seduction of Effie is, at least in part, meant to shame her, and he never recovers from the guilt he feels when she dies. Another crucial episode involves the killing of a pig. David's sensibilities are put on edge by the contrast between the agonizingly drawn-out slaughter of the pig and the jocular mood of the men standing around (p. 185). When Chris makes a casual remark about David's nervousness, David becomes defensive and decides to prove that he is both *one* of them and *superior* to them by climbing to a beam across the roof. Ironically, he suffers from vertigo and falls, scarring himself for life. When Chris visits him to apologize, David wilfully refuses the opportunity for reconciliation (p. 194), and, significantly, it is at this point that David takes up writing.

His attempts at composition, however, are still ego-centred. Writing is a therapeutic escape from his pain into a realm of pure equations and possessions:

Suddenly he knew how to surmount everything. . . . There was only one way to possess anything: to *say* it exactly. Then it would be outside you, captured and conquered. (p. 195)

At the same time, he realizes that his "equalizing weapon" separates him from the spontaneous (Dionysian) experiences of his neighbours, so he destroys his writings and feels "the pain returning" (p. 199). He becomes an observer and an outsider, self-deluded, self-destructive, never able to reconcile his divided allegiances to his family and to the outside world, to Chris and to Toby, to Effie and to Anna, to Martha and to Ellen, to kitchen and to attic, to rock and to keel tree, to life and to art (each pair is parallel to the others) — to mountain and to valley. Even when he writes a story about "how a man could be trapped by his own nature," he is ashamed of its inadequacy to portray life, and he burns it (p. 261).

The final episodes in the novel are both ironic and tragic in every detail. When Toby leaves for the war in Europe, David, whose weak heart keeps him at home, runs to see the train take his friend away. He has reached a crisis in his life:

> This was the toppling moment of clarity which comes once to everyone, when he sees the face of his whole life in every detail. He saw then that the unquestioned premise all his calculations had been built on was false. He realized for the first time that his feet must go on in their present path, because all the crossroad junctions had been left irretrievably far behind. . . . You could build a wall about yourself for safety's sake, but whenever you chose you could level it. That wasn't true, he saw now. After a while you could beat against the wall all you liked, but it was indestructible. The cast of loneliness became pitted in your flesh. . . .
>
> I will always be a stranger to everybody, he thought — the others know that I don't know what any of their things is like. My own life brimmed and emptied so soon, I could never fill it again. (pp. 274–75)

The realization drives him into a rage; he hacks at roots the way he longs to uproot himself. His old vindictiveness returns, and he vows he will someday snub Toby if he ever gets the chance, even if it means he will punish himself for the guilt he will feel, as he has done in the past. "But then he knew that nothing he could ever do would put Toby outside as *he* was outside this. He knew that even if Toby was killed — more than ever, if Toby should be killed — he was beaten" (p. 277). As David sobs for Toby's "stolen life," his [David's] "scar burned white as moonlight in the chill afternoon" (p. 278). And Toby *is* killed.

The second last chapter describing Anna and Toby's walk to the top of the mountain casts David's dreams into an even more ironic and tragic light. Anna, as David's alter-ego who gets to the outside world, also reaches the top of the mountain in David's place. She experiences the completeness and ecstasy which he has always expected. Toby thinks how sad it would be to walk to the top *alone* (as David does later). Anna feels that standing with Toby on the top of the mountain is "the peak of her whole life" (p. 269). Yet in the next minute, she has a premonition that Toby will be called away to die. The weather changes from Indian summer to the chill of winter, and back in the valley "the mountain was a single great cloud of night" (p. 271). So, even though Anna reaches the top of the mountain, her epiphany (in archetypal terms, a sense of being between the world of the gods and the world of nature), inevitably is fleeting. And even though Toby is carried to the outside world, he is also rushing to be drowned. David rages when the train passes him by. The irony is that the train carries Toby to the city and ultimately to his death. David's frustration and anger are self-deluding and tragically misdirected.

At the end of "Part Six: The Train," David and Anna are both left in the farmhouse consoling one another, so that his individual tragedy is fitted inside the larger human predicament that Anna's journey has presented. The twins' lives have become reflections of each other. Taken together, their lives evoke individual and universal sadness — David is unable to satisfy his longings for completion; Anna finds completeness only to realize once again that it lasts but an instant.

In the Epilogue, David moves outside of the house and up the mountain. Subjective self and objective reality begin to merge:

> Even the sensations of his own flesh had become outside. The inside was nothing but one great white naked eye of self-consciousness, with only its own looking to look at. . . . And then . . . it was as if the outline of the frozen landscape *became* his consciousness: that inside and outside were not two things, but one — the bare shape of what his eyes saw. (p. 281)

As he climbs, his weak heart is strained until every detail in his memory and in his immediate environment swims around in his head and clamours for articulation: "The swarming multitude of all the voices it was physically impossible to attend to gave him a sense of exquisite guilt" (p. 291). The sensations and memories heighten in intensity until David feels that he is being called upon "to give the thought to exactly how each of them was" (p. 295); and at that point he sees the downed keel-piece which killed his father — an ironic reminder of the lurking danger of romanticism. When he reaches the mountaintop, he realizes how the power of words can be used to "*become* the thing you told" (p. 298). His leap for absolutes carries him too far once more, and Buckler's own voice intrudes to make the irony plain:

It wouldn't be necessary to take them one by one. That's where he'd been wrong. All he'd have to do . . . oh, it was so gloriously simple . . . was to find their single core of meaning. It was manifest not differently but only in different aspects, in them all. That would be enough. A single beam of light is enough to light all the shadows, by turning it from one to another.

He didn't consider how he would find it. . . . Nor how long it might take . . . He knew only that he would do it. . . . It would make him the greatest writer in the whole world. (pp. 298–99)

He will be the voice of the valley, and that is how his life will have meaning. Time, his own nature, and circumstances have conspired against him, however, and his heart gives out. His crowning moment of "translation" (p. 299) is also one of self-delusion. He sees "an absolute white" in death (p. 300), and is finally covered with snow. He merges with the white centre of Ellen's rug made of lace from her own dress. Buckler fuses tragedy and irony in his portrait of the buried artist, who, in refusing to accommodate himself to the limitations of words, betrays their power and loses his life.

It would be a mistake to emphasize the novel as tragedy *or* as irony, for its power lies in the fact that both are there in equal measure. The prose style of the novel reinforces the reader's sense of pity because its tropes draw us into David's emotional centre. At the same time, this richly figurative prose constantly reminds us that David lives in a fragile escapist's world which cannot be integrated (through David, at least) into his life in the valley. The crowning irony, however, is that Buckler writes the book that David could not write.

The novel has been analyzed as a study of the working of time in both its diachronic and synchronic dimensions. The constant references to seasons, weather, and farm routine, as well as the evolving relationships among characters, emphasize the passing of (diachronic) time in daily life and imply that the direction of one's life is fixed to its destiny.[67] Counterpointing diachronic time in the novel is the presence of synchronic time embedded in Buckler's use of tropes — especially similes and metaphors — which have the effect of linking the specific and concrete to a transcending universal, outside of quotidian experience. This treatment of time includes: how children's perception of time is different from that of adults; how time destroys hope; how the gradual separation and ineluctable death of the individual parallels the decline of the community and its way of life. This counterpointing of diachronic and synchronic aspects of time gives the novel its universal (timeless) appeal. The prose style demands a slow (one might say Maritime) reading pace, which encourages contemplation of the operation of time itself and of how we lose the rich textures of our sensory and emotional experiences. In this union of theme and style, Buckler has created a novel which will probably endure time itself.

Buckler's next novel, *The Cruelest Month*, has not received much critical attention since its publication in 1963 and its republication in paperback in 1977. The reviewers who disliked it generally felt that its pace was too slow, that there was too much talk and too little action, and that the style of the prose was too elaborate in detail and syntax. The reviewers who were more favourable in their assessments liked the delineation of complex relationships among the characters, the intensity and depth of their portrayal, and the intricate interweaving of symbols in the novel's design. The confusion among reviewers may be the consequence of the novel's form and structure. The novel's structure is close to that of many plays. A number of characters flee their circumstances and gather in a pastoral retreat called "Endlaw." As in many plays based on this same premise, the characters' lives become entangled, and each one reveals his or her innermost anxieties, opinions, and traumas in long dialogues and monologues which also serve as repositories for ideas the author is trying to work out. Eventually the characters are transformed and disperse back to the "real" world. Because so many issues are debated in the course of this novel, Gregory M. Cook describes it as an *anatomy* and Robert Chambers suggests symphony and opera analogies for its structure.[68] Since it also contains some of the more conventional structuring devices of novels — intersecting love triangles, coincidence, a forest fire that brings about a climax — readers may become confused as to what response is being demanded of them. On top of the complicated structure of the novel, there is an overlay of symbols and allusions from T.S. Eliot's *The Waste Land* as well as recurring symbols which seem to be tacked on to the novel rather than to emerge from its episodes naturally and spontaneously.

In general, then, one can say that the novel's greatest strengths sometimes conspire against the novel itself. As *anatomy*, for example, the novel raises some fascinating ideas about the social function of the artist and critic, the purposes of art, the problems of evaluating art, the self-deluding properties of love, and the terror of death — all of which, Buckler himself acknowledges, is "too much . . . in the one mouthful of a book."[69] So many ideas also slow down the pace of the novel and seriously interfere with its plot. And yet it is a device of *plot* (a forest fire which threatens the lives of the characters who now have to take risks to escape their "Walden") that is used to bring many of the issues raised in the *anatomy* to a climax. Because it is a plot device, it tends to push aside all of the previous discussions as either empty or irrelevant. Although one could argue that the irony implicit in this device is the whole point of the novel, the reader can be excused if he is confused as to how to respond, simply because there is so much that has been absorbed that now has to be cast overboard.

The same kind of problem arises out of the dramatic structure of the novel. When the relationships form new configurations at the end of the novel and the characters leave their pastoral retreat, one expects that moral conflicts have now been resolved. But have they? Buckler himself has indicated that he does not think so. Even the union of Paul and Letty at the end (which seems to be the moral centre of the novel), is ironical, Buckler suggests, because they both "continue to fool themselves."[70] The April lilacs in the final section of the novel are equivocal symbols at best, and the Letty and Paul of the last paragraphs are apparently *not* significantly different from the Letty and Paul of the opening paragraphs. They are playing the same tune (or at least this is a possibility) but in a different key. If one allows for ambiguity and irony in the ending of the novel, then both the dramatic design and the plot have in a sense been contradicted by the themes. Perhaps one explanation is that all of Buckler's aesthetic instincts and training as a novelist enticed him to resolve the tensions and conflicts by completing the structures he had set up. His intellect and his mature experience of modern life, however, would allow him no such tidy resolutions because they would ring false to life. Hence various elements of the novel are made to qualify (perhaps undermine) each other, and thus the reader is led into a maze of contradictory responses. Depending on your point of view, this "problem" may be the novel's greatest strength or its greatest weakness.

The difficulties of structure aside, it must be stressed that *The Cruelest Month* is a mature work by a serious, skilled novelist who has moved from investigations of the world of childhood and adolescent romantic idealism to a dissection of the dilemmas of adult experience in the contemporary world. There are many sections of the novel which are genuinely moving, and some of the separate features of the novel are fascinating. Morse, for example, is a writer who decides to describe all of the people at Endlaw, but each time he thinks that he has an ending for *his* novel, the people under observation resist his schematizations. *The Cruelest Month* becomes the novel he was trying (and failing) to write, but, at the same time, his failures provide an ironic note for the ending of the novel in which he is a character. Buckler's use of symbolism is also often fascinating. At the "geometric centre" of Endlaw's lake there is an island, suggesting that the hidden depths of each character will be brought to the surface. A deer, a lilac bush, fire, rain, and various kinds of illness are some of the recurring symbols tying the book together and linking it to T.S. Eliot's *The Waste Land*. Rex's mangled foot, symbolizing his spiritual and intellectual impotence, takes on added significance when he shoots himself (he had shot himself in the foot to escape the war). Sheila shoots a hole through the heart on Rex's jacket, and the noise interrupts Morse and Kate's love-making. These are only a few isolated examples of how a complicated network of symbolism is woven into the novel's design.

Buckler himself has accurately assessed why all of the separate parts of the novel fail to knit together organically:

> It was written too deliberately — so that it became (what a novel never should become) point-y, Q.E.D.-y. Most of the characters were drawn too verbatimly from people I've known, without proper digestion and transmutation of them (with the paradoxical result that they may sound unreal). . . . The interlocking was too intricate by half. A sentence on page 215, say, is tied up with one which heralds it on page 6, say . . . Themes (and there are dozens of them, count them) get in the way of the movement. I guess I got the themes and then cast them, as it goes in the theatre. But in novels it should be the exact opposite. Characters are all, should come first, and let the themes fall where they may.
>
> Another thing that misfired: Often I thought the subtlest way to let some of the characters hang themselves was to have them think that what wasn't witty at all in them was very witty, that what they took for sentiment was either sentimentality or over-

blown guff, that what they took to be their great problems were merely minor balls. But everyone thought they were speaking for *me*, straight.[71]

There are also a number of places in the novel where Buckler's style tends to sacrifice character differences (they all seem to speak and think alike) to exactness of phrase or to clarity of emotion. The prose style tends to obtrude, and many passages create a wide gap between character and language. Here, for example, is part of a six-page-long description of a psychological crisis in the mind of the childish and rather dull Rex Giorno:

> And now the transubstantiation took another form.
> The quintessential perfume of loneness and apprehension had been like a vapour so attenuated that even the naming of it with noun or the description of it with adjective would make it sound too falsely substantive.[72]

The style of writing in the novel is also rather different from that in the previous works. Buckler's fondness for unusual metaphors is evident on almost every page. Take, for example, ". . . her voice walking on eggshells" (p. 22); ". . . a lake still as theorems" (p. 8); ". . . the space in the room was full of the moth holes of where his body had stood" (p. 122); or

> His head was splitting. Trawl hooks of ache were in past their barbs in his eyes and everywhere behind his skull. All the other particles of his body were trembling without movement, grasping at each other for stability but their reaches just failing. (p. 242)

He chooses many of his images from mathematics and philosophy, and his diction is far more abstract than usual. This kind of prose is useful in a novel of ideas or for the *anatomy* form but it tends to interfere with the dramatic dimension of this novel. Despite the uneven quality of the style, there is enough in the novel to interest most adult readers.

The original title of the novel was "Cells of Love" (Morse's successful book in the novel is called *Each In His Narrow Cell*). As Buckler himself explains, the title "was supposed to cover (in a kind

of double, somewhat ironic, application) both the cellular variegation of love and love's sometimes prisoning aspects."[73] In Parts I and
II, the first love triangle involving Paul, Kate, and Morse is developed. Paul hides any love he feels for Kate because he cherishes his
independence. Kate is worried about becoming a lonely spinster
because she feels obligated by her love for him to care for her ailing
father (who dies in Part II and leaves his daughter to forge a new
identity). Morse is trying to cover up and escape from his artistic
impotence which is partly the result of his inability to love. Then Rex
and Sheila Giorno, who have come to Endlaw in an attempt to save
their dying marriage, are added to the group, along with Bruce, who
is guilt-ridden over the accidental death of his wife and child. He is
looking for his "lost" wife and finds her counterpart in Sheila, thus
filling out the second triangle.

Parts III and IV depict the transformations taking part in each
character because of "the kind of thing that happens to them," as
Morse puts it (p. 14). Along the way, there are many long conversations about urban blight, death, the inadequacy of words, time, love,
guilt, youth, alienation, and a host of related topics. At one point,
Morse itemizes the losses suffered by each character: Kate has lost
youth, Morse has lost talent, Sheila love, Rex self-esteem, Bruce his
family, and Paul his identity. Concerning a rural character named
Letty, Morse remarks "I don't think she's ever lost a thing" (p. 118).
Evidently Letty is supposed to be a still centre in the novel's moral
design, but Buckler seems very tentative about her ability to act in
this capacity. At any rate, each character comes to realize that past
memories do not fulfill present desires, as the novel's epigraph from
T.S. Eliot implies: "April is the cruelest month . . . mixing memory
and desire" (p. vi).

Near the end of the novel Rex accidentally starts a forest fire which
the others then confront. Sheila decides to stay with Rex. As they
leave Endlaw escaping the fire, she tells him of their expected child
and sees the deer she had missed seeing in Part I. The symbols of the
fire and the deer inform the ending. Sheila sees the deer bound away
with "one last transcendental parabola" and experiences "a vaulting
insight" that stoicism and resignation are at least as valuable as
happiness (p. 264). Bruce also sees the deer while deciding to become
a psychiatrist for children, thus atoning for his lost child through an
act of altruistic love. Morse and Kate see the deer when they are
stopped on a bridge, and he then rushes through the fire, knowing

he can now write a novel based on these experiences and his consequent vision of hope. After a brief temptation to return to nurse Paul, Kate follows Morse. Her decision inspires the ending for Morse's novel. As Morse explains, each of his characters will be

> ... made to see each other's homely, individual ... lighting ... by the light of a common overbearing fate. ... Love can be burned or broken. But this business of seeing each other's *lighting* plain, that's the only fibre in the world that's indestructible. (p. 283)

In some respects, Morse's previous discussions of art (pp. 149–54) extend those of David Canaan in *The Mountain and the Valley*. His failures stem from his disappointment in the power of words, much as David's do. Kate's insistence on the reality of love liberates his vision, but there is genuine irony in their final conversation:

> "Darling, will you help me get it down absolutely true? Once and for all?" ... You'll never get it right, she thought. No writer ever gets it right. How can they get it true to life when life's not true or faithful to itself? ... or people to themselves? (p. 284).

Kate will have to nurse Morse's self-delusion the way she nursed her father, so her flight through fire from Endlaw may not signal any real change for her.

When Paul sees the deer, he is destroying the notes for a novel he has been drafting. He is forced to fight the fire with Letty and collapses in the process. Watching Letty fight the fire alone, he comes to the sudden realization that his pseudo-existentialism is really cynicism and that Letty has an ability to "reduce the mythographic to the magnificently ordinary" (p. 294). Like the others, he develops his own particular variegation of love. His loss of Kate is a release (p. 234), and his love for Letty is "like that of pairs whose two equations may contain quite different powers and arrangements of the x and y and z, but in whose feeling there's the recognition that in either case the *value* for each basic variable is the same" (p. 294). Paul's recognition of Letty's worth brings with it a spring rain which extinguishes the forest fire. He makes love with Letty that night and catches "a glimpse of Death's losing face" (p. 296).

It is indeed difficult to know what to make of each of the character's final insights, especially those of Paul. The design of the novel itself suggests that each has ended his or her sojourn to Endlaw transformed for the better. They are complicated characters, however, who may not be true to art, life, or themselves. Buckler himself comments on this:

> The question of change; do people, ever, much? The tempering of the fire, and its somewhat ironic results. (When you see someone maybe made over the way you'd thought you wanted them to be, do they seem suddenly worse? Kate's reaction to Morse's almost "soft" idealism at the end, her notice of her almost silliness with love; the irony that Paul thinks he's found an answer in Letty — when, anyone should see, particularly with Letty changing herself ("proper" speech, etc.), that this is maybe an *ignis fatuus* too).[74]

Alan R. Young interprets the ending as nihilistic and bitter: "The whole redemptive process, the primary concern of the novel, is exposed as self-deception"; thus, the irony and ambiguity of the ending are thrown off-balance.[75] In fact the novel may contain just the opposite problem. It seems to be heading for an ending in which each of the characters experiences a positive transfiguration. At the last moment, however, Buckler seems to have had doubts about the possibility or plausibility (given the way his characters have turned out) of those changes or of a "happy" ending. So he leaves room for ambiguity of interpretation. If, after all, we are to rest finally with Paul and Letty, who have abandoned words and art to a considerable degree, then what are we to think of a narrator whose language most of the other characters imitate? At every point, this novel turns back on itself and becomes a maze without an exit.

Buckler's next two books, *Ox Bells and Fireflies: A Memoir* and *Nova Scotia: Window on the Sea*, are essentially lyrical impressions of rural areas of Nova Scotia written in the form of poetic prose sketches. If David Canaan had been able to write the novel inside of him at the end of *The Mountain and the Valley*, it would have been *Ox Bells and Fireflies*. In fact both of the books begin with dreams and the death of a neighbour. Both books investigate the same phenomena: memory, community, time, death, and (by implication) art. Both books are richly laden with images which blend to form similes, metaphors, symbols, personification, and, consequently, a Zen-like concentration on detail. The prose is full of onomatopoeic verbs, phonetic intensives, alliterations, catalogues, and abstract words linked to concrete images to form startling conceits. As the narrator notes, from the artist's perspective through his "shaft of clarity," as it is called in *The Mountain and the Valley* (pp. 13, 297), everything can be seen in its own light:

> Light, finding things, draws their shadows from them slantwise on the ground, then gives them light. The tin pails shine. Diamonds are discovered in the pebbles on the road, emeralds in the branch tips of the firs, rubies in the idol eyes of roosters, ebony in the black horse's glistening flank. Dandelions dazzle themselves with yellow. Shingles glow gray, with fatherly knowledge. Thistles sparkle with a family wit. Spider bridges, cantilevered as light as glances, twinkle between the plum twigs. Auntly hens shine brown on the glinting straw. Swallows shimmer, hills kindle, and the fields sheen themselves with resurrection and internal rhyme. . . . Kingfishers bright as rings draw perfect parabolas on the air and sing of them. Clocks brighten at the thought of company, the bread knife awakens, and plates become transitive. A hush of freshness walks on the air like Christ. (pp. 8–9)

The narrator shifts from first-person to second- and to third-person points of view, and this technique helps to abstract the personal and the concrete — to indicate the universal in the particular, to imply the macrocosm in the microcosm.

By choosing what he calls a "fictive memoir" form, which includes such things as sketches, anecdotes, folklore, local jokes, and caricature, Buckler is free to explore a large variety of themes without running up against the structural limitations he faced in *The Cruelest Month*. Instead, this novel (if it can be called that) is loosely organized around the development of the narrator as he grows from the age of ten, "when Time is young" (p. 3), through school, puberty, work, marriage, and parenthood, and then back to childhood memory again at the end (p. 293). Time is presented as both linear and cyclical in this arrangement of events. Death is a presence which defines time throughout the book, and it is associated with ox bells and crows. However, both death and time are ultimately defeated by memory and imagination which are associated with the lighting up of the dark by fireflies. As such, fireflies symbolize freedom (p. 302).

Mark, the narrator and the artist figure in this work, seems to divide the working of the imagination into two categories — "the mind" and "the heart." The "mind" can mislead or be overly sentimental but not the heart:

> The heart, far less misty-eyed than the mind, despite its senti-mental name, is a far sounder witness. Once in a while it leaps of its own accord — through the skin, through the flesh, through the bone — straight back to the pulse of another time, and takes all of you with it. You are not seeing this place again through the blurred telescope of the mind: you are standing right there. Not long enough to take it all down, but long enough to give memory a second chance. (p. 21)

The working of the heart furnishes what Buckler elsewhere calls "the author's ability to catch the essence of time, place and human equation."[75] His concept of the "heart" seems to carry with it the power of the imagination to focus or clarify experiences so that an essential truthfulness of feeling is perceived.

As his career develops, Buckler moves further away from the rhetorical nature of fiction and moves towards a poetic vision. This is not to say there are no rhetorical patterns in this work. The past and present are always compared, and the past is presented as a better time, partly because the narrator was young then, but also because values were rooted in the family and community then, and because he felt close to nature, experiencing a sense of wonder at the unfolding of all things and stoically accepting the outcome of that process. The "Norstead" (No More Place) of youth is gone. The marigolds of his youth, which "radiate from the center to form a perfect circle" (p. 11), have given way to the lilies of his current age, which always close up at night (p. 18). Death, loss, sorrow, and loneliness are always present in the book. Often they are parenthet-ical (especially at the beginning), but their presence is inevitable and pervasive:

> I see the hardwood hills blazing (though not yet haunted) with remembrance. Golden light plates the skin of everything.
> (Not yet is the skin of things seen through the naked viscera

beneath; the light itself not yet a skin of burning sadness that casts those invisible bars of shadow on the heart.) (p. 33)

Even the joy of artistic creativity is qualified in a passage reminiscent of the first two novels. As a child, Mark remembers playing with alphabet blocks and learning to form words:

> I think, glancingly, how strange it is that everything in the world could be spelled out with these twenty-six little pine blocks. To chance on small wonders like that makes a fine sparkle in the blood.
> (Not yet the compulsion to think hard. Not yet the discovery that too much thought about things stirs them up, until they dismay you with their infinite clamor.) (p. 37)

Much like *Ox Bells and Fireflies*, *Nova Scotia: Window on the Sea* is a eulogy for Buckler's province, except that here the emphasis is more on the present than on the past. Because it is meant to accompany Hans Weber's photographs, Buckler has developed his aphoristic, anecdotal style to a pitch that resembles free verse. Even in the short story "Man and Snowman," the prose lines resemble photo captions. The experience of reading the text is similar to that of watching a slide show or a film of shifting scenes accompanied by snatches of dialogue. The catalogues of details seen close-up, the proliferation of adjectives, adverbs, similes, metaphors, sensory images, balanced opposites, and all the other familiar techniques of Buckler's style are pushed to their limits. The results are necessarily uneven, because many risks have to be taken in this kind of writing, but on the whole, the prose-poetry can be savoured and enjoyed again and again. A representative example from the text sums up in its last line Buckler's expectations for his own art:

> They are not giants or heroes in any way (they'd laugh if you told them they were) — but their essences are richer than most. And what any account of them must recurrently come back to is the constant interplay of their senses with what is everlastingly intrinsic and near; until finally they come as if to have a common bloodstream with it. A current that puts them in the presence, at least, of all the vastnesses of implication in each particle (each a universe) that surrounds them. This, if not in their head, is in

their bones, in instance after instance.

The crowing of the rooster is thus shorthand for all the trumpets of Morning.

The blackening of the night-struck brook is all sorcery.

The smell of the auger shavings all willingness.

The clench of ice upon itself all strength.

The clench of rocks upon themselves all fortitude.

The touch of firewood the key to satisfaction.

The taste of ruby-red beet wine all expectation.

The fern-shaped patterns the frost draws with its diamond on the moonlit pane all grace.

The chaliced lichen on the stone all courage.

Some snows, the way they lie, hinting all gain.

Some snows, the way they lie, all loss.

Some hills all Easters, some hills all judgments.

Whatever flaw is just missing in the perfect flower paradoxically all love.

Some sundowns (striking their endless and perfect sets from second to second) all hope; some all defeat.

Shadows that can't be held, distances of field that yield no answer to the heart's vain questions, shores that watch the gulls fly out of sight — all yearning.

Heads of ripened wheat (and wild cherry blossoms that extol the air) all joy.

The funeral hush in the spokes of the motionless wheel that the snow sifts through saying more about Death than the dead.

The spiral marking on the snail's snug house infinity . . . .[78]

It is interesting to note in this context that the figure of old Ellen from *The Mountain and the Valley* (here called Esther) returns in this work. She is still hooking a rug from fragments of family members' clothes, and her last words are that an old woman knows "that 'yes' is more than 'no' . . ." (p. 108).

Failing health slowed down Buckler's work considerably. His eyesight was poor, so he wrote very little. *Whirligig*, a collection of humourous essays and verses written over the years, is his only work published after 1974. This book displays in distilled form the wit and gentle mockery that is so carefully controlled in the five serious books. Buckler's eye for irony, hypocrisy, and sham, his occasional whoop into sheer nonsense, his distaste for the superficial and the urbane, and his straightforward sexuality earned the book the Stephen Leacock Award.

Claude Bissell, in his tribute to Buckler in 1982, mentioned that only the natural reticence of the local people prevented them from showing their affection towards Buckler and their pride in his work. Nova Scotians have every right to laud a man who was so much a part of his region. He spent his life connecting it with the rest of us, while in the process asserting its timelessness. In *Nova Scotia: Window on the Sea*, Buckler is no doubt talking about himself:

> Nova Scotia has no linear equalities within itself, but (taking the sea as base) it forms an isosceles triangle with the man who loves it; welding him, where their equal sides converge, to the universals. And though itself the least given to hyperbole, of nowhere can it be said with more truth that here is where the heart meets its match in every sense of the word. (p. 112)

NOTES

[1] Ernest Buckler, *Ox Bells and Fireflies: A Memoir*, introd. Alan R. Young, New Canadian Library, No. 99 (Toronto: McClelland and Stewart, 1974), pp. 3–78. All further references to this work appear in the text.

[2] Ernest Buckler, "Last Stop before Paradise," *Maclean's*, 1 June 1949, pp. 22–23, 49; "School and Me," *Maclean's*, 1 Sept. 1949, pp. 30, 44, 47–48; and "A Little Flag for Mother," *Farm Journal*, 87 (May 1963), 69–70.

[3] Ernest Buckler, quoted in "The Winners of the *Maclean's* Fiction Contest," *Maclean's*, 1 Jan. 1949, p. 3.

[4] Ernest Buckler, "Others Support Compulsory P.T.," *Dalhousie Gazette*, 10 Feb. 1928, p. 3; "The Chase," *Dalhousie Gazette*, 18 Jan. 1929, p. 2; "What Price Freedom?" *Dalhousie Gazette*, 15 Feb. 1929, p. 2; "Why?" *Dalhousie Gazette*, 22 Feb. 1929, p. 2; "Music," *Dalhousie Gazette*, 15 March 1929, p. 2; "Visions," *Dalhousie Gazette*, 15 March 1929, p. 2; and "Thought," *Dalhousie Gazette*, 22 March 1929, p. 2.

[5] Handwritten versions of these essays are part of the Ernest Buckler Manuscript Collection, Thomas Fisher Rare Book Library, University of Toronto.

[6] Ernest Buckler, "The Best Place To Be," *Graduate* [University of Toronto], 4, No. 3 (1977), 32–33.

[7] Ernest Buckler, "No Second Cup," *The Trinity Review*, 46 (Dec. 1933), 74–76; and "Always Old Ending," *The Trinity Review*, 46 (June-July 1934), 246–49, and 46 (Oct. 1934), 16–21.

[8] Arnold Gingrich, *Nothing but People: The Early Days at Esquire: A Personal History* (New York: Crown, 1971), p. 253.

[9] Ernest Buckler, "Notable Spring Fiction," rev. of *They Wanted to Live*, by Cecil Roberts, *New York Herald Tribune Book Review*, 2 April 1939, p. 16. A notation on the author's copy of this review in the Ernest Buckler Manuscript Collection reads: "My first paid for article."

[10] Ernest Buckler, "One Quiet Afternoon," *Esquire*, April 1940, pp. 70, 199–201. For a complete listing of Buckler's published stories, see John Orange, "Ernest Buckler: An Annotated Bibliography," in *The Annotated Bibliography of Canada's Major Authors*, ed. Robert Lecker and Jack David, III (Downsview, Ont.: ECW, 1981), 18–21.

[11] For a listing of Buckler's radio plays broadcast on CBC, see Orange, "Ernest Buckler: An Annotated Bibliography," pp. 27–28.

[12] Ernest Buckler, "The Quarrel," *Maclean's*, 15 Jan. 1949, pp. 5–6, 26–27; rpt. in *Chatelaine*, July 1959, pp. 65–68; rpt. in *Maclean's Canada*, ed. Leslie F. Hannon (Toronto: McClelland and Stewart, 1960), pp. 146–51; rpt. in *The Rebellion of Young David and Other Stories*, ed. Robert D. Chambers (Toronto: McClelland and Stewart, 1975), pp. 41–53.

[13] Ernest Buckler, "Anything Can Happen at Christmas," *Chatelaine*, Dec. 1957, pp. 66–68; and "The Dream and the Triumph," *Chatelaine*, Nov. 1956, pp. 12, 33–36, 38, 40–44; rpt. in *The Rebellion of David and Other Stories*, pp. 67–80.

[14] For a short history of the publication of the novel, see Gregory M. Cook, Introd., *Ernest Buckler*, ed. Gregory M. Cook, Critical Views on Canadian Writers, No. 7 (Toronto: McGraw-Hill Ryerson, 1972), pp. 4–5. For a record of dramatic adaptations of this novel for broadcast on CBC, see Orange, "Ernest Buckler: An Annotated Bibliography," pp. 46–47.

[15] Quoted in Claude Bissell, *Ernest Buckler Remembered* (Toronto: Univ. of Toronto Press, 1985), p. 139.

[16] See, for example, Ernest Buckler, "Thinks Dos Passos Opaque," *Esquire*, March 1937, p. 178. For a complete listing of Buckler's letters published in *Esquire*, see Orange, "Ernest Buckler: An Annotated Bibliography," p. 27.

[17] Dorothy Van Ghent, *The English Novel: Form and Function* (New York: Holt, Rinehart and Winston, 1953), p. 264.

[18] For a list of reviews and notices of this novel in American newspapers and journals, see Gregory M. Cook, "Ernest Buckler: His Creed and Craft," M.A. Thesis Acadia 1967, pp. 326–31. Cook lists 73 reviews and notices.

[19] See, for example, William Arthur Deacon, "Every Little Movement Has a

Meaning All Its Own," rev. of *The Mountain and the Valley*, *The Globe and Mail*, 29 Nov. 1952, p. 13; rpt. in *Ernest Buckler*, ed. Gregory M. Cook, pp. 29–31. See also Katherine Douglas, rev. of *The Mountain and the Valley*, *The Dalhousie Review*, 32 (Winter 1953), iii, v; rpt. in *Ernest Buckler*, ed. Gregory M. Cook, pp. 38–40.

[20] See, for example, Edmund Fuller, rev. of *The Mountain and the Valley*, *Chicago Sunday Tribune*, 26 Oct. 1952, p. 2; Stuart Keate, "Good Earth, Good People," rev. of *The Mountain and the Valley*, *New York Times Book Review*, 26 Oct. 1952, p. 5; rpt. in *Ernest Buckler*, ed. Gregory M. Cook, pp. 28–29.

[21] See, for example, William Arthur Deacon, p. 13.

[22] See, for example, Katharine Douglas, pp. iii, v.

[23] Warren Tallman, "Wolf in the Snow: Part One: Four Windows onto Landscapes," *Canadian Literature*, No. 5 (Summer 1960), pp. 7–20; and "Wolf in the Snow: Part Two: The House Repossessed," *Canadian Literature*, No. 6 (Autumn 1960), pp. 41–48.

[24] R.E. Watters, "*The Mountain and the Valley*," in *Ernest Buckler*, ed. Gregory M. Cook, pp. 41–48. This paper was first delivered as a lecture in 1954 at Victoria, British Columbia, and again in 1955 at Nanaimo, British Columbia. See also R.E. Watters, "Unknown Literature," *Saturday Night*, 17 Sept. 1955, pp. 31–33, 35–36; rpt. in *Ernest Buckler*, ed. Gregory M. Cook, pp. 49–54.

[25] See, for example, Anne Montagnes, "Buckler Encore No Classic," rev. of *The Cruelest Month*, *The Globe Magazine* [Toronto], 18 Jan. 1964, p. 15. See also Robert Harlow, "Sound and Fury," rev. of *The Cruelest Month*, *Canadian Literature*, No. 19 (Winter 1964), pp. 58–59; rpt. in *Ernest Buckler*, ed. Gregory M. Cook, pp. 86–88.

[26] Claude Bissell, rev. of *The Cruelest Month*, *Dalhousie Review*, 43 (Winter 1963–64), 566–69; rpt. in *Ernest Buckler*, ed. Gregory M. Cook, pp. 82–86. R.G. Baldwin, rev. of *The Cruelest Month*, *Queen's Quarterly*, 71 (Summer 1964), 277; excerpt rpt. in *Ernest Buckler*, ed. Gregory M. Cook, 91–92. Dave Godfrey, "Buckler and Allen," rev. of *The Cruelest Month*, by Ernest Buckler, and *The High White Forest*, by Ralph Allen, *The Tamarack Review*, No. 36 (Summer 1965), pp. 82–86.

[27] D.O. Spettigue, "The Way It Was," *Canadian Literature*, No. 32 (Spring 1967), pp. 46–56; rpt. in *The Canadian Novel in the Twentieth Century: Essays from* Canadian Literature, ed. George Woodcock, New Canadian Library, No. 115 (Toronto: McClelland and Stewart, 1975), pp. 145–60; rpt. in *Ernest Buckler*, ed. Gregory M. Cook, pp. 95–115.

[28] See, for example, Gregory M. Cook, rev. of *Ox Bells and Fireflies: A Memoir*, *Dalhousie Review*, 48 (Autumn 1968), 413–14; rpt. in *Ernest Buckler*, ed. Gregory M. Cook, pp. 121–24. See also D.O. Spettigue, rev. of *Ox Bells and*

Fireflies: A Memoir, Quarry, 18, No. 4 (Summer 1969), 53–54; rpt. in *Ernest Buckler,* ed. Gregory M. Cook, pp. 129–31.

²⁹ Claude Bissell, "A Masterly Return to Innocence and Wonder," rev. of *Ox Bells and Fireflies: A Memoir, The Globe and Mail,* 9 Nov. 1968, p. 27; rpt. in *Ernest Buckler,* ed. Gregory M. Cook, pp. 119–21.

³⁰ Ian A. Atkinson, *"The Mountain and the Valley:* A Study in Canadian Fiction," M.A. Thesis Guelph 1969; rpt. (in part) "Imagery and Symbolism" in *Ernest Buckler,* ed. Gregory M. Cook, pp. 132–36.

³¹ Bernita H. Harris, "A Comparison of the Symbolism and Imagery of Ernest Buckler's *The Cruelest Month* with T.S. Eliot's *The Waste Land,*' " M.A. Thesis New Brunswick 1969.

³² John C. Orange, "Ernest Buckler: The Masks of the Artist," Phil. M. Thesis Toronto 1970; rpt. (in part) "In *Oxbells and Fireflies*" in *Ernest Buckler,* ed. Gregory M. Cook, pp. 137–42.

³³ Richard Reichart, *"The Mountain and the Valley,* Reconsidered," M.A. Thesis New Brunswick 1971; Einhard F.H. Kluge, "The Artist in Modern Canadian Fiction," M.A. Thesis Alberta 1972; Jean Huntley Willmott, "A Writer's Crucible: The Short Stories of Ernest Buckler," M.A. Thesis Sir George Williams 1974; Rhonda Hustler, "Irony and Isolation in the Fiction of Ernest Buckler," Diss. McMaster 1985.

³⁴ William French, "Ernest Buckler: A Literary Giant Scorned?" *The Globe and Mail,* 24 June 1972, p. 23.

³⁵ See, for example, Issac Bickerstaff, "Running Blue Noses," rev. of *Nova Scotia: Window on the Sea, Books in Canada,* July–Sept. 1973, p. 35. See also William French, "In Buckler Country, Neighbour Is a Holy Word," rev. of *Nova Scotia: Window on the Sea, The Globe and Mail,* 2 June 1973, p. 36.

³⁶ Alan R. Young, "The Pastoral Vision of Ernest Buckler in *The Mountain and the Valley,*" *Dalhousie Review,* 53 (Summer 1973), 219–26.

³⁷ Clara Thomas, "New England Romanticism and Canadian Fiction," *Journal of Canadian Fiction,* 2, No. 4 (Fall 1973), 850.

³⁸ Eileen Sarkan, *"The Mountain and the Valley:* The Infinite Language of Human Relations," *Revue de l'Université d'Ottawa,* 44 (July–Sept. 1974), 354–61.

³⁹ J.M. Kertzer, "The Past Recaptured," *Canadian Literature,* No. 65 (Summer 1975), pp. 74–85.

⁴⁰ Douglas Barbour, "David Canaan: The Failing Heart," *Studies in Canadian Literature,* 1 (Winter 1976), 64–75.

⁴¹ Alan R. Young, "The Genesis of Ernest Buckler's *The Mountain and the Valley,*" *Journal of Canadian Fiction,* No. 16 (1976), pp. 89–96; "A Note on Douglas Barbour's 'David Canaan: The Failing Heart' (*SCL,* Winter 1976),"

Studies in Canadian Literature, 1 (Summer 1976), 244–46; and *Ernest Buckler*, New Canadian Library, Canadian Writers, No. 15 (Toronto: McClelland and Stewart, 1976), pp. 29–37.

[42] Bruce F. MacDonald, "Word-Shapes, Time and the Theme of Isolation in *The Mountain and the Valley*," *Studies in Canadian Literature*, 1 (Summer 1976), 194–208; Robert D. Chambers, "Notes on Regionalism in Modern Canadian Fiction," *Journal of Canadian Studies*, 11, No. 2 (May 1976), 27–34; Andrew Thompson Seaman, "Fiction in Atlantic Canada," *Canadian Literature*, Nos. 68–69 (Spring–Summer 1976), pp. 26–39; and Sister A.M. Westwater, "Teufelsdrock Is Alive and Doing Well in Nova Scotia: Carlylean Strains in *The Mountain and the Valley*," *Dalhousie Review*, 56 (Summer 1976), 291–98.

[43] Gerald Noonan, "Egoism and Style in *The Mountain and the Valley*," *The Marco Polo Papers One: Atlantic Provinces Literature Colloquium, Colloque Littérraire Des Provinces Atlantiques*, ed. Kenneth MacKinnon (Saint John: Atlantic Canada Institute, 1977), pp. 68–78; and D.J. Dooley, "Style and Communication in *The Mountain and the Valley*," *Dalhousie Review*, 57 (Winter 1977–78), 671–83; rev. and rpt. as "*The Mountain and the Valley*: The Uncreated Word," in his *Moral Vision in the Canadian Novel* (Toronto: Clarke, Irwin, 1979), pp. 49–59.

[44] Laurence Ricou, "David Canaan and Buckler's Style in *The Mountain and the Valley, Dalhousie Review*, 57 (Winter 1977–78), 684–96.

[45] Sarah Dyck, "In Search of a Poet: Buckler and Pasternak," *Germano-Slavica: A Canadian Journal of Germanic and Slavic Comparative Studies*, 2 (Spring 1978), 325–26.

[46] Marilyn Chapman, "The Progress of David's Imagination," *Studies in Canadian Literature*, 3 (Summer 1978), 186–98; Robert J. Stewart, "Buckler's David Canaan and Joyce's Stephen Dedalus," *Canadian Notes & Queries*, No. 23 (June 1979), pp. 5–6; and L.M. Doerksen, "*The Mountain and the Valley*: An Evaluation," *World Literature Written in English*, 19, No. 1 (Spring 1980), 45–56.

[47] John Orange, "Ernest Buckler," in *Profiles in Canadian Literature*, ed. Jeffrey M. Heath (Toronto: Dundurn, 1980), pp. 17-24.

[48] Andrew Thompson Seaman, "Visions of Fulfillment in Ernest Buckler and Charles Bruce," *Essays on Canadian Writing*, No. 31 (Summer 1985), pp. 173, 159.

[49] Lawrence Mathews, "Hacking at the Parsnips: *The Mountain and the Valley* and the Critics," in *The Bumper Book*, ed. John Metcalf (Toronto: ECW, 1986), p. 198.

[50] See, for example, D.O. Spettigue, rev. of *The Rebellion of Young David and Other Stories, Queen's Quarterly*, 82 (Winter 1975), 657–59. See also Miriam Waddington, "Ernest's Importance of Being," rev. of *The Rebellion of Young David and Other Stories, Books in Canada*, July 1975, pp. 6–7.

[51] Alan R. Young, Introd., *The Cruelest Month*, by Ernest Buckler, New Canadian Library, No. 139 (Toronto: McClelland and Stewart, 1977), pp. vii–xiii; and *Ernest Buckler*, pp. 37–44.

[52] Robert D. Chambers, *Sinclair Ross and Ernest Buckler*, Studies in Canadian Literature (Toronto: Copp Clark, 1975; Montreal: McGill-Queen's Univ. Press, 1975), pp. 84–92.

[53] Alan R. Young, Introd., *Ox Bells and Fireflies: A Memoir*, by Ernest Buckler, New Canadian Library, No. 99 (Toronto: McClelland and Stewart, 1974), pp. xi–xvi; Chambers, *Sinclair Ross and Ernest Buckler*, pp. 53–102, 107–09; and Orange, "On *Oxbells and Fireflies*," pp. 137–42.

[54] See, for example, William French, "Buckler in an Unbuttoned Mood Plays a Little Ragtime, But Not Always Well," rev. of *Whirligig*, *The Globe and Mail*, 15 Oct. 1977, p. 45. See also Jon Kertzer, "Windmills and Turnpikes," rev. of *Whirligig*, *The Canadian Forum*, Dec.–Jan. 1977–78, p. 39.

[55] See, respectively, Ernest Buckler, "No Second Cup"; "Always Old Ending"; and "What Is Coronet?" *Coronet*, 25 Jan. 1938, pp. 191–94.

[56] Ernest Buckler, "How To Write an Artistic Novel," *Saturday Night*, 3 May 1941, p. 25.

[57] Ernest Buckler, "Casting Suspicion on an Adage," *Saturday Night*, 14 Dec. 1940, p. 41.

[58] See, for example, Spettigue, "The Way it Was," in *Ernest Buckler*, ed. Gregory M. Cook, pp. 97–99; Young, *Ernest Buckler*, pp. 21–27; and Chambers, *Sinclair Ross and Ernest Buckler*, pp. 55–65.

[59] Ernest Buckler Manuscript Collection.

[60] Ernest Buckler, *The Rebellion of Young David and Other Stories*, pp. 31–32. All further references to this work (*RYD*) appear in the text.

[61] Ernest Buckler, Letter to Dudley H. Cloud, 24 March 1951, Buckler Manuscript Collection.

[62] Ernest Buckler, Letter to Dudley H. Cloud, 15 May 1951, Buckler Manuscript Collection.

[63] Ernest Buckler, *The Mountain and the Valley*, introd. Claude Bissell, New Canadian Library, No. 23 (Toronto: McClelland and Stewart, 1961), pp. 13–14. All further references to this work (*MV*) appear in the text.

[64] J.A. Wainwright, "Fern Hill Revisited: Isolation and Death in *The Mountain and the Valley*," *Studies in Canadian Literature*, 7, No. 1 (1982), 65.

[65] For a psychoanalytical analysis of the relationship between these twins, see John Moss, *Sex and Violence in the Canadian Novel: The Ancestral Present* (Toronto: McClelland and Stewart, 1977), pp. 90–94.

[66] For a study of this side of David's personality, see Barbour, "David Canaan: The Failing Heart."

[67] For a study of time in this novel, see MacDonald, "Word-Shapes, Time and the Theme of Isolation in *The Mountain and the Valley*."

[68] Cook, Introd., *Ernest Buckler*, p. 3; and Chambers, *Sinclair Ross and Ernest Buckler*, pp. 84, 86.

[69] Ernest Buckler, "My Second Book," in *Ernest Buckler*, ed. Gregory M. Cook, p. 81.

[70] Buckler, "My Second Book," p. 81.

[71] Letter received from Ernest Buckler, 11 Feb. 1970.

[72] Ernest Buckler, *The Cruelest Month*, introd. Alan R. Young, New Canadian Library, No. 139 (Toronto: McClelland and Stewart, 1977), p. 166. All further references to this work (*CM*) appear in the text.

[73] Ernest Buckler, Letter to John Rackliffe, 14 Oct. 1961, Buckler Manuscript Collection.

[74] Buckler, "My Second Book," pp. 80–81.

[75] Young, *Ernest Buckler*, pp. 42–43.

[76] Ernest Buckler, quoted in Donald Cameron, "Ernest Buckler," in *Conversations with Canadian Novelists 1* (Toronto: Macmillan, 1973), p. 9.

[77] Ernest Buckler, "My Third Book," in *Ernest Buckler*, ed. Gregory M. Cook, p. 118.

[78] Ernest Buckler and Hans Weber, *Nova Scotia: Window on the Sea* (Toronto: McClelland and Stewart, 1973), pp. 109–10. All further references to this work appear in the text.

[79] William French, "A Literary Feat at Harbourfront," *The Globe and Mail*, 5 Oct. 1982, p. 15.

SELECTED BIBLIOGRAPHY

Primary Sources

Books and Manuscripts

The Mountain and the Valley. New York: Henry Holt, 1952.

————. Toronto: Clarke, Irwin, 1952.

————. New York: New American Library, 1954.

————. Introd. Claude Bissell. New Canadian Library, No. 23. Toronto: McClelland and Stewart, 1961.

The Cruelest Month. Toronto: McClelland and Stewart, 1963.

————. Introd. Alan R. Young, New Canadian Library, No. 139. Toronto: McClelland and Stewart, 1977.

The Rebellion of Young David and Other Stories. Ed. Robert Chambers. Toronto: McClelland and Stewart, 1975.

Ox Bells and Fireflies: A Memoir. New York: Knopf, 1968. Drawings by Walter Richards.

————. Toronto: McClelland and Stewart, 1968.

————. Introd. Alan R. Young. New Canadian Library, No. 99. Toronto: McClelland and Stewart, 1974.

Whirligig. Introd. Claude Bissell. Toronto: McClelland and Stewart, 1977.

Nova Scotia: Window on the Sea. Toronto: McClelland and Stewart, 1973. Photographs by Hans Weber.

Buckler Manuscript Collection, Thomas Fisher Rare Book Library, University of Toronto, Toronto, Ontario.

Secondary Sources

Books

Bissell, Claude. *Ernest Buckler Remembered*. Toronto: Univ. of Toronto Press, 1989.

Cook, Gregory M., ed. *Ernest Buckler*. Critical Views on Canadian Writers, No. 7. Toronto: McGraw-Hill Ryerson, 1972.

Young, Alan R. *Ernest Buckler*. New Canadian Library, Canadian Writers, No. 15. Toronto: McClelland and Stewart, 1976.

Articles, Sections of Books, and Theses

Atkinson, Ian A. "*The Mountain and the Valley*: A Study in Canadian Fiction." M.A. Thesis Guelph 1969.

Barbour, Douglas. "David Canaan: The Failing Heart." *Studies in Canadian Literature*, 1 (Winter 1976), 64–75.

———. "The Critic Criticized: A Reply to Bruce MacDonald." *Studies in Canadian Literature*, 2 (Winter 1977), 127–28.

Bickerstaff, Isaac. "Friends, S.O.B.'s and Critics." *Books in Canada*, Jan.–Feb. 1973, pp. 20–21, 23.

Cameron, Donald. "Letter from Halifax." *Canadian Literature*, No. 40 (Spring 1969), pp. 55–60.

———. "Ernest Buckler: A Conversation with an Irritated Oyster." *The Mysterious East*, Jan. 1970, pp. 21–24. Rpt. "Don Cameron Interviews Ernest Buckler." In *Quill & Quire*, July 1972, pp. 5, 8. Rpt. in *Conversations with Canadian Novelists — 1*. Toronto: Macmillan, 1973, pp. 3–11.

Chambers, Robert D. *Sinclair Ross and Ernest Buckler*. Studies in Canadian Literature. Toronto: Copp Clark; Montreal: McGill-Queen's Univ. Press, 1975, pp. 1–5, 53–102, 105–07.

———. "Notes on Regionalism in Modern Canadian Fiction." *Journal of Canadian Studies*, 11, No. 2 (May 1976), 27–34.

Chapman, Marilyn. "The Progress of David's Imagination." *Studies in Canadian Literature*, 3 (Summer 1978), 186–98.

Cook, Gregory M. "Ernest Buckler: His Creed and Craft." M.A. Thesis Acadia 1967.

Dawson, Anthony B. "Coming of Age in Canada." *Mosaic*, 11, No. 3 (Spring 1978), 47–62.

Doerksen, L.M. *"The Mountain and The Valley*: An Evaluation." *World Literature Written in English*, 19, No. 1 (Spring 1980), 45–56.

Dooley, D.J. "Style and Communication in *The Mountain and the Valley*." *The Dalhousie Review*, 57 (Winter 1977–78), 671–83. Rpt. (rev. "*The Mountain and the Valley*: The Uncreated Word"). In *Moral Vision in the Canadian Novel*. By D.J. Dooley. Toronto: Clarke, Irwin, 1979, pp. 49–59.

Dyck, Sarah. "In Search of a Poet: Buckler and Pasternak." *Germano-Slavica: A Canadian Journal of Germanic and Slavic Comparative Studies*, 2 (Spring 1978), 325–36.

French, William. "Ernest Buckler: A Literary Giant Scorned?". *The Globe and Mail*, 24 June 1972, p. 23.

Gingrich, Arnold. "Promoting Mr. Ernest Redmond Buckler." *Esquire*, Jan. 1939, pp. 5, 10.

———. "Publisher's Page." *Esquire*, Oct. 1958, p. 6.

Harris, Bernita H. "A Comparison of the Symbolism and Imagery of Ernest Buckler's *The Cruelest Month* with T.S. Eliot's 'The Waste Land.' " M.A. Thesis New Brunswick 1969.

Jones, D.G. *Butterfly on Rock: A Study of Themes and Images in Canadian Literature*. Toronto: Univ. of Toronto Press, 1970, pp. 11, 23–25, 26, 27, 37.

———. "Myth, Frye and Canadian Writers." *Canadian Literature*, No. 55 (Winter 1973), pp. 7–22.

Kertzer, J.M. "The Past Recaptured." *Canadian Literature*, No. 65 (Summer 1975), pp. 74–85.

Kluge, Einhard F.H. "The Artist in Modern Canadian Fiction." M.A. Thesis Alberta 1972, pp. 52–66.

Lyon, John E. "The Challenge of Nihilism: Problems of the Artist in the Works of Ernest Buckler." M.A. Thesis Waterloo 1975.

MacDonald, Bruce F. "Word-Shapes, Time and the Theme of Isolation in *The Mountain and the Valley*." *Studies in Canadian Literature*, 1 (Summer 1976), 194–209.

Moss, John. *Patterns of Isolation in English-Canadian Fiction*. Toronto: McClelland and Stewart, 1974, pp. 9, 106, 110, 118, 122, 197, 225–26, 228, 229, 237.

———. *Sex and Violence in the Canadian Novel: The Ancestral Present*. Toronto: McClelland and Stewart, 1977, pp. 36, 48, 55, 84, 87, 90–95, 102, 189, 308.

Noonan, Gerald. "Egoism and Style in *The Mountain and the Valley*." *The Marco Polo Papers One: Atlantic Provinces Literature Colloquium, Colloque*

Littéraire Des Provinces Atlantiques. Ed. Kenneth MacKinnon. Saint John: Atlantic Canada Institute, 1977, pp. 68–78.

Orange, John C. "Ernest Buckler: The Masks of the Artist." Phil.M. Thesis Toronto 1970.

——. "Ernest Buckler." In *Profiles in Canadian Literature.* Vol. II. Ed. Jeffrey M. Heath. Toronto: Dundurn, 1980, pp. 17–24.

——. "Ernest Buckler: An Annotated Bibliography." *The Annotated Bibliography of Canada's Major Authors,* Vol. 3. Ed. Robert Lecker and Jack David. Downsview, Ont.: ECW, 1982, pp. 13–56.

Pacey, Desmond. *Creative Writing in Canada: A Short History of English-Canadian Literature.* Toronto: Ryerson, 1952, pp. 252, 256, 266–67.

Reichert, Richard. "*The Mountain and the Valley,* Reconsidered." M.A. Thesis New Brunswick 1971.

Ricou, Laurence. "David Canaan and Buckler's Style in *The Mountain and the Valley.*" *The Dalhousie Review,* 57 (Winter 1977–78), 684–96.

Savage, David. "Not Survival but Responsibility." *The Dalhousie Review,* 55 (Summer 1975), 272–79.

Sarkar, Eilen. "*The Mountain and the Valley:* The Infinite Language of Human Relations." *Revue de l'Université d'Ottawa,* 44 (July–Sept. 1974), 354–61.

Seaman, Andrew Thompson, "Fiction in Atlantic Canada." *Canadian Literature,* Nos. 68–69 (Spring–Summer 1976), pp. 26–39.

Spettigue, D.O. "The Way It Was." *Canadian Literature,* No. 32 (Spring 1967), pp. 40–56. Rpt. in *The Canadian Novel in the Twentieth Century: Essays from* Canadian Literature. Ed. George Woodcock. New Canadian Library, No. 115. Toronto: McClelland and Stewart, 1975, pp. 145–60.

Stewart, Robert J. "Buckler's David Canaan and Joyce's Stephen Dedalus." *Canadian Notes & Queries,* No. 23 (June 1979), pp. 5–6.

Tallman, Warren. "Wolf in the Snow. Part One: Four Windows onto Landscapes." *Canadian Literature,* No. 5 (Sept. 1960), pp. 7–20, and No. 6 (Autumn 1960), pp. 41–48. Rpt. in *A Choice of Critics: Selections from* Canadian Literature *1964–74.* Ed. George Woodcock. Toronto: Oxford Univ. Press, 1966, pp. 53–76. Rpt. in *Contexts of Canadian Criticism: A Collection of Critical Essays.* Ed. Eli Mandel. Patterns of Literary Criticism, No. 9. Chicago: Univ. of Chicago Press, 1971, pp. 232–53. Rpt. in *Ernest Buckler.* Ed. Gregory M. Cook. Critical Views on Canadian Writers, No. 7. Toronto: McGraw-Hill Ryerson, 1972, pp. 55–79. Rpt. in *Open Letter,* 3rd Ser., No. 6 (Fall 1977), 131–49.

Thomas, Clara. "New England Romanticism and Canadian Fiction." *Journal of Canadian Fiction,* 2, No. 4 (Fall 1973), 80–86.

Walker, William Ronald. "The Theme of the Artist in the Novels of Ernest Buckler." M.A. Thesis Windsor 1972.

Watters, R.E. "Unknown Literature." *Saturday Night*, 17 Sept. 1955, pp. 31–33, 35–36.

Wainwright, J.A. "Fern Hill Revisited: Isolation and Death in *The Mountain and the Valley*." *Studies in Canadian Literature*, 7, No. 1 (1982), 63–89.

Westwater, Sister A.M. "Teufelsdrock Is Alive and Doing Well in Nova Scotia: Carlylean Strains in *The Mountain and the Valley*." *The Dalhousie Review*, 56 (Summer 1976), 291–98.

Willmott, Jean Huntley. "A Writer's Crucible: The Short Stories of Ernest Buckler." M.A. Thesis Sir George Williams 1974.

Young, Alan R. "The Pastoral Vision of Ernest Buckler in *The Mountain and the Valley*." *The Dalhousie Review*, 53 (Summer 1973), 219–26.

————. "The Genesis of Ernest Buckler's *The Mountain and the Valley*." *Journal of Canadian Fiction*, No. 16 (1976), pp. 89–96.

————. "A Note on Douglas Barbour's 'David Canaan: The Failing Heart' (*SCL*, Winter 1976)." *Studies in Canadian Literature*, 1 (Summer 1976), 244–46.

*Morley Callaghan
and His Works*

Morley Callaghan (1903–90)

GARY BOIRE

Biography

MORLEY EDWARD CALLAGHAN was born in Toronto on 22 February 1903; he grew up there in an ambience of literary and political awareness (both parents were active in liberal causes, read poetry to the family, and his father, Thomas, regularly contributed satirical verse to *The Telegram* and *The Moon*).[1] Callaghan was educated at Withrow Public School (1909–16), Riverdale Collegiate (1916–21), and St. Michael's College, University of Toronto (1921–25). In this last year he entered Osgoode Hall, where he stayed until 1928 when he was admitted to the Ontario Bar. Although in the late 1920s Callaghan viewed Toronto as something of a cultural wasteland, it was nonetheless the locale of his own formative experiences, the inspiration for and scene in many of his stories and novels, and the place of initial contact with international magazines and writers. Despite the prestige of Paris, which he visited in 1929, and the publishing convenience of the United States, where he lived briefly in 1930, Toronto was the home he accepted, when in 1952 he settled permanently in the neighbourhood of Rosedale.

Callaghan's early life might be viewed as a series of vocational and ideological flirtations which in turn moved towards an undivided and passionate devotion to writing fiction. Most significant for Callaghan amidst the usual middle-class tangle of primary and secondary education, summer jobs (selling magazines in the Ottawa Valley), athletics (baseball, boxing, and hockey), hobbies (debating), and so on, were three principal influences: his Torontonian background; his seminal experience during university as a part-time reporter for *The Daily Star*; and his early interest and study in law.

In many ways Toronto was Callaghan's own *fons et origo*. Edmund Wilson's 1960 description, "Morley Callaghan of Toronto," seems now paradoxical: odd, yet singularly apropos.[2] On one hand Callaghan was resolutely international, hostile to what he saw as misguided definitions based solely on nationality. He stated bluntly in *That Summer in Paris*, "[Toronto] was a very British city. I was intensely North American. . . . Physically, . . . I was wonderfully at home in my native city, and yet intellectually, spiritually, the part that had to do with my wanting to be a writer was utterly, but splendidly and happily, alien."[3] And yet as a writer Callaghan chose to remain "alien" in Pound's "Tomato, Can." Prideful, at times sentimental quotations abound; in 1958 he remarked to Robert Weaver of the war years, ". . . in those ten years, God forgive me, I began to take a great interest in Canada. I mean, I say this with tears in my eyes and on my knees, but I began to think this was my country — to look at it for whatever it is — and God help me it's my country — and I began to take a great interest in it."[4] Such an ambivalence characterized Callaghan's entire career. He was at once a world writer, a compeer of Tolstoy, Flaubert, or Anderson; but he was also a *Canadian* writer whose life and work must also be considered in specifically *Canadian* contexts.

The importance of Callaghan's early avocations, journalism and the law, cannot be over-emphasized. Both exerted artistic influence: stylistically the lean prose belied the journalism which in turn partly motivated his well-known assertion, "I'd be damned if the glory of literature was in the metaphor. . . . Tell the truth cleanly" (*TSP*, p. 20); thematically the novels returned continuously to the question of real justice, natural versus legalistic, personal versus institutional. Equally important, moreover, is the fact that both interests provided the young Callaghan with a liberal dose of experience, the chance to use his Canadian training to develop international contacts, and the opportunity to explore those necessary intellectual flirtations preparatory to a writing career.

Concerning his experience as a part-time reporter for *The Daily Star*, Callaghan remarked, "[I was] vaguely aware that I might be coming to a turning point in my life" (*TSP*, p. 17). While on staff at *The Daily Star*, for example, Callaghan not only honed his distinctive reportorial style, but faced the grim task of distilling human experience (much of it painful) into a verbal form for public perusal. He began writing his first stories around 1923, and in 1924 met the first of his important literary contacts, Ernest Hemingway, who showed Callaghan's stories to both writers and publishers in Paris. During his Osgoode years Callaghan continued to write (he began "An Autumn Penitent" in 1925 while articling under Joe Sedgewick), and in 1925 published his first story, "A Girl with Ambition," in *This Quarter*; with Art Kent in Toronto he opened the Viking Lending Library; he met Raymond Knister (one of the few Canadian writers who interested him); he began correspondence with Hemingway, Robert McAlmon, and Yvor Winters; and in both 1926 and 1928 he visited New York where he met American literati like Josephine Herbst and John Herrman, Nathan Asch, William Carlos Williams, Allen Tate, and Katherine Ann Porter. In this latter year Callaghan met Max Perkins of Scribner's who accepted for publication the first of his novels, *Strange Fugitive* (1928) and commissioned a subsequent collection of stories, *A Native Argosy* (1929). Also in 1928 Callaghan appeared for the first of fourteen consecutive times in Edward J. O'Brien's *The Best Short Stories*.

Following this initial breakthrough Callaghan established a publishing record impressive by any standard.[5] The 1930s, regarded by some critics as his most successful period, witnessed a spate of novels and stories; these include the early toyings with naturalism, *It's Never Over* (1930) and *A Broken Journey* (1932), the at-the-time risqué *No Man's Meat* (1931), privately printed by Edward W. Titus for his Black Manikin Press, the biblically titled triad, *Such Is My Beloved* (1934), *They Shall Inherit the Earth* (1935), and *More Joy in Heaven* (1937), as well as his second collection of stories, *Now That April's Here and Other Stories* (1936).

In 1939, depressed by recent events in Spain, political developments in Europe, and the certainty of world war, Callaghan entered what he has referred to as "the dark period of my life."[6] Fiction writing faltered. He wrote instead two plays, "Just Ask for George" and "Turn Again Home" (an adaptation of *They Shall Inherit the Earth*). Neither were staged until 1949 and 1950 respectively, under the titles *To Tell the Truth* and *Going Home*. Throughout the forties there appeared first sports and then editorial columns for E.P. Taylor's *New World Illustrated* (1940–48); there were only occasional published stories or essays.[7] In 1943 Callaghan turned to radio work with the CBC; from 1943 to 1947, he chaired the community series, "Of Things to Come" (later called "Citizen's Forum"); he then became a panel member for the quiz show, "Beat the Champs," and in 1950 he hosted the series, "Now I Ask You." Association with the CBC continued intermittently: through the 1950s Callaghan served as a panel member on the television series "Fighting Words"; in 1962 he narrated "A Tale of Three Cities" for *Camera Canada*. In 1963 he appeared for a literary discussion with Nathan Asch on *Quest* and in 1964 CBC Television presented a five-part serialization of *More Joy in Heaven*, directed by Ron Weyman. (This was later done over when Weyman re-made a two-hour feature film of the same novel.) The 1970s and 1980s saw Callaghan frequently on CBC Radio's *Anthology*, discussing (amongst others) such writers as Samuel Beckett and Gabriel García Márquez. In 1970 CBC Television produced four half-hour shows of Callaghan's short stories, "Very Special Shoes," "Rigmarole," "Father and Son," and "The Magic Hat." Finally in 1971, CBC Television presented an hour-long documentary, "The Life of Morley Callaghan" — an honourable gesture repeated in 1986 on CBC's *Lifetime*.

1948 saw a renaissance of sorts with the publication of two novels and the start of a third: *Luke Baldwin's Vow*, a novel for young readers based on a 1947 short story of the same name (later reprinted as "The Little Business Man" in *Morley Callaghan's Stories* [1959]); *The Varsity Story*, a fictional tale about the University of Toronto (a fund-raising gambit for the university); and *The Loved and The Lost* (1951). The subsequent three decades saw Callaghan experiment with both larger and more ambitious formats: the 1955 novella, "The Man with the Coat," was thoroughly recast in *The Many Colored Coat* (1960); and in 1961 there appeared the critically controversial *A Passion in Rome*. At wider intervals there followed the memoirs of 1929, *That Summer in Paris* (1963); a commentary on a book of John de Visser's Canadian photographs, *Winter* (1974); the amusing *roman à clef*, *A Fine and Private Place* (1975); a revised version of *Going Home, Season of the Witch* (1976); the mystical *Close to the Sun Again* (1977); and in 1978 a reprint of *No Man's Meat*, coupled with *The Enchanted Pimp*.

This latter text seemed to be something of an irresistible topic for Callaghan; he first began the story in 1963 under the working title of "Thumbs Down on Julien Jones." In 1973 he published a reworked excerpt in *Exile* as "The Meterman, Caliban, and Then Mr. Jones," and in 1974, CBC produced a film version entitled *And Then Mr. Jones*. In 1979 Callaghan published two further revised chapters of *The Enchanted Pimp* in *Exile*, this time as part of a projected new novella called *The Stepping Stone*. The most recent instalment was Callaghan's 1985 novel, *Our Lady of the Snows* — a book described on the dustjacket as "A new novel, suggested by the story *The Enchanted Pimp*"!

During all of this revision Callaghan had time to produce three further books: in 1983 he published *A Time for Judas* (a revisionist look at the crucifixion); in 1985 *The Lost and Found Stories of Morley Callaghan* (an anthology of stories left out of the 1959 collection); and in 1988 *A Wild Old Man on the Road* (a thinly disguised blending of Callaghan's interviews, earlier novels, and reminiscences).

Morley Callaghan died in Toronto on 26 August 1990, at the age of 87. At his death, he was at work on at least two projects: a book involving his early non-fiction about writers and writing, and a further collection of "lost and found" stories.

Despite the ebb and flow of Callaghan's critical reputation, his record did not go unrewarded. As well as having been nominated for the Nobel Prize in Literature, he received many awards, both honourary and highly remunerative. These included the Governor-General's Award for Fiction for *The Loved and The Lost* (1951); the *Maclean's* novel prize of $5000 for "The Man with the Coat" (1955); the "Celebrity of the Day" from Celebrities Services International, New York (1960); the Lorne Pierce Medal of the Royal Society of Canada in recognition of distinguished services to Canadian litera-ture (1960); the City Award of Merit, City of Toronto (1962); a D.Litt. from the University of Western Ontario (1965); an LL.D. from the University of Toronto (1966); an offer of the Medal of Service of the Order of Canada which he rejected in 1967 as a second-class honour inferior to the Companion medal earlier awarded to other writers (like Hugh MacLennan); the $15,000 Molson Prize and the $50,000 Royal Bank Award (1970); and in 1973, a D.Litt. from the University of Windsor. Late in 1982 Callaghan was awarded the full Companion Medal by a repentant Canadian government and in 1983 received the Booksellers' Award as Author of the Year for *A Time for Judas*.

Tradition and Milieu

It is a critical commonplace that every artist, to some degree, must come to terms with the awful spectre of influence. Influences — historical and contemporary, local and international — converge within the individual who may then either develop his art by engaging in a creative dialectic with these influences (either adapting or rejecting), or surrender conformingly to them, submitting to what he or she feels is superior perception. Callaghan states the case clearly in a 1958 interview with Robert Weaver:

CALLAGHAN . . . well, literature is a kind of muddied stream. As you grow older, you read more and more, and you get interested in the way other writers write, and you get interested in problems of writing, and you get interested in the way other writers see things. And in the course of time . . . this begins to make writing more difficult. You become aware of problems that never existed as problems before.

WEAVER You can't get the direct feeling of experience as easily?

CALLAGHAN That is true. Because the eyes of a hundred other writers are in your way. You have a tendency to pick up their glasses and put them on. (Weaver, pp. 4–5)

As Harold Bloom tersely remarks in *The Anxiety of Influence: A Theory of Poetry*, "Weaker talents idealize; figures of capable imagination appropriate for themselves."[8] Just how capable Morley Callaghan is remains a moot question. Admittedly he is well known for his motto, that artists must always "see the world with their own eyes" (Weaver, p. 7). But how well does he apply theory to practice? How original is he? How triumphantly does he confront his own precursors? Indeed, how important a writer is he and where does he belong in modern literary history?

Within Canadian contexts Callaghan is something of a monumental renegade. He has steadfastly refused to join the mainstreams of Canadian fiction (let alone the various nationalist movements of the past sixty years), and even today he has little affinity with the majority of Canadian writers. During his most prolific period in the late 1920s and 1930s, for example, when Canada was, in Desmond Pacey's words, a "virtual monopoly of romanticism,"[9] Callaghan countered with deceptively simple, ironic stories told in a crisp, neo-imagistic prose. Anticipating the more politicized writings of Patrick Anderson, Hugh MacLennan, and F.R. Scott, Callaghan introduced serious themes and ideas that seem today to have been more appropriate, more intellectually relevant to post-war Canadian society than the misty nostalgia of *Jalna*. As F.W. Watt, one of Callaghan's shrewdest critics, has argued, Callaghan's fiction is "a coherent, developing *oeuvre* in which leading ideas of the 'twenties, 'thirties, and 'forties are used in exploring individual and social life in this country and in shaping it into artistic patterns"[10] — leading ideas like the extent of scientific and economic determinism, the validity of a religious response to social problems, the feasibility of the Left, the desirability of a personalistic "love," and most recurrent of all, the moral role of the imagination in a society dominated by immoral concerns. This last in particular has dominated virtually the entire canon, underlying works as diverse as *Strange Fugitive* and *A Wild Old Man on the Road*.[11]

Like Raymond Knister and Frederick Philip Grove, Callaghan eschewed the proliferation of escapist fiction in Canada and took his cue from developments in American and, to a lesser degree, European literature. In this larger context he appears less as a monolithic revolutionary presence than as a competent workman participating in recognizable mainstreams of modern world fiction. Although not in any strict sense of the word a "realistic" writer (on the whole he has produced moralistic romances that use realistic details), Callaghan was influenced by the thematic and stylistic innovations of the major European "realists." He has declared a temperamental sympathy with Leo Tolstoy and Gustav Flaubert; from Émile Zola he derived an early interest in naturalism; he shares with Anton Chekhov a delicate sense of compassionate irony; and like Guy de Maupassant and Katherine Mansfield (both of whom he admires) Callaghan viewed his own stories as tightly woven objects comprised of integrated parts, fiction wherein nothing is superfluous, wherein everything tells. As Callaghan remarked in an undated letter to Raymond Knister (probably written in the early 1930s): "As for literary style, I have no awareness of it, or the lack of it. Sometimes there is a piece of work that strikes me as being good writing in a kind of way that an organism is good."[12] Over thirty-five years later Callaghan wrote in the *Times Literary Supplement*: ". . . I wanted a novel to have an impact as a whole — to offer some one vision of life, giving the whole thing its own reality."[13]

In the same essay, Callaghan admired H.G. Wells's *Tono-Bungay*, and Arnold Bennett's *The Old Wives' Tale* and *Clayhanger* series, as well as the work of Lawrence, Woolf, Conrad, Joyce, Yeats, Synge, Moore, O'Casey, and O'Neill. Expressing aversion to what he saw as a modern "Puritan" school of writing — Greene, Golding, Pinter — Callaghan favoured Camus' spiritual conviction that "man, just being what he was, had the possibilities for dignity and responsibility."[14] Most significant among any "spiritual" influences (aside from his Roman Catholic upbringing) were the teachings of the French neo-Thomist, Jacques Maritain, whom Callaghan met in 1933. (The former was beginning a six-year association with Toronto's Pontifical

Institute.) Critics now debate both the extent and duration of Maritain's importance, but the fact is that Callaghan's fiction of the 1930s displays a marked awareness of Maritain. Callaghan has implied that he was aware of Maritain well before 1933 (*TSP*, p. 94); and indeed he uses Maritain's theories of Christian personalism as his own argument against the persuasions of Marxist thought.[15]

Believing as Callaghan does that "Canada is part of the North American cultural pattern" (Weaver, p. 5) (and not, in any case, an English colony with inherited English cultural assumptions), he turned naturally and most receptively to the mid-war circle of American writers. In general he displays little interest in radical European artistic experimentation (he seems untouched, for instance, by Surrealism or Dada), preferring instead more accessible developments like the use of vernacular language, simple descriptions of ordinary locations, or a prose stripped down with a minimum of symbol or metaphor. "The words," argued Callaghan in *That Summer in Paris*, "should be as transparent as glass, and every time a writer use[s] a brilliant phrase to prove himself witty or clever he merely [takes] the mind of the reader away from the object and direct[s] it to himself; he [becomes] simply a performer" (p. 21).

In this sense Callaghan's most immediate milieu lies with such writers as Sherwood Anderson (whom Callaghan considered his literary "father" [see Weaver, p. 15]), Sinclair Lewis, H.L. Mencken, and Stephen Crane, as well as with the little magazines like *The Smart Set*, *Adelphi*, and *The Dial*. Callaghan himself drew the obvious conclusion: "I guess I was an American writer, and I am an American writer now" (Weaver, p. 5). Hemingway — "No man had meant more to me than Ernest" (*TSP*, p. 10) — was Callaghan's single most potent American precursor; a covering cherub of sorts, he not only encouraged the young Callaghan to continue writing, but in his own works provided a model of prose form and subject matter which Callaghan would copy, perfect, and "capably appropriate" for his own fictional purposes.[16]

But of all the influences that impinged on the young Callaghan, perhaps none exerted so far-reaching an effect as the imagist movement of the early 1900s. Although Callaghan in no way possesses the theoretical acumen of either F.S. Flint or Pound, there is nevertheless an essential unity of impulse that underlies the aesthetic judgements of the three men. Consider these excerpts from the "Imagist Manifesto":

1 Direct treatment of the "thing," whether subjective or objective.

2 To use absolutely no word that did not contribute to the presentation. . . .
   Use no superfluous word, no adjective, which does not reveal something . . . the natural object is always the *adequate* symbol. . . .
   Use either no ornament or good ornament.[17]

Fifty years later Callaghan published *That Summer in Paris*. Sprinkled throughout are "theoretical" statements like the following:

I remember deciding that the root of the trouble with writing was that poets and storywriters used language to evade, to skip away from the object, because they could never bear to face the thing freshly and see it freshly for what it was in itself. (p. 19)

But I knew what I was seeking in my Paris street walks. . . . It was this: strip the language, and make the style, the method, all the psychological ramifications, the ambience of the relationships, all the one thing, so the reader couldn't make separations. Cézanne's apples. The appleness of apples. Yet just apples . . . the thing seen freshly in a pattern that was a gay celebration of things as they were. (p. 148)

In all America how many critics were there who were capable of submitting themselves to the object — the thing written — and judging it for what it was? (p. 205)

On one level such comments merely reflect a general reaction against what was perceived as the literary excesses of one's Victorian precursors (colonial forebears in Callaghan's case). Part of the modernist move away from an inherited Victorian idiom, the imagists not only acknowledged the legitimacy of using the language and rhythm of common speech (compare Callaghan: "the language of feeling and perception, and even direct observation had to be the language of the people I wrote about, who did not belong in an English social structure at all"[18]), but the imagists also approved the artist's rejection of the audience's expectations in favour of pursuing his or her own vision (more of which in a moment). Cézanne's apples, in other words, are decidedly Cézanne's and not the more "realistic" Rembrandt's; yet they are apples, vividly created by the artist to convey the appleness of apples. In both these senses, then, Callaghan is part of that wave of later writers who gained impetus from the earlier movement which, as a formal movement itself, was relatively short-lived.

Stylistic theory and the practical application of it, however, have more than "literary" implications. Callaghan's decision to convey clearly the object as he alone sees it, constitutes an essentially anarchic attitude to language. Witness these remarks from *That Summer in Paris*:

> Tell the truth cleanly. Weren't the consequences of fraudulent pretending plain to anyone who would look around? Hadn't the great slogans of the First World War become ridiculous to me before I had left high school? Wilsonian idealism! Always the flight of fancy. And Prohibition. Another fantasy. It was hilarious, a beautiful example of the all-prevailing fraudulent morality . . . (p. 20)

Here is the awareness of how the uncritical acceptance of formulaic slogans in place of a clear and (theoretically possible) original use of language becomes an abnegation of one's political responsibility. Like George Orwell, Callaghan recognizes quite shrewdly the potential of language both to express but more perniciously, to formulate the thoughts of an individual. (This notion resurfaces in *A Fine and Private Place* when Al Delaney thinks that most people "register" even their words with the state authorities.) These similarities between Orwell and Callaghan are more than superficial and both are worth quoting at length. Orwell states his case with characteristic vigour:

> . . . modern writing at its worst does not consist in picking out words for the sake of their meaning and inventing images in order to make the meaning clearer. It consists in gumming together long strips of words which have already been set in order by someone else, and making the results presentable by sheer humbug. . . .
> Orthodoxy, of whatever colour, seems to demand a lifeless,

imitative style. . . . A speaker who uses that kind of phraseology has gone some distance towards turning himself into a machine. The appropriate noises are coming out of his larynx, but his brain is not involved as it would be if he were choosing his words for himself. . . . And this reduced state of consciousness, if not indispensable, is at any rate favourable to political conformity. . . .

This invasion of one's mind by ready-made phrases . . . can only be prevented if one is constantly on guard against them, and every such phrase anaesthetises a portion of one's brain.[19]

Throughout his career Callaghan has likewise emphasized the need to stop precisely this kind of "invasion" of one's mind. Interviews, commentaries, memoirs, columns, stories, the novels themselves — in each case he returns to a central imperative: the individual, and especially the artistic individual, must not surrender himself (in Callaghan the artist is usually male) to inherited language, popular movements, other individuals, or ideologies. As Callaghan remarks,

The weakness of an economic democracy is that it tends to produce mass thinking, mass reactions, mass reading. The whole productive machinery of the economy is geared up to produce a common appetite for a common commodity. What used to be called the great common touch is reduced to a dreary mediocrity of vision. . . . It seems to me that the writer, since his material is human beings, and since his special equipment is for having his own vision, has an enormous responsibility. He is concerned with the heart of man . . . and he is a fool if he is seduced by the latest fashions in knowledge, the psychological jargon, the sociological jargon, and chatter about the meaning of meaning.[20]

The artist, in other words (taking Harold Bloom one step further), is in continual dialectic not only with the myriad influences that surround him — struggling to maintain the purity and autonomy of his own vision — but the artist must also struggle always with his audience itself, forcing them to relinquish their own inherited ways of perception in order to entertain the possibility of seeing the world (and its ideologies) afresh. Callaghan's critique of Sinclair Lewis epitomizes the argument:

. . . it seemed to me that his grand success was based on one of his weaknesses as an artist: he gave the reader a chance at too quick a recognition. This kind of writing always puts the writer and the reader in a comfortable relationship, neither one being required to jar himself, or get out of this groove of recognition. A writer who has this gift is always meeting his reader and reviewers on their terms, and it should always be the other way around. (*TSP*, pp. 68–69)

Callaghan is thankfully not so dogmatic as his rhetoric would imply. In practice his fiction is neither idiosyncratic nor intrusively homiletic, it contains figurative language which he skilfully controls, and as an *oeuvre*, the fiction is admirably dynamic. It has evolved over a sixty-year period through a variety of different phases. Callaghan himself is neither a rarefied isolato, nor a partisan objector to mainstream literary developments. Remembering that the artist must always look outward, he has obviously been influenced by what he sees — from literary movements to political events to cultural changes — but he has always tried to capably appropriate the objects of his perception, placing them under strict criticism before deigning to adapt. An ironic testimony to this fierce belief in individual autonomy is the fact that Callaghan, like his own Eugene Shore, has remained singularly uninfluential both at home and abroad. Neither strikingly radical nor yawningly derivative, Callaghan remains a lonely figure of major importance in Canadian literature, but an overlooked minor personality in the international literary history of this century.

Critical Overview and Context

Debate about the nature and quality of Morley Callaghan's achievement has been both varied and extreme; the dispute calls to mind the aphorism "One man's meat is another man's poison" which is echoed in his 1931 novella *No Man's Meat.* His prose style has been praised as clear and direct, condemned as prolix and clumsy; his novels and stories have been touted as architectonic masterpieces, scorned as ramshackle; his ideas applauded as profoundly humanist, dismissed as cloying and sentimental. Generally, Canadian critics agree that his internationalist stance "broke open for us the egg-shell of our cultural colonialism,"[21] but disagree whether he is a realistic writer or a symbolist/allegorist, a shrewd observer of human nature or a weaker talent content to create cardboard cut-outs of humanoid figures. On this basis Callaghan's critical heritage has been one of ebb and flow, marked by both ebullient acclaim and fierce disparagement.

Until the 1950s Callaghan usually meets with enthusiastic critical responses — most notably for his short stories. Jazz and swing age critics never tire of comparisons: Callaghan is another Maupassant, Chekhov, Crane, Hemingway, or Anderson; he is praised for such qualities as technical expertise, social realism, and especially his insightful representation of life-like characters. All are qualities that place Callaghan securely in the vanguard of younger writers, and for the most part, early critics like Cleveland Chase suffer "a momentary urge to place the laurel crown on his brow without more ado."[22]

Chase is a typical example, particularly in his commendation of *Strange Fugitive*. The novel has a "clear, deep, slightly hard-boiled comprehension" and Callaghan is incomparable in his portrayal of psychologically convincing characters. He is also an able "disciple" of Hemingway, his style is "fresh and vivid," his dialogue "sparkling" (an allegation that has met with much critical dubiety), and his representation of the world characterized by a "clear, sharp objectivity."[23] Admittedly there was some dissent: Jonathan Daniels, in his 1932 review of *A Broken Journey*, notes unhappily Callaghan's tendency toward mystical and psychological obscurity;[24] in 1934 Mary M. Colum remarks upon the "queerly pedestrian style" of *Such Is My Beloved*;[25] and in 1937 J.R. MacGillivray complains in the *University of Toronto Quarterly* of Callaghan's dull style, simple-minded plots, and incredible characterizations.[26] These latter, however, were in the minority and subsequent critics shared with Chase a curiously uncritical fervour.

Of particular interest in these early reviews is the fact that although critics may begin by considering Callaghan's technical proficiency and stylistic clarity, they inevitably conclude with praise for his catholic compassion and its potential to effect a benign change in the reader. R.P. Blackmur, for example, observes that "The reader is able to adopt the curious equanimity of the characters and to share intimately in the inner consecration."[27] Similarly, Wyndham Lewis praises the effects of Callaghan's fiction: "As a result of such reading your behavior might grow more temperate and more charitable, your outlook more philosophic."²⁸ This early view of the reader's response to the Callaghan text not only corroborates Callaghan's view of fiction as essentially heuristic (as well as anticipating the reader-response criticism of our own time), but more immediately, it also looks forward to the view of Callaghan as a religious novelist, a view that occupies critical discussion intermittently over the next four decades.

Such a view underlies the first important surveys of Callaghan's work that appear during the 1950s. Claude Bissell's remarks on *The Loved and the Lost* might well be taken as synecdoche for the whole of this period's criticism: Callaghan "is still fascinated by the dialectics of good and evil, by the contrast between the society's easy moral dichotomies and the sensitive observer's tortured sense of life's complexity."²⁹ The moral ambiguities involved in action and choice. The autonomy of the self. Hostile social forces. But most important, the imperative to quest after insight, to seek a state of intellectual and spiritual freedom which subsequently, at least from the point of view of a conservative and capitalistic society, must constitute an anarchic threat to that society's easy definitions.

These are the topics that intrigue major critics of the 1950s, particularly Desmond Pacey, Malcolm Ross, Hugo McPherson, and Frank Watt. In each case these critics concentrate less on stylistic manner than on intellectual content. Privy to a developing historical perspective denied earlier reviewers, they arrive at a general consensus accommodating individual critical differences. Most readily admit Callaghan's obvious early defects: a poor control of language, the bungling structure and derivative thought of the early novels, and an occasional clumsiness of characterization, particularly in *Strange Fugitive* and *A Broken Journey*. Such faults notwithstanding, Callaghan appears at this time as a *thinking* novelist above all, one who deals with the moral complexities arising from the apparently trivial events of everyday life. A sort of little man's T.S. Eliot, he is a moralist who probes the grey areas of human reflection and action, who, despite an annoying ambiguity and failure to provide clear-cut solutions, does at least make us "think" (Pacey); a thinker who responds intelligently to major options of the age like Naturalism, Radicalism, and Personalism (Watt); a religious novelist (Ross); but one whose traditional Christian worldview has profound artistic effects (McPherson).³⁰

This last point underlies McPherson's "The Two Worlds of Morley

Callaghan," perhaps the most important essay of the decade (and one of the few to earn Callaghan's personal approval). To Mc-Pherson, Callaghan's fiction rests on a conventional Christian dualism which posits two realms: the earthly in which human beings live and the spiritual to which they aspire. Such dualism is evident in Callaghan's style and structure:

> he has wrought out a fictional form in which the surface events function simultaneously as realistic action and symbolic action, revealing both the empirical and the spiritual conflicts of his protagonists. This duality, moreover, is never merely a tricky fictional device calculated to entertain both the naïve and the knowing; it is fundamental to Callaghan's perception of the interdependence of the spiritual and empirical realms. Man's career occurs in the imperfect world of time, but its meaning (man's dignity or "place") depends finally on a larger reality *out of time*. To escape the first world is physical death; to ignore the second is to embrace the condition of the Waste Land — life-in-death. This tension, to which Callaghan's best fiction gives dramatic form, is the fundamental tension of life.[31]

Given the nature of our own survey, the operative words here are "realistic" and "symbolic" — for these are the crucial concepts around which revolve many of the critical debates of the 1960s.

This latter period emerges in retrospect as a time of intense polarization in Callaghan studies; although earlier critics (with few exceptions) disagree over the extent of Callaghan's obvious talents, those of the 1960s dispute not only his talents, but also the essential nature of his fiction. Callaghan himself, in a 1958 interview with Robert Weaver (much of which anticipates *That Summer in Paris*), expressed his enthusiasm for American "realists" like Mencken, Suckow, Anderson, and Hemingway — but flatly denied any indebtedness to them (Weaver, p. 14). Prompted partially by these statements and partially by the critiques of McPherson and Watt, critics now begin re-questioning, re-examining the problematic bases of interpretation. Is Callaghan, in fact, a realist? Or a symbolist? Neither or both? A moralist with psychological insight? Or an allegorist who manipulates stock types through a landscape of moral abstracts?

On one hand, Callaghan enthusiasts continue with, by now, standard defences: Callaghan is a traditional writer of realistic novels which probe the social and psychological ambiguities of humanity's quest for meaning; in so doing he displays a compassionate humanitarianism which derives from an unconventional, undogmatic Christian point-of-view. Taking this tack, Edmund Wilson makes his famous remark in 1960: "Morley Callaghan ... is today perhaps the most unjustly neglected novelist in the English-speaking world," "a writer whose work may be mentioned without absurdity in association with Chekhov's and Turgenev's."[32] An overstatement to be sure, Wilson's assertion nevertheless corroborates both the earlier and contemporary views of most Canadian critics, particularly those of Brandon Conron. The latter emphasizes Callaghan's mastery of symbol and irony within a predominantly realistic mode and remains even now Callaghan's most relentless defender; apparently unchanged in his opinions since 1966, he reprinted in 1975 and 1980 his praise of Callaghan's uniqueness as well as his "wistful lyric quality, Celtic fancy, supremely ironic point of view, and his insight into the significance of the minutiae of ordinary life."[33]

Less fervent in their admiration are Victor Hoar and Desmond Pacey, both of whom adopt the moralist-realist approach while trying to place Callaghan in his proper historical contexts. Hoar cites as influential the general inclinations to literary realism in North America during the late nineteenth and early twentieth centuries, post-World War 1 cultural malaise, and Callaghan's own newspaper experiences during the 1920s. Dividing his sensitive and witty study into two sections on techniques and themes, he emphasizes throughout the inseparability of the two.[34] Pacey, writing in the *Literary History of Canada: Canadian Literature in English*, places Callaghan in a modern great tradition of short story writers, viewing him as a compeer of Flaubert, Maupassant, Chekhov, Mansfield, Anderson, and Hemingway. He argues for an evolving Callaghan who moves gradually away from the naturalism of the 1930s toward the symbolism of the 1960s, and detects a triadic pattern to the whole career: the first phase in which Callaghan is struggling to establish his own view of the world, warring with perceptions inherited from other writers and his own culture and time; a second phase of intense Christian personalism initiated by his meeting with Maritain; and finally a third phase in which Callaghan continues to explore the same themes, but unfortunately moves away from the brevity and succinctness of the early works, experimenting as he does with more complicated plots, more complex structure.[35]

Most provocative of all the 1960s' critics is George Woodcock who argues passionately that Callaghan is neither a realist, a masterful technician, nor a prose stylist of any exceptional merit. He is rather a competent moral parabolist, a fantasist who partakes in a tradition of fabulist-parable writings. In "The Callaghan Case" (a review of *A Passion in Rome*), Woodcock states that

> it is impossible to accept even the best characters in Callaghan's novels as plausible in a realistic manner; their very simplicity gives them a curiously obsessional quality, and they only become plausible if we regard them — as we regard the characters of Balzac — as symbolic figures within the structure of moral parables. For Callaghan is, essentially, a moralist; he uses his works to make certain clear statements about the problems that afflict man once he becomes aware of himself as an individual, which usually implies the discovery that he is in opposition to society.[36]

Two years later Woodcock would repeat the moralist charge and in his influential essay, "Lost Eurydice: The Novels of Callaghan," remarks that "[Callaghan's] view of style is essentially moralistic, and every one of his works fails or succeeds according to the success with which he manipulates the element of parable within it."[37] Like Pacey, Woodcock deplores Callaghan's gradual complication of plot and structure throughout the 1950s and 1960s, preferring instead the biblically entitled "parables" of the mid-thirties: "as a group these three novels . . . represent Callaghan's best work outside some of his short stories, and one of the real achievements in Canadian writing."[38]

Recent critics have begun the necessary task of revision, re-examining and re-esteeming both the canon and its reputation. Admittedly many of Callaghan's recent critics merit the author's contempt: dully conservative, they remain safely within the broader contexts established by McPherson, Watt, Conron, and Woodcock. William Walsh, studying Callaghan's Commonwealth connections, reiterates the tired formulas about simple style and moral themes;[39] Fraser Sutherland, in an otherwise intelligent and lively study, follows Woodcock's parable argument while re-exploring the stylistic influences of Hemingway.[40] D.J. Dooley predictably includes Callaghan in his very modest book, *Moral Vision in the Canadian Novel*;[41] John Moss praises Callaghan's "exploration of the moral patterns encompassed by individual isolation" and feels that he "is not writing realistic fiction."[42] John Orange has written practically the only intelligent study of *Luke Baldwin's Vow*, relating it to the rest of Callaghan's fiction.[43] And in her 1978 booklet, Patricia Morley reassesses the phases of the fiction, suggesting an alternative triad to Pacey: phase one in which the redemptive power of love is paramount (1928–39); phase two in which Callaghan stresses the need of worldly prudence (1945–60); and phase three where he embraces a new philosophy of vitalism (1970 –present).[44]

Thankfully, however, the late 1970s also witness a gradual dwindling of such persistent (and mundane) thematizing of Callaghan's fiction. Much of the most interesting current work on Callaghan participates in the historical and theoretical revolution occurring in Canadian criticism itself. In 1979 Judith Kendle published in *Canadian Literature* the first important bibliographical study of Callaghan's journalism, "Callaghan as Columnist, 1940–48."[45] This move toward solid bibliographical research was followed up by both David Latham ("A Callaghan Log," 1980) and David Staines ("Morley Callaghan: The Writer and His Writing," 1981) whose excellent research was finally superseded by Kendle herself in 1984 in her exhaustive annotated bibliography of all Callaghan's known published work (i.e., written, televised, and broadcast).[46]

In 1980, four articles were devoted to Callaghan in the *Journal of Canadian Studies*, and although critics such as Brandon Conron and Patricia Morley continue to follow well-established thematic paths, Ina Ferris directs a tough-minded critique towards both inherited critical assumptions *and* Callaghan's major novels. In the process she develops a startling new perception of the Callaghan "hero" — a modern questor to be sure, but one uncomfortably reminiscent of Ayn Rand's fascist-heroes who seek above all else an "imperialistic" assertion of the self.[47] This new, more historical, more willingly theoretical approach to Callaghan is partially evident in the 1981 collection of essays, *The Callaghan Symposium*, edited by David Staines as part of the Ottawa Symposium series. Certainly the thematic (and "parabolic") tendency is still played out in essays by Leon Edel, Patricia Morley, and Barry Cameron; but there are also important indicators here of a growing new approach.[48] Barbara Godard expertly explores the problematics involved in translating Callaghan into French.[49] Larry McDonald, concentrating on the early fiction, tackles the critical "slough of Christian personalism" which has deluged the Callaghan industry. He re-examines the overshadowing trinity of Freud, Darwin, and Marx, arguing that the early Callaghan is by far the more revolutionary writer than the author of *A Fine and Private Place*.[50]

By the mid 1980s, however, McDonald's position appears perhaps more vulnerable, given Callaghan's publication of *A Time for Judas*, *Our Lady of the Snows*, and *A Wild Old Man on the Road*. Although space prohibits a detailed discussion of these novels, suffice it to say that critical reviews, following Callaghan's own drift, have begun to concentrate on his growing "metafictional" experimentation. As Graham Carr remarks in his review of *A Time for Judas*, "perhaps the most significant departure . . . is [Callaghan's] overt concern with aesthetic issues."[51] Interestingly, however, given this new concentration, reviews in both the popular and academic presses have nevertheless also begun to return to precisely those complaints made in the 1930s and 1940s! Mark Abley, in *Canadian Literature*, reckons that *A Time for Judas*, though subtle and intriguing, is nonetheless "prosaic," the language flat and uninspiring (and this is a judgement shared and expanded upon by Carr in *Essays on Canadian Writing*).[52] Anthony John Harding, in his review of *Our Lady of the Snows*, though he praises Callaghan's narrative prowess, confesses that the ending is ultimately "disappointing."[53] Callaghan's works, in other words, continue to elicit mixed responses, his refractory fictions resisting still the easy categorization, the unambivalent response.

Callaghan's Works

Just as Callaghan's interviews reveal a marked anxiety of influence, so his fictions contain as their real subject the tension inherent between self and other: the antagonism between the self-conscious individual and the world of non-self that continually impinges. Thematically the stories and novels continually examine the conflicts arising between the individual and ideology, personal desire and public need, individual *eros* and a society that seeks to influence, to create obstacles to the fulfilment of that *eros*. Throughout his career Callaghan has intelligently considered the shortcomings of ideologies that offer, through the abnegation of self-reliance, either escape or oblivion from self-consciousness. He offers no easy answers (or difficult ones for that matter). He poses the questions, sets characters in motion, and reports. The reader, as always in Callaghan, is forced to scrutinize; the reader must synthesize his or her own meaning from the fictional dialectic, using the imagination to learn.

In terms of technique Callaghan's works also reveal the tension between individual expression and external, impinging (usually inherited) forces. Although realism as a decision may well have constituted a subversive act (political-literary-psychological) against one's intellectual and creative precursors, it too becomes, like any movement that fossilizes into a doctrine, inhibiting and restrictive. Callaghan's responses to this inescapable fact of cultural development are particularly interesting; for throughout the canon we witness an ever-present internal dissension between the theoretical adherence to radical realistic principles and the opposite impulse toward romance and symbol, away from the orthodox demands of the radical realist school. As a result we get the distinctive type of "Callaghanese" fiction: essentially a moral tale, structured like a romance, embroidered with realistic details, and lacking a definitive conclusion.

Because of the sheer bulk of Callaghan's output the following essay is by necessity highly selective. I have tried to reach a happy medium between sticking with the established novels and exploring the virtues of lesser-discussed ones. Hence I concentrate on six representative books from across Callaghan's long career: *Strange Fugitive*, *Such Is My Beloved*, *Luke Baldwin's Vow*, *The Many Colored Coat*, *A Fine and Private Place*, and *A Time for Judas*. Reluctantly, again because of space limitations, I give only a token bow in the direction of the short stories and, sadly, no attention at all to Callaghan's journalistic writings or the radio and television works of the 1940s and 1950s.

If not exactly synecdoche, Callaghan's earliest writings provide something of a canonical overview in terms of both theme and technique. Apprenticeship by nature means a process of appropriation, and from 1921 to 1932 Callaghan is no exception; he carefully tries to evolve by adaptation his own artistic voice and the forms in which to embody it. Unfortunately at this point the American influence, especially of Anderson, threatens overkill, and what emerges is really a derivative fiction trying desperately to be itself. Crammed with contemporary clichés about the "plight of modern man," the fiction of this time seems obsessed with the image of the helpless individual buffeted by one or more of scientific determinism, socialism, orthodox Christianity, Freudianism, and the like.

"A Windy Corner at Yonge-Albert" (1921), Callaghan's first publication, is interesting because it establishes from the outset both a theme and a structure that will dominate his subsequent fiction. The episode, in fact, is adapted in *Strange Fugitive*.[54] On Sunday evening the narrator saunters to his local "Speaker's Corner," seeking "the magnetic goal that draws all lovers of street-corner oratory."[55] Here, at a Toronto street corner, Callaghan's narrator, an early analogue for the reader, *must choose where to stand*:

> Here, however, a problem confronts us. On the very corner, an intensely religious circle is formed by a considerable crowd: some hundreds of paces along Albert Street, a rapidly swelling group, socialistic in character to judge from the outcries invokes the aid of the elements and between these centres of friendly dispute, a third circle, rather sparsely attended, continues to gather admirers of a somewhat independent bolshevik nature, if such an expression may be used. Where shall we set our weary feet? . . . We are somewhat confused, a trifle dizzy . . . but the spirit of compromise prevails and draws us to the human magnet in the centre. From this place of vantage we can hear the loudest outcries from the two extremes. (p. 17)

Significantly enough, given the inconclusivity of most of Callaghan's novels, the piece ends with no conclusion at all. The speakers are sent on their way by a policeman; and the narrator leaves pondering his own ambivalence as a "proletariat with a bourgeois mind" (p. 17).

Most important here is the fact that Callaghan places in dialectical confrontation two mighty opposites, Christianity and socialism, both of which command a submission of the self to the larger whole. This confrontation, itself confronted by a confused narrator who ultimately opts to stand with those of "a somewhat independent bolshevik nature," develops into one of Callaghan's fiercest *bêtes noires*, obsessing his talents in one form or another over the next six decades. I will discuss this tension more thoroughly at the appropriate point; suffice it to say now that from as early as 1921 Callaghan is using fiction as a heuristic device (albeit very rudimentary), but he is using it to illustrate a moral puzzle which is left deliberately for the reader to solve.

Callaghan's early phase, like that of many artists, is notable less for what is accomplished than intended. By now it is commonplace to remark on this period's clumsy characterization, stilted colloquial dialogue (always a problem for Callaghan), and at times maniacal emphasis on the subnormal or retarded (e.g., "Amuck in the Bush," "A Country Passion," "An Autumn Penitent," and "In His Own Country"). Never a realistic writer *per se* though, Callaghan is at his best here when experimenting with methods of symbolic structure, probing the ways by which shape can echo or "participate" in meaning (something he develops superbly in the 1930s). How does one form a story in order to continue its content? George Woodcock has convincingly argued that Callaghan — for all his protests against in *That Summer in Paris* — does rely on traditional literary devices: image, symbol, patterns, spatial metaphor, irony, frustrated expectations of the reader, and so forth.[56] Most notable, and this is true of the entire canon, is Callaghan's "constitutive" detail: a form of fiction in which "everything tells." As Brandon Conron rightly observes, in Callaghan the apparently trivial detail is virtually always significant, if not momentously so.[57] "A Girl with Ambition" (1926), Callaghan's first published story, is a case in point.

Like many of the stories collected in *A Native Argosy* (1929), this tale deals ironically and compassionately with the folly of "great expectations." Epiphanic by nature, the story has the simplest of plots: Mary Ross is working-class, pedestrian, and ambitious. She leaves public school at sixteen, wanting to be a famous dancer. Her parents object, she then gets a job selling shoes at Eaton's, meets Harry (who is middle-class and wants to be a lawyer), fraternizes with "tough" company, marries Wilfred Barnes the grocer's son, gets pregnant, and exits the story on a grocery cart, bitter and watched by both a puzzled Harry and an equally puzzled reader. What is the point of this "broken journey"? The significance of Callaghan's many incidental descriptions?

From the outset Callaghan lays imagistic and thematic frameworks within which this ironic drama will occur. Consider the opening paragraphs with their vague fairy-tale echoes (both "village queen" and Tom Thumb are later mentioned explicitly):

After leaving public school when she was sixteen Mary Ross worked for two weeks with a cheap chorus at the old La Plaza, quitting when her stepmother heard the girls were a lot of toughs. Mary was a neat clean girl with short fair curls and blue eyes, looking more than her age because she had very good legs, and knew it. She got another job as cashier in the shoe department of Eaton's Store, after a row with her father and a slap on the ear from her stepmother.

She was marking time in the store of course, but it was good fun telling the girls about imaginary offers from big companies. The older salesgirls sniffed and said her hair was bleached. The salesmen liked fooling around her cage, telling jokes, but she refused to go out with them; she didn't believe in running around with fellows working in the same department.[58]

Even at this point of his career Callaghan makes everything connect, leaving nothing superfluous. The story begins and ends on the topic of education, albeit a bitter lesson of life's arbitrary unfairness. Callaghan's ironic use of "respectable" throughout the story is here carefully prepared for by the implicit contrast between "cheap chorus" and Mary's coy decorum with workmates. Mary, moreover, who is to be victimized by her sexuality, ambition, and economics is here introduced as sexually self-conscious, theatrically pining, and best of all, working inside a symbolically resonant cashier's "cage."

Most engaging of all is Callaghan's apparently gratuitous remark about the shoe department. Why not cosmetics which would complement the bleached hair motif and further the notion of self-deception? The answer, of course, is that we are here witnessing an ironic re-telling of "Cinderella," complete with evil stepmother. Hence the bathetic, dislocated emphasis on that romance's significant "shoe" (a motif Callaghan returns to in More Joy in Heaven and The Loved and The Lost). Mary works in "the shoe department" (p. 84); she confronts a "fat man with a limp" (p. 89) (a grotesque de-idealization of her Prince Charming); Harry "tore loose a leather layer on the sole of his shoe" with which he later "beat time as they walked, flapping the loose shoe leather on the sidewalk" (p. 92). Mary herself is fired from a theatrical troupe because "She wasn't a good dancer" (p. 93). And like Cinderella, Mary also dreams of "imaginative offers" and inherits her very own pumpkin coach, albeit Wilfred's literal grocery wagon.

By itself Callaghan's Cinderella story is an interesting exercise in ironization. Taken in context of oeuvre, however, the story is significant for a number of reasons. Like so many stories from A Native

Argosy, it shows Callaghan working out his own anxiety of influence: here in pristine form is the internal tension between American realism and Callaghan's own impulses toward romance and symbol. Like his short stories in general, it relies for its effect on the masterful handling of the epiphanic moment, the significant detail. For example, not only does Callaghan use repetition (Mary is continuously described in theatrical or fairy-tale terms), but also ironic foreshadowing, as when Mary rudely shouts early on, "Oh, have an apple" (p. 87) — a rather nice anticipation of Wilfred's own later shout of "Grocer" (p. 95). Also, like Callaghan's entire canon, the story indicates his strong interest in the fragility of the self when it confronts the grim realities of the outer world. As Callaghan was to remark years later, "It's just too bad that as you grow older you get beaten up. We all get beaten up one way or the other."[59]

"A Girl with Ambition" depends for its success finally on the reader's "completing" its tensions in his or her own mind, synthesizing each of its component parts in order to empathize with the magic of the whole. This kind of entirety continues to fascinate Callaghan throughout his career and is present, however moderately, in his first novel, *Strange Fugitive*.

Hugo McPherson correctly describes the book as "the uncertain attempts of a young artist to say something that he has felt profoundly."[60] The plot is vintage Jazz Age and has much in common with classic films like *Underworld*, *Little Caesar*, and *Scarface*. Something of a gangster classic itself, the novel traces the initial social fall, criminal rise, and final deadly fall of Harry Trotter. Again, Callaghan's protagonist is simple and uneducated, a "little guy" who falls prey to forces and impulses greater than himself. Harry is strongly marked by a "will to power" — lording it over both underlings at work and his wife Vera at home. He is fired from his foreman's job and in rapid succession he leaves his wife, provokes an anti-Semitic brawl, hijacks a truckload of illegal liquor, becomes a powerful bootlegger (competing with characters vaguely based on Al Capone, Bugsy Seigel, and Hymie Weiss), assassinates an Italian rival, and is gunned down finally in revenge. Throughout the narrative Harry becomes progressively more isolated and lonely, vacillating continually about whether to return to Vera or remain with his blonde-bombshell floozie.

Like the classic gangster films, Callaghan's novel, for all its spectacular episodes, is a serious attempt to dramatize the effects of modern social pressures (and determining historical influences) on individual lives. Thomas Schatz, in his fine study of American film genres, makes a number of directly relevant comments on the gangster:

> The gangster's setting, like that of the Westerner, is one of contested space where forces of social order and anarchy are locked in an epic and unending struggle. But whereas the Western depicts the initial and tremendous struggle to establish social order, the gangster film deals with an organized society's efforts to maintain that order. The urban environment is not merely an ideological frame of reference to be accepted or rejected by the hero as it is for the stoic, detached Westerner; instead, the city represents a complex, alienating, and overwhelming community that initially creates the gangster and eventually destroys him. . . . Not only is this city an extension of the gangster's imagination, but of the viewer's as well.[61]

Contested space which is the hero's imagination. Self versus overwhelming community. The hero as reader. *Strange Fugitive*, in a similar manner, uses the extravagance of its gangster plot as a means to study in Harry Trotter the extent and nature of these topics. With Freud well in hand, Callaghan makes much of Harry's unfreedom: his mother fixation, the continuing influence of his childhood, his idealizing memories; with Marx he examines the arguments pro and con a socialist revision of the state which theoretically could accommodate Harry's urges for power; and with the naturalists, Callaghan stresses Harry *Trotter*'s — with all its animalistic implications — imprisonment to heredity and environment. Society here, as in so many inter-war novels, emerges as the urban jungle, the dark underworld, alienating and impersonal, that creates and destroys its Trotters.

On this last point of unending repetition Callaghan's structure is of particular interest. Critics have suggested a number of readings: to Brandon Conron, Callaghan uses a four-part structure grounded on the central symbol of the Cathedral (and, I suggest, its ironic counterpart, the Labour Temple); George Woodcock suggests the motif of a Canadian Rake's Progress; Victor Hoar suggests a two-movement, before-and-after-success, pattern; while Patricia Morley sees the narrative as an archetypal quest of the prodigal son.[62] All these patterns are contained by the novel's overall shape which graphically appears as an inexorable turning of Fortune's wheel that contains within itself multiple journeys in multiple directions. Harry's circular rise and fall includes within its arc a number of spatial and conceptual movements: journeys either backward (memorially to his childhood, physically to his hometown, or intentionally to his wife), or ironically forward (the novel is filled with cars, trucks, vans, and trains — all involved in either short-lived or aborted journeys).

Like a hamster in a wheel, Harry spends his futile little life running furiously to arrive nowhere. This inexorable and meaningless turn is represented finally in a curiously cinematic fashion; Callaghan uses a gradual close-up to conclude the novel with an image that not only recalls the way Harry killed Cosantino, but that also reflects Harry's fragile self colliding with the ever-present and hostile macrocosm of the outer world. Callaghan offers his own "hard-boiled" version of the impersonal turn of the wheel:

> The men in the car fired. Sam grunted. Harry dropped his gun, hit in the neck, his head dropping down slowly till his forehead rubbed against the pavement. He saw the wheels of the car going round and round, and the car got bigger. The wheels went round slowly and he was dead. (p. 264)

Rudimentary as it is, *Strange Fugitive* nonetheless charts the directions in which the young Callaghan was (and would be) going. Harry Trotter — as clumsy and automatic as he is — does look forward not only to Callaghan's later criminal-outsider-saints, but more intriguingly to Callaghan's self-portrait in *A Fine and Private Place*: the little subversive, the criminal at odds with his own culture. As the "cop" in this later book remarks about Callaghan's surrogate, Eugene Shore, he is "a traitor to his class."[63] Something of a pathetic quester, Callaghan's gangster also anticipates his later reader-seducing outlaws: anarchists who function in the text as reader-analogues, characters whose experimentations with both power and revolt force the reader to respond heuristically, to question his or her own attitudes to state, authority, and personal freedom.[64]

Whereas these earlier characters seem overall to be helpless victims of hostile irresistible forces, those of the mid-1930s possess a certain degree of responsibility, a greater self-awareness, a limited freedom to partially control their own destinies. As Nathaniel Benjamin remarks in *They Shall Inherit the Earth*, "You might be just free enough to have just a little influence on whatever happened."[65]

Callaghan has by no means abandoned his fascination with the influencing factors in individual lives (notably biology, economics, and psychology), but like the Church fathers on astrology, he now preaches that while such influences may very well incline, they by no means completely determine.

Ever the thinking novelist, Callaghan himself begins to re-question (as do his characters) many of the older wisdoms, the inherited ideas so apparent in *Strange Fugitive, A Broken Journey*, and *It's Never Over*. On this last point *Such Is My Beloved* and *More Joy in Heaven* represent two sides of the same coin: the sacred and the profane, the saintly and the criminal. Both novels examine the plight of the outsider, the subversive innocent whose behaviour throws the rules of society under the most stringent glare of critical scrutiny.[66] Though each novel examines only one side of the criminal-saint archetype, both posit similar questions that undermine the complacent ideas of hero and reader. What is the nature of innocence? Is it a virtue or a vice? As Al Delaney ponders in *A Fine and Private Place*, "In a world full of criminals who is the criminal?" (p. 100). Finally, is it possible, let alone desirable, to go one's own way in a society that demands "mass thinking" (and run the risk of anarchy), or is it better simply to capitulate, throw in with the common lot (and relinquish one's own modicum of freedom)?

Against a Depression era background, a modern world bereft of viable and unquestionably trustworthy "forms," Callaghan now places an increased emphasis on the value and desirability of form-making. Hence the virtual array of form-makers who now begin to populate the fiction: priests, artists, magicians, criminal-saints, circus performers, pimps, politicians, ideologues — characters who in one way or another hold up an image, a form for the hero (and reader) to contemplate. What emerges is Callaghan's typically modernist view of the imagination as a potentially healing energy that creates forms which render tolerable an existential world of unemployment, exploitation, and oppressing hierarchical structures. The imagination is both a retreat and a womb; somewhere to flee, somewhere from which to be reborn. What we have, in effect, is Callaghan's growing belief in the spiritually liberating powers of an articulated aesthetic humanism.

At this point we should note what will also develop into the typical Callaghan situation: an isolated figure suddenly experiences an unexpected crisis which throws into uncertainty his unthought-out, usually inherited, beliefs and values. Callaghan's healthy scepticism is here most evident, for there follows a period of intense critical introspection. The hero (and by implication the reader) must then evaluate a number of options or "forms" which seem to offer resolutions to the problematic crisis. Callaghan consistently uses his hero's foils to illustrate the limited success of what had become the 1930s' governing ideologies: orthodox Christianity, Marxism, bourgeoisie materialism, a cold behaviourism — in each case a *systematic* form of perception that contrasts to the hero's eventual solution of personalistic imagination, an individual form of compassion and pragmatism. Michael Aikenhead, for example, in *They Shall Inherit the Earth*, has his own set of orbiting options/foils: the religious orthodoxy of Nathaniel, the individualism of Huck Farr, the Marxism of William Johnson, the materialism of Jay Hillquist. Unlike the earlier Father Dowling, though, Michael does triumph tangibly. He is "healed," in the company of his loving Anna and compassionate doctor brother-in-law, "healed" by imaginatively rejecting the ideological and inhuman forms of his society (including legal justice) and embracing in their place a form of subversive, imaginative loving, something that anticipates Eugene Shore's anarchic Church in *A Fine and Private Place* — not to mention Simon's "love" in *A Time for Judas* and Ilona's "sympathy" in *Our Lady of the Snows*.

In terms of technique and structure the novels of this period mark a definite maturation. No longer the novitiate, Callaghan is well on his way toward developing a novelistic idiom of his own. The zippered effect of the earlier fiction is lessened, and component parts now blend more fluidly to create what Callaghan himself would describe as an organic type of style. Most admirable are Callaghan's continued efforts to integrate structure with theme, to use the shape of his fictions as a part, rather than complement, of his meaning.

The 1930s' hero, for example, is engaged always in an exploration that goes both inward and outward, in toward the soul, out toward the existential world with its governing ideologies. A quest, in effect, for some kind of *prudentia*, a coping but never static personality. Predictably, Callaghan experiments here with conventional quest structures — most obviously the ever-present circular pattern that has dominated Western literature since Homer's *Odyssey*. The hero, the self, the mind, leaves the security and complacency of home, the family, the womb of inherited ideas and journeys out into the world and time. The accumulation of experiences then constitutes some kind of regeneration that enables the hero to return, to reintegrate as part of the social body. Hence, Callaghan bases much of this fiction on motifs like the centripetal journey, images of the prodigal son, cyclical Christian symbolism of rebirth and renewal, seasonal patterns — in effect, conventional forms of the circular rites of passage.

Callaghan's experimentation is by far more appropriative than idealizing, and the borrowings are never dull or static. On the contrary, his adaptation of conventional forms is decidedly subversive, and the conventional is always twisted toward a new reading, a subtle, new meaning. The great circle, for example, never quite closes in rapturous harmony, the hero never triumphs by means of simple social reintegration. Callaghan's centripetal movements always spiral inward at the critical moment, the circle transformed into a swirling vortex. The typical Callaghan hero, quiet anarchist that he is, triumphs by recognizing the inhibiting enclosures of society, the limitations of its "forms," opting instead for an inner freedom, a psychological or spiritual wholeness that may exist inside, but is always independent of the social body.

Narratively the novels of this period operate in a like manner of dialectic. The central internal dialectic faced by the characters and contained within the plot is reflected in the containing shape of the novel itself. This, in turn, is also based on a dialectical form. That is, on one level (say, the alluded text) the narrative suggests a traditional comic movement towards the promise of fruition, marriage, union, some sort of including or integrating celebration. Callaghan usually accomplishes this by consistent references to church holidays or social carnivals, temporal celebrations of resurrection or harmony. In direct contrast he posits yet another narrative line (say, linear) which, at least in the cases of *Such Is My Beloved* and *More Joy in Heaven*, moves inexorably in the opposite direction, towards a traditional tragic exclusion, isolation, and loneliness. In other words, Callaghan places at the centre of his fiction a character engaged in a series of moral dialectical questions. This opposition between inside and outside, selfhood and community, is repeated in the very shape of the discourse, usually two ironically discrepant streams moving in opposite directions, one toward a conventional closed circle of happiness and community, the other toward the broken shards of tragic despair and isolation.

Such Is My Beloved illustrates precisely this kind of ironic interplay between narrative threads, an interplay that results in an equivocal resolution to the novel's moral dialectic. Perhaps Callaghan's most beloved novel, it traces the inevitable fall of Father Stephen Dowling in his attempts to save two prostitutes of his parish, Ronnie and Midge. In this quest for redemption he encounters various solutions put forward by a variety of foils: the orthodoxy of his Church, the socialism of his medical friend Charlie Stewart, the deterministic arguments of the wealthy Mrs. Robison, and the materialistic pay-off-mentality of her lawyer husband. Gradually the young priest opts for a form of personalistic compassion, of imaginative loving sympathy. Father Dowling finally comes to the attention of his scandal-fearing Bishop who pulls the appropriate strings: the women are arrested and sent out of town, Father Dowling goes mad with depression, and the novel concludes with the isolated priest confined to an asylum, working on the Song of Songs in his lucid intervals.

On one level *Such Is My Beloved*, like a classic comic structure, moves inexorably and promisingly toward a final fruition, an inclusive wholeness or unity of characters. Throughout the story the narrator refers continually to the approaching Easter season, the growing warmth of the days, the change in people's clothing from winter coats to spring dresses. Even Father Dowling plays in this "comic" anticipation of renewal: riding in a taxi with Ronnie, Midge, and Mr. Robison he remarks, "Easter is a full week earlier this year. Does anybody know how you tell when it's Easter each year?"[67] Continual mention is made of the Cathedral and from start to finish *Such Is My Beloved* moves inextricably along with the church calendar toward the final joyful celebration of Christ's bodily Resurrection. (The body, in fact, is one of Callaghan's central metaphors, more of which in a moment.)

In direct opposition to this mythical "alluded text" is the novel's "linear narrative," the pathetic relation of Father Dowling, Ronnie, and Midge and the daily realities that they face. Opposed to the grand scale of the Christian Easter ritual (with all its earthly pomp and finery), Callaghan meticulously constructs a world of slushy streets and wet boots, flimsy coats and empty bellies, cheap hotels and hardened emotions. As Father Dowling meditates in an oft-quoted passage:

. . . there was a whole economic background behind the wretched lives of these girls. They were not detached from the life around them. They had free will only when they were free.

He remembered suddenly, with a quick smile that brightened his face, how he had learned in the seminary that St. Thomas Aquinas has said we have not free will when we are completely dominated by passion. Hunger was an appetite that had to be satisfied and if it was not satisfied it became a strong passion that swept aside all free will and rational judgement. (p. 42)

Significantly enough, as Father Dowling strengthens his devotion to the two women he loses contact literally with his own mother, and symbolically with his spiritual Mother Church. Like Kip Caley, the deeper Father Dowling becomes involved with his moral problem, the more distant he moves away from community and cohesion. His innocence threatens the social norms so much so that he is ultimately crushed in self-defence by society's threatened ideologies themselves.

Callaghan maintains balance throughout his story by carefully mirroring aspects of each narrative thread in the other. Most obvious is his use of architectural metaphor, juxtaposing the Cathedral and the Standard Hotel, the Bishop's palace, and the Robison home. In each case prostitution of human values runs rampant and between the Bishop, the Robisons, and Lou the pimp, there is but a fine line indeed. But this use of parallelism is not confined to mere montage. Callaghan subtly rounds up a series of juxtapositions each of which is meaningless in itself and which throws light, usually ironically, on the others. To illustrate, *Such Is My Beloved* is a novel that, on one level at least, traces how each of society's ideologies, if not corrupt, is at least perverted, prostituted from its original ideal. In this sense the physical bodies of the two women, economically locked in their hotel and exploited daily, become a synecdoche for the whole of this particular fictional world.[68] As such they reflect critically on the series of real and metaphorical bodies which Callaghan places in direct opposition: the physical body of the risen Christ, the mystical cosmic Body of Christ, the body of Mother Church, the social body, the body politic, the intellectual bodies of thought examined (or encountered) by Father Dowling. Given this interrelatedness of metaphors Midge's hinted disease emerges in general as a profound indictment as well as an ironic foreshadowing of Father Dowling's psychiatrists' diagnosis: "[they] were of the opinion that some local infection was the cause of his malady" (p. 283).

In many ways, Father Dowling is Callaghan's first major fictional artist, an analogue for Callaghan himself who looks outward to his world and tries compassionately, through his fiction, to mediate the intellectual diseases of his own readership. A form maker *par excellence*, Father Dowling is not only the ultimate artist-magician-saint who transmogrifies matter into divinity, but on a lower, less grand scale he is the heroic anarchist-artist who rejects society's accepted "forms" and opts instead for a more personal, more humane (hence, subversive) saintliness. Kip Caley's remarks about Father Butler in *More Joy in Heaven* might equally apply here:

> ... Butler's a saint, see. But what does that mean? He's against the field, he plays it his own way — a guy like him has to be against the field. If they catch up to him, they'll destroy him.[69]

In his attempts to save his prostitutes Father Dowling, like Father Butler, tries to make known to them a "human presence" — what Kip in *More Joy in Heaven* describes as touching somebody "magically."[70] Like Callaghan, like Eugene Shore the wizard-artist of *A Fine and Private Place*, like Christ, and Judas, and Philo in *A Time for Judas*, Father Dowling opts for imagination in place of ideology.

Significantly, given the importance in the text of these two central image patterns, the body and the re-forming artist, *Such Is My Beloved* coheres to a great degree by means of Callaghan's many images of clothing, of garments, dresses, vestments, shirts, robes, cloaks, hats, and so on — clothes to ornament the temple of the spirit as the Bishop remarks in *More Joy in Heaven* (p. 54). There are of course the characteristic Callaghan jibes against pomposity and pretension: the Robisons' clothing, for example, like their car, simply reveals their crass materialism (as well as their bad taste which, in a universe governed by aesthetics, constitutes a moral flaw of the worst kind). But there are also the symbolic garments: Father Dowling's Easter vestments, ironically symbolic of resurrection; Ronnie's gift of a shirt to Lou who destroys it in a rage; and undoubtedly the most profound example, Father Dowling's gift of dresses to the women, symbolic images of his attempted re-formation:

> ... the girls picked up the dresses and went silently into the other room, and for a long time Father Dowling waited, glancing impatiently at the door every time he heard a sound. Closing his eyes, he kept on waiting with a strange breathlessness, as if some transformation in the girls, far deeper than a mere change of clothing, would be effected there before his eyes. (p. 119)

In one sense all these various motifs cohere within the grand narrative scheme outlined above. Artistic re-forming, clothing, Easter ritual — all these are subsumed under the "comic" movement toward the holy (and holistic) celebration of Resurrection: the body reintegrated, risen, clothed in the Grace of God. But in dark, ironic contrast we have the linear movement away, toward fragmentation, and undress, the body shattered. Poignantly Callaghan uses these clothing patterns to give us our last glimpse of the two women before they are exiled from town and novel:

> In the courtroom, among the lawyers, the other vagrant women and the constables, Ronnie and Midge looked plain, shabbily dressed and almost unnoticeable. Ronnie had her old red coat thrown over her arm and was standing there in the black silk dress the priest had given her, which was spotted now and badly wrinkled; Midge, too, wore Father Dowling's gray dress and badly discolored gray shoes. (p. 227)

Is Father Dowling a failure? Does his quest end here, in dullness, squalor, and exile? Critics have argued vehemently on both sides of the fence since the novel first appeared in 1934. Conservative traditionalists like Malcolm Ross, Hugo McPherson, and Brandon Conron have argued for a religious reading which, not surprisingly, tries hard to both have its cake and eat it too. To these critics Father Dowling is a Catholic "beautiful loser" — an earthly flop but a heavenly success. Less spiritualized readers like Judith Kendle and Ina Ferris have pushed for Father Dowling as a monstrously egotistical saint, one obsessed with an assertion of self, a madman who fails.[71] Is there no solution possible?

Surely the best approach is that of Callaghan himself who has always regarded fiction as primarily a heuristic device and not as a medium through which to dictate yet another ideology at the beleaguered reader. Certainly each novel of this period has a conclusion in which choices are made and problems apparently resolved. But in each case Callaghan deliberately blurs the final choice, deliberately leaving his readers faced with an unresolved ambiguity. Is Father Dowling an idiot or a saint? Has Kip been a fool or a criminal saint? Is Michael Aikenhead deluded or redeemed? The dialectics of Callaghan's fictions, in effect, have not been comfortably solved: on the contrary, they've burst through the bounds of fiction, into the reader's world. Callaghan is hardly evading the issue; what he is doing, not unlike a good Brechtian, is setting up before his audience a thesis, an antithesis, and one of many possible syntheses. Once again, like Callaghan's very first readers, we find ourselves left on the windy corner of doubt and irresolution. We, the critical, synthesizing readers, have been implicated by both Callaghan's ironic narratives and plot. The result is plain: we are now expected to engage the ideas of the text, to go on intellectual journeys of our own, to enter into our own dialectics with ideology and system (including the novel we've just finished reading). We are forced to see the outer and inner worlds for ourselves, through none but our own eyes. Compare Frank Kermode's statement in his *The Sense of an Ending: Studies in the Theory of Fiction*:

> We have to distinguish between myths and fictions. . . . Myth operates within the diagrams of ritual, which presupposes total and adequate explanations of things as they are and were; it is a sequence of radically unchangeable gestures. Fictions are for finding things out, and they change as the needs of sense-making change. Myths are the agents of stability, fictions the agents of change.[72]

This kind of heuristic dialectic characterizes the fiction of Callaghan's next phase which begins roughly in 1948 after a hiatus of ten years, and continues unabated until 1963 with the publication of his autobiographical memoir, *That Summer in Paris*. Throughout this period the moralist's hand is still ever-present: Callaghan still pursues the unanswerable questions posed in the earlier fiction. His ten-year break proved fruitful and we now witness a more sophisticated form of moral speculation. The fiction is not merely old wine in new bottles, but rather we have a new shift of focus onto old material, a new examination of the complexities of the old themes. "Wonder," "mystery," and "magic" are words that begin to recur frequently; in *Luke Baldwin's Vow*, for example, Alex Kemp, in a virtual paraphrase of Callaghan's artistic credo, praises the kind of observation that looks at things as "if [it] had never seen [them] before."[73]

This renewed complication is most evident in Callaghan's reconsiderations of innocence and prudence, his by now favourite conundrum. Innocence had never been viewed as a virtue; as early as 1921 in "A Windy Corner at Yonge-Albert," the Callaghan persona had stressed the need for worldly prudence, a knowledge of men and manners. If not exactly the "vice" portrayed in *The Many Colored Coat* — "innocence was like a two-edged sword without a handle, and if you gripped it and used it, it cut you so painfully you had to lash out blindly, seeking vengeance on someone for the bleeding"[74] — it had nonetheless always been a liability for the character involved. During this period the innocence-prudence relationship is still put forth as something to be considered, but Callaghan now prizes a more fluid kind of prudence — the worldly wisdom of the *picaro* — a subversive virtue that, taking its cue from Michael Aikenhead in *They Shall Inherit the Earth*, allows one to maintain an "innocent awareness" within a world of oppressive ideologies, a world capable of Hiroshima or Nagasaki, Auschwitz or Dachau.

Callaghan still regards fiction essentially as a verbal medium for moral thought; author and reader are still engaged in a heuristic dialectic where the text is merely the starting point for moral change. Callaghan now pursues the logical implications of his favourite slogan: as Alex Kemp advises Luke in *Luke Baldwin's Vow*, "You think your own thoughts, Luke, and rely on your own experience" (p. 75). The relativity of human experiences, in effect, now becomes one of Callaghan's recurrent themes. If we do live in a relativistic world where every individual's perceptions are both valid and desirable, how do we avoid a breakdown into isolated particles? Indeed, what happens to morality in such an anarchic world where value itself becomes a relative concept? The Callaghan hero, now as before, does endure crises which threaten his beliefs and values. But now Callaghan abandons his past-favourite quartet of options — Marx, Freud, Darwin, or Christ — and has his hero alone, facing an ever-shifting world that is objectively unknowable. At this point, at the edge of despair, Callaghan puts forward a renewed and reinvigorating concept of the imagination, virtually Blakean in its championing of energy, delight and union — qualities embodied earlier in the regenerative sexuality of Anna in *They Shall Inherit the Earth* and now with Annie Laurie in *The Many Colored Coat*.

Certainly the imagination for Callaghan had always been a humanist and humanizing faculty of the self; both Father Dowling and Kip Caley use the imagination to make known "a human presence" to other people. Even Harry Trotter displays an elementary form of imagination in his construction of a monument to his dead parents. Now however, Callaghan stresses the synthesizing capacities of the imagination; not unlike Locke, he sees it as a faculty of the mind that coheres, configures, a "magic" that can join disparate and apparently unlike parts into a coherent and whole entity.[75] Callaghan's concept of the imagination, moreover, is a moral as well as humanizing faculty and as such it fulfils a redemptive role, redeeming people from the hell of an isolated consciousness into the haven of a sympathetic, but never bullying, community. To Callaghan, the imagination is not merely an ability to rhyme or to sketch (like Jim McAlpine's in *The Loved and the Lost*), but is rather the ability or the potential to go beyond the stupidities and oppressions of which individuals, societies, and ideologies are so capable: to empathize, to be compassionate, to be human and "comfortable together," to use a phrase from *The Many Colored Coat* (p. 318).

This concept of the imagination underlies *Luke Baldwin's Vow*, a book particularly valuable for the literary critic. A child's-eye view of the artist at work, it provides a blue-print of Callaghan's more sophisticated adult experiments. Thematically the book offers simplified treatments of ideas like the primacy of the imagination, the need for prudence, the liability of innocence, the need to see the world through your own eyes. Technically it exteriorizes what is usually implicit in Callaghan's fiction — myth, foreshadowing, the telling image — and by so doing, reveals Callaghan for the romancer that he is, the fabulist who uses realistic detail for symbolic purposes. Structurally *Luke Baldwin's Vow* is a beginner's guide to reading Callaghan's dialectical fiction: for once the Callaghan narrator condescends to resolve the internal conflict. We, the readers, for once, get an unequivocal statement regarding the proper dialectical synthesis.

Like Dickens' *Hard Times*, which it resembles throughout, the novel posits a binary division between imagination and utilitarianism, between fact and fancy. Luke's father, an easy-going doctor who taught "that the world was bright and mysterious and not to be easily understood" (p. 9), who "was careless with his accounts and yet took an extraordinary interest in the petty ailments of his patients" (p. 2), dies, and Luke is sent to live with his practical Uncle Henry who, though kind, has no time for the imagination. "Always the facts" (p. 28), he argues; and in direct contrast to his dead brother, he values people "by [their] value to me" (p. 85). What emerges is a conflict between the imagination and a neo-Gradgrindian world of fact.

Indeed, Uncle Henry uses the word frequently. The focus of the main conflict is Dan, an old collie who is crippled and blind in one eye (prefigurative of the seer, old Mr. Kon in *The Many Colored Coat*). He is worthless to Uncle Henry who arranges for the dog to be drowned. Luke rescues it in a dramatic swimming scene, but then faces the dilemma of how to convince Uncle Henry to allow him to keep this "worthless" dog. Alex Kemp provides the solution by advising him to make an offer his uncle can't refuse: by beating him at his own game. Luke offers to pay for Dan's upkeep with the salary he will earn using Dan to collect Kemp's cows in the evening. Imagination in other words adapts utilitarianism to preserve itself. The novel then ends with Luke's vow — a vow, as Patricia Morley observes, that contains the wisdom so obviously lacking in *The Loved and the Lost* and so painfully acquired in *The Many Colored Coat*:

> In the world there were probably millions of people like Uncle Henry who were kind and strong and because of their strength of character and shrewdness, dominated and flattened out the lives of others. Yet it was possible not only to protect yourself against such people but also to win their respect. It all depended on the weapons you used. If you knew how to handle yourself, there were fascinating ways of demanding respect for the things that gave your own life a secret glow.
>
> Putting his head down on the dog's neck, he vowed to himself fervently that he would always have some money on hand, no matter what became of him, so that he would be able to protect all that was truly valuable from the practical people in the world. (p. 187)[76]

This kind of binary division, a dialectical opposition in need of a synthesis, forms the basis of Callaghan's highly schematized, carefully balanced shape of the novel. Structurally, *Luke Baldwin's Vow* centres on the striking differences between the two worlds of the imagination and utilitarianism, made manifest in the novel's two most notable spaces: Uncle Henry's realm and the home of his Polish immigrant employee, Willie Stanowski.

The world of Uncle Henry is characterized by factuality, functionalism, and most interesting, a staunch Canadian Puritanism. (There are few Callaghan fictions that do not take a swipe at the WASP mentality.) Callaghan presents Uncle Henry's house as a charming, warm, and friendly barracks. It is run on the principles of order, cleanliness, neatness, serviceability, and unequivocal moral definitions. The furniture is solid and functional. Aunt Helen, lambent in her cleanliness and soapy aura, wears a sensible black dress on Sundays, prizes reputation and efficiency, and is content to have Uncle Henry run the house like a domestic arm of the sawmill. The sawmill itself, an Ontario version of Dickens' Coketown, whines "like an agonized shriek" (p. 20) as it mangles trees from the mysterious forest (which Luke associates with his dead father). It drowns out Luke's pleas for mercy and kindness (p. 164), and in a fine leap of Freud, Uncle Henry's saw terrifies Luke as he "imagin[es] what would happen to him if he were ever caught on one of the logs and drawn toward the spinning saw" (p. 36).

The values underlying this kind of mechanistic nightmare are evident in the transformation of man to machine. Uncle Henry values Sam Carter as his best worker (the one he asks to destroy Dan); the narrator, however, leavens such praise with irony for his juvenile reader:

> He lived alone in a rough cast cottage a half mile along the road to town and never talked with his neighbours and never went anywhere in the company of another man. He had never been married, never drank, never spent much money, needed little to live on. He was an excellent workman but no one had ever heard him laugh out loud. He was not an unhappy man, but the only kind of happiness he had known came from doing exactly what he was told to do. (p. 20)

> But no matter how closely he looked at Sam Carter [Luke] couldn't understand Uncle Henry's appreciation of him ... even if he did the right thing around the mill he did it in a mechanical way. His eyes never glowed, he never moved quickly or joyfully, he never made much conversation with the other men. (p. 85)

Henry himself emerges as an ambiguous "villain." Although he is doubtless kind and well-meaning, he does actively oppose imagination (he takes Luke's collection of fairy-tales and recommends sensible biographies instead).[77] Moreover, in an action that recalls so many of Callaghan's "form-makers," he tries to re-dress Luke in his own image. Recalling Father Dowling and the women, Senator McLean and Kip, Kip and Julie, McAlpine and Peggy (and anticipating both Sam and Carla in *A Passion in Rome* and Edmund Dubuque and Ilona in *Our Lady of the Snows*), Uncle Henry replaces one set of clothes (and all that they represent) with his own kind of taste:

> "I want the most serviceable pair of shoes you've got.... I want pants, heavy serviceable stuff, and a sweater or two, and a windbreaker." Turning to Luke he explained carefully, "Don't ever buy shoddy stuff, Luke. You might as well keep your money in your pocket. You've got to learn to recognize a real value."
> (pp. 38–39)

This kind of spiritual and physical appropriation is most powerfully evoked when Aunt Helen forbids Luke to play with the Stanowski children. Willie "drinks," the children are brats, and Maria, especially, "goes places she shouldn't go and sees people she shouldn't see, and gets a bad name and it all means that she'll come to a bad end" (pp. 92–93). A graphic image of Canadian Puritanism at its judgemental worst, Aunt Helen's ban effectively denies the exuberance and unconventionality of the anarchic imagination. For if Uncle Henry's world is of the Gradgrindian mould, the Stanowski household derives directly from Mr. Sleary's hilarious and vital circus. In an almost point-by-point contrast Callaghan posits a house of wonder and joy, vitality and disorder, music and sloppy exuberance. In place of Aunt Helen's black dress Maria wears a "white apron"; the respectable church organ is replaced with a tinkling piano; cleanliness is replaced with an earthy dirtiness; and even the work of Uncle Henry's place is here substituted with play. The house itself seems to Luke to contain "all the wild happiness . . . [that] was never to be touched by him" (p. 94). Like the black family Johnson in *The Loved and the Lost*, the Stanowski's are among Callaghan's outsiders, marginal inhabitants whose socially inferior vitality is placed in ironic juxtaposition to the flattening banality of the middle-class Canadian Puritan.

Moving in and out of these different houses, positioned between apparently dichotomous poles, Luke is the novel's questing Everyman, the fictional analogue for the questing reader faced with the difficulty of choice. What must he do to save and be saved? William

Walsh answers the question shrewdly in some remarks on "The Little Business Man" (Callaghan's original short story version first published in 1947 and reprinted later in 1959):

> The story poses in opposition, disinterested love and practical use, and the subtlety comes in the revelation of how the boy learns to defend the first by adopting the technique of the second. But this triumph is also in a sense an ironic comment on his education because it teaches him that 'love' must be flawed by 'use,' and the intrinsic value if it is to be preserved in a world set to destroy it, cannot avoid being infected by the efficient means.[78]

Callaghan, in other words, solves his dialectical opposition by suggesting a synthesis of his two discrete, but paradoxically interrelated realms. One must make prudential use of the factual world in order to preserve the impractical but invaluable world of the imagination. Just as Luke uses Uncle Henry's "serviceable pair of shoes" (p. 38) to boot a vicious dog who threatens to kill Dan in a dogfight! Or, foreshadowing this conclusion, how Luke initially uses his imagination to transform Uncle Henry's piles of sawdust into piles of gold — which they are symbolically: not only money to Uncle Henry, but also potential paper for Luke's books of imaginative literature.

What is most important to acknowledge in this explicit resolution is that Luke's final proposition is not his at all, but Alex Kemp's, a shadowy character who is an important member of Callaghan's list of magus-figures. He is a story-teller, a champion of the imagination; it is Alex who inspires Luke to play and to fantasize when bringing in the cows. More importantly, he is a man who synthesizes the two extremes of the book: a magical median of sorts. Not only is he similar in appearance and outlook to Luke's father (and to Callaghan), but he is also *respected* by Uncle Henry for his clean and efficient farm. "Another kind of wise man," he fulfils the Callaghan ideal set out in all the fictions, especially of this period; the ideal blend of fact and fancy, worldly wisdom and divine innocence. What Patricia Morley rightly describes as the wisdom of the serpent and the innocence of the dove.[79]

As simplified as they are in *Luke Baldwin's Vow*, these fundamental themes and methods of structural composition underlie the more complex experimentation of Callaghan's adult fiction. The primacy of the imagination, the necessity of prudence over innocence, the imperative to form an "anarchistic" self; the dialectical opposition of desirable and undesirable realms, the use of symbolic realism, the forming of a fictional wholeness wherein everything tells — these are the ideas and techniques honed throughout this period, which characterize *The Many Colored Coat*, perhaps Callaghan at his most intriguing. For here he recasts a five-year-old novella, radically restructuring, revising, and rethinking "The Man with the Coat" into a monumental novel of almost Jamesian subtlety. Callaghan no longer asserts bluntly, he now implies.[80] And in the process he creates a Janus-like novel that harkens back thematically to the moralistic parables of the 1930s, yet looks forward in structure to the aestheticist fiction of the 1970s and early 1980s.

Based loosely on the Old Testament story of Joseph and his brothers (Genesis 37–50), the novel has a characteristically simple plot which contains almost limitless complications. Scotty Bowman is a plain banker respected for his honesty and upright character. He is secretly unhappy, however, and wishes to participate in the jet-set world of Harry Lane, a peculiarly "innocent" PR man for a local distillery. Mike Kon, a thick-witted ex-boxer, present tailor, and friend of Scotty's, scoffs at his admiration (an ironic foreshadowing of one of Mike's roles as one of the novel's "Kon-sciences"). Scotty fiddles a loan for Harry's stock purchases, but the latter is unaware of the fraud. The stocks crash, Scotty is arrested, tried, and imprisoned. In despair, he commits suicide.

As a result of all this melodrama Harry begins his inexorable fall from popularity. At the trial he loyally withheld evidence damaging to Scotty and he subsequently appeared to be the villain of the piece. Obsessed with regaining his reputation he goads Mike Kon into an assault in order to reclaim the stand to clear the air. He does so by constantly wearing a shabby suit made by Kon, damaging the latter's business reputation and public esteem. The ruse succeeds only too well and Mike puts Harry into the hospital after knocking him down some stairs. The second "direction" of the novel now moves toward yet another dramatic trial scene. By this time Harry has, through the imaginative sympathy and love of Annie Laurie, a prostitute, become one of Callaghan's clown-outsiders. He gives over his quest for revenge and fails to show at the trial. Annie delivers the truth of what happened, Mike Kon retracts his initial accusations, and the novel ends with Harry peacefully in possession of his own soul, exulting in his new-found freedom from a dangerous innocence.

So bald a paraphrase does little justice to Callaghan's masterful orchestration of such a large, symphonic novel. Themes and structures are carefully interwoven to the point that we have a book of many structures which in turn contain or continue a number of various but interrelated themes. On one level of reading, for example, *The Many Colored Coat* is a modern tale of exclusion and alienation, of the innocent self in dialectical relationship with a corrupt and corrupting society. In this sense the ironized tale of Joseph and his brothers can be seen as a governing structure: the biblical story is always just under the narrative, directing, prodding the reader. Joseph's coat is ironized into Harry's tattered suit jacket with the rotten lining (a pattern redesigned in *Our Lady of the Snows*), and comes to stand in the novel as the central, most important metaphor. Not only an image of Harry's tattered reputation, or of Scotty's deceptive exterior and real interior, or of the innocence/guilt problem, the coat is the most obvious "object" in the book about which no two characters can agree. The coat itself proves that "everyone has their own angle" (p. 107), that truth is indeed a relative term. It is important to note at this juncture that Callaghan made a particularly significant revision here: in "The Man with the Coat" Mike Kon accepts responsibility for the damaged lining; in *The Many Colored Coat* he does not — and no one, for that matter, can determine who *is* responsible. Such a revision is hardly gratuitous fudging; on the contrary Callaghan's revision subtly reinforces this notion of relativity, how the world itself is a many coloured object with no definitive interpretation.

Callaghan's image of a many coloured garment about which no one can agree might easily be referred back towards the text itself which discloses a many hued range of readings and structures. Here is a novel intensely concerned with justice, innocence and *prudentia*. Hence it is, on yet another level, structured as two broad movements that culminate in two separate but interrelated trial scenes. It is also a novel about the need for metamorphoses, for imaginatively transforming our selves as we grow older and, it is to be hoped, wiser: hence, it is also a novel structured around the exchange of roles of Harry and Mike. *This* broad shape then contains a number of smaller, reinforcing structures of transformation, from a minor remark about a minor character — "Joe had straightened up and joined Alcoholics Anonymous and had become another man" (p. 157) — to some of the major set pieces like the comeback and reformation of a burnt out singer (pp. 205–14), to the painting and redecoration of living quarters (pp. 246–49). Subsidiary, complementary structures abound: Harry's transformation into a clown-outsider is carefully supported by continual colloquial expressions — "a clown" (p. 183), "The poor fool" (p. 183), "a slap-happy martyr" (p. 184); his social fall, the fall of the hero-king, is illustrated in his shift from his upper-crust flat on Sherbrooke Street to a cheap room *down Mountain* street (p. 233). Significantly the novel had opened with Scotty wistfully standing *outside* the *entrance* to the *Mount Royal* Hotel (emphasis added). The list could be extended for pages.

But of all these various and interrelated threads perhaps the best one with which to conclude, the one that most contains the essence of the whole (possibly because it contains the essence of so much of Callaghan's debunking spirit) is the synecdochic opposition of the novel's two principal female characters: Harry's girl, Mollie Morris, and the hardly respectable prostitute, Annie Laurie. Callaghan's women have always been problematical, both for author and critic. As George Woodcock somewhat brusquely retorts, "Callaghan has always had difficulty in portraying women except as types — the cold, proud pseudo-saint and the easy-hearted, loose-legged floozie; the leading women in *The Many Colored Coat* represent these types at their worst, Mollie an insufferable prig and Annie a kind of soft-centred candy doll."[81] The comment is only partly just for Callaghan's two heroines represent, if anything, a symbolic juxtaposition of a deadening, unimaginative Canadian Puritanism with an artistic exuberance, an imaginative delight that transforms, liberates the self from the former's stupid and restrictive censures.

From the very outset Mollie can be seen for the prude she really is. Upper middle-classed like Catherine Carver in *The Loved and the Lost*, she is a weak willed Daddy's girl subsumed by the ideologies of her family: their class, and that class's bourgeois cultural assumptions. Callaghan meticulously aligns Mollie with a Puritan heritage which imprisons her within its iron grasp. Typically the alignment takes place over the whole novel, but one example will suffice. Early on she slights Annie Laurie and Harry jokingly banters as follows:

"Now, now, darling," Harry said, and he turned, laughing. "Don't get it wrong, Scotty. This isn't Molly now. It's her Baptist grandmother."

"It's not my Baptist grandmother. It's me, and I'm not ashamed that it's me." (p. 18)

Forty pages later the reader is told that Mollie "was going over to Birks' jewelry to leave a silver necklace that had belonged to her grandmother, to have the clasp repaired" (p. 57). This kind of burdening heritage is consistently built up — through the Morris' antique furniture, their abortive and miserable sexuality, and Mollie's own resounding statement: "I'm a little puritan, Harry, it's ground into me, and I can't forget it" (p. 100). In Callaghan such admission is paramount to declaring one's own intellectual, imaginative, and spiritual deficiency. Virgin and puritan to the end, Mollie exits the fiction bitter, twisted, and restricted, clinging desperately to her little world of reputation, respectability, and Junior League ethics.

If Mollie is the novel's real moll, the establishment whore who infects with her diseased imagination, Annie Laurie is one of Callaghan's inverted hero/heroines, an anarchic outsider who heals through a healthy, regenerative imagination, who redeems through loving compassion. Like many of Callaghan's outsider-saint-clown-outlaws (all members of Eugene Shore's/Morley Callaghan's private "Church" in *A Fine and Private Place*), Annie possesses a wisdom of the heart that is neither tainted by worldly cynicism nor plagued with the liability of a naïve innocence. Appropriately enough she is far removed from Mollie's world, both physically and mentally; in contrast to Mollie's cold superior looks, she is continually associated with light, warmth, joy, and laughter; and in place of Mollie's neurotic virginity (and in contrast to the preponderance of broken or dull marriages in the book) Annie offers a pleasurable sexuality, a healing "delight." These redemptive powers are appropriately portrayed in artistic terms; with Harry she redecorates an old and shabby flat — an activity of reformation, or replacing a rotten lining, that draws Harry in, refreshes him, and sends him back to the world renewed and alive (pp. 246–49).

Most striking in this presentation of Annie as the outsider-artist-redeemer is the fact that Callaghan emphasizes that it is only through the imagination that one can perceive "the mysterious wholeness of things." Of all the characters in the novel it is only Annie who can give full testimony at the final trial, a testimony that paradoxically accuses everyone of complicity yet absolves everyone of guilt. Like Bouchard in *The Loved and the Lost*, Annie quite simply and openly sees (her eyes are described continually) and accepts humankind for what it is. In all its glory and degradation, in all its guilt and innocence. As a dialectical opposite to Mollie, she offers a more congenial *modus vivendi*, but one which is necessarily synthesized in Harry's final redemption. Interestingly, Callaghan himself had radically rewritten the conclusion: whereas Harry dies in "The Man with the Coat," here he survives in exultation and joy — perhaps the ultimate testimony of the imagination's regenerative powers.

It is this kind of vital imaginative response which Callaghan prizes in all the fiction of his most current, "metafictional" phase, begun in 1975 with the self-reflective, *A Fine and Private Place*, and continued in the eighties with *A Time for Judas* and *Our Lady of the Snows*. Because of space limitations it is impossible to examine each of these later books in any great detail; however, *A Fine and Private Place* is singularly appropriate with which to conclude this discussion. A delicately astringent *roman-à-clef*, it provides *both* a critical retrospective of Callaghan's career — an introspective meditation on "what he was up to" (p. 1) — as well as a proleptic view of what, by 1990 at least, is a continued and resilient examination of the storyteller's art.

As a self-reflective *roman-à-clef*, *A Fine and Private Place* offers a complicated series of readings that spring from a masterfully interwoven web of separate narrative threads. On one level there is the comparatively straightforward story of Eugene Shore, a character based obviously on Callaghan himself. A Toronto writer long valued by American critics but overlooked by local pundits, Shore "was a man who delighted in criminals and sometimes got them mixed up with saints" (p. 1) (which is precisely what Philo — another Callaghan analogue — does in *A Time for Judas*). He is suddenly praised in *The New Yorker* by the critic Starkey Kunitz as a "master who ought to be read wherever the English language was spoken" (p. 36). (Read Edmund Wilson on Callaghan: "Perhaps the most unjustly neglected novelist in the English-speaking world.") A second thread now comes into play: Al Delaney, a brilliant analytical graduate student, is committed to his thesis on Norman Mailer (who, of course reviewed *That Summer in Paris* and who, like Callaghan in *A Time for Judas*, turns to an ancient locale in *Ancient Evenings*). Through a number of flukes Al becomes obsessed with Shore's novels, especially with how Shore himself is something of an artist-magus who founds his own "Church of the Imagination" which inverts or parodies the established rules of society. *This* thread then traces a dual development wherein Al grows to appreciate the "wholeness," the "mystery" of both Shore's fiction and of his own lover, Lisa Tolen. (The textualization of human beings, especially women, is a recurrent motif in Callaghan, most notably in *A Passion in Rome*.) Lisa comes to embody the typical Callaghan/Shore principles of creative anarchy — not only does she recall the virtues of Anna Prychoda, Annie Laurie, and Peggy Sanderson, she also looks directly forward to such fecund female characters as Mary of Samaria, Ilona Tomoroy, and Cretia Sampari. As Shore remarks on meeting her, "You don't need to bother reading [my novels]. You're in them" (p. 26).[82]

As Al becomes more obsessed with Shore's fiction, its valuation of a kind of anarchy, and the effects it has on the reader (*and* as his relationship with Lisa moves forward, each growing toward independence), Callaghan introduces yet another character: a belligerent and unhappy policeman, Jason Dunsford, who accidentally shoots and kills a young Panamanian boy. With Al, Shore attends the inquest and resolves to get the "whole" story for *The World*. By this time Dunsford has read one of Shore's novels (obviously *Such Is My Beloved*) and feels threatened by Shore whom he sees as a "traitor to his class" (p. 177). In a contorted mélange of events Shore is eventually killed in a hit-and-run accident (presumably by Dunsford), and the novel concludes with Shore's funeral and a new, promising relationship between Al and Lisa, both of whom have learnt through Shore to recognize the complex tissues which make up the entire "rotten human stuff" (p. 142).

As a watershed type of novel, *A Fine and Private Place* contains if not the precise techniques and ideas of the earlier fiction, at least logical permutations of them. Through Shore and Al, Callaghan delivers a punchy lecture to his insipid Canadian critics, detailing what for him are important overlooked aspects of his own work. Admittedly many of the ideas are by now familiar ones to readers of Callaghan: natural versus legalistic justice, exuberant criminality versus staid respectability, the need for an anarchic imagination, the limitations of ideologies, the hazily defined ideal of an organic oneness or "wholeness," and above all else the desirability of becoming an outsider-clown-hero.

Interestingly, Callaghan also here introduces what, in the eighties, will become a recurrent technique (and theme): a recycled version of his own aesthetic statements published in a variety of sources throughout the 1940s, 1950s, and 1960s. Not only does Eugene Shore resemble Callaghan in age, appearance, and publishing record, he also — like Philo in *A Time for Judas* — functions as an aesthetic mouthpiece. Consider, for example, Shore's remarks to Al:

> ... one night after midnight, I was at my window. It overlooked a little park flooded with moonlight, and I stood idly looking out. In my line of vision there was a tree and a drinking fountain. Suddenly that tree was there with an astonishing reality — coming right up close to me. I saw it as I had never seen it before, and I was moved, deeply moved and then fascinated. Why this moving clarity? Then I realized that I hadn't been saying to myself, "There's a tree. How should I see it? How would Flaubert see it?" No, standing at the window without a thought in my head, I had forgotten I existed, so I was there. All of me exposed to that object, all of me there without any awareness of myself, all of me hanging together, receptive just to the thing as it was — and the wonder of it — being just as it was. The wonder of separate things. And this is funny, Al. Not thinking about myself, I seemed to come all together . . . it's the truth. (pp. 163–64)

The passage recalls, of course, Callaghan's infamous modernist manifesto in *That Summer in Paris*, a manifesto wherein he praises the kind of writing and thinking open to the "thinginess" of things. Recall the following:

> I remember one time at twilight, sitting at the typewriter in the sunroom of my parents' home. I could smell the lilacs. A night bird cried. A woman's voice came from a neighbor's yard. I wanted to get it down so directly that it wouldn't feel or look like literature.
>
> Wandering around Paris I would find myself thinking of the way Matisse looked at the world around him and find myself growing enchanted. A pumpkin, a fence, a girl, a pineapple on a tablecloth — the thing seen freshly in a pattern that was a gay celebration of things as they were. Why couldn't all people have the eyes and the heart that would give them this happy acceptance of reality? (pp. 21–22, 148)

Callaghan is here surrendering to the autobiographical impulse which was present as early as 1928 in *Strange Fugitive*, but which is here — in this later phase — integrated into the attempt to re-justify those aesthetic principles dominating Callaghan's writing career. One more example will suffice. In a 1956 piece (quoted above), Callaghan complained about the recent trends that take the artist away from his true calling: "[The writer] is concerned with the heart of man ... and he is a fool if he is seduced by the latest fashions in knowledge, the psychological jargon, and the chatter about the meaning of meaning." Compare now a scene from *A Time for Judas* where Philo, like Callaghan, meditates on the nature of writing and reading:

> Coming to myself, angry and rational again, I thought, all this silly talk in Jerusalem about "as it was written." Too much poring over the meaning of the word, the meaning of the meaning, then the meaning behind the meaning. When I hear someone say "as it was written," I say cynically, "Well, who wrote it and why?"[83]

Whereas earlier Callaghan would comment on fiction-writing in his published non-fiction, now he seems to have deliberately reversed his tack. This later fiction contains a number of "writer" characters who, in their frequent manifestos, sound transparently like the Callaghan of *That Summer in Paris*. In this way Callaghan has begun not only to rebut his various critical detractors, but to offer a reassessment of his own theories and practices since 1928! Within the multiple folds of an increasingly complex narrative style he has also moved towards a more overt interest in readerly participation. The standard themes remain — an anarchic vitalism, regenerative imagination, the outsider-clown-heroes, etc. — but overall the later fiction returns again and again to the role of the reader: how the reader is affected and changed through the experience of fiction.[84]

This latter concern is by far the most intriguing aspect of Callaghan's *A Fine and Private Place*, his now explicit interest in the heuristic nature of his own fiction; i.e., how does fiction mean in the mind of the reader? How does the reader use fiction in order to learn, to develop, to change? Indeed, how does the imaginative wonderment contained inside the fiction get transferred to inside the mind of the reader so that he or she might move from the text to life with a new "wondering awareness"? Throughout the novel one of Callaghan's major *topoi* is the writing and reading of texts and their subsequent effects on both creators and audiences. The book opens, for instance, with one of Shore's neighbours complaining about the effect on her of one of Shore's books; a local reviewer is "so exasperated [by one of Shore's novels] that he . . . hurled the book across the room" (p. 5); Al becomes obsessed with both reading Shore's fiction and describing their "magic" in a book of his own; Jason Dunsford reads what is obviously *Such Is My Beloved* and immediately feels ill at ease; Lisa reads, revises, and disorders Al's manuscripts; Al continually reads the newspapers; critics read Shore; critics read critics on Shore and then publish their own responses which are then read by Al — all of which is read by the reader of Callaghan's novel. *A Fine and Private Place*, in effect, is a book *about* reading and its effects, about how the text is completed by the reader by applying its information and lessons to his or her own life.

Not at all unlike some contemporary phenomenological criticism — most especially Georges Poulet's notion of "interiority" — Callaghan's main theme stresses the need for an open reader-response, a submission of the self to the magical wholeness of the fiction.[85] To Callaghan, experience of this wholeness is redemptive — a subversive redemption no doubt — and one which allows the reader to perceive subversively the wholeness of things, not the fragmented particles of truth perpetuated by state ideologies. As Al discovers, his reading of Shore implicates him irrevocably to the point where he, as reader, becomes part of Shore's parodic and anarchic circus-church:

. . . Shore's kind of criminals — they were like lovers knowing only the law of their own love, their actions surely rooted in a common criminality whether they were boundless lovers like that priest who had to be caught by the little cops of his own tribe and put away, or the bank robbers.

High towers shone suddenly in the early light. The street he was in now was a great dark gully, yet he felt he was up there in the light, big with his own power, big with imagination, while down in the dark gullies, on their stilts 40 feet high, came all Shore's great clowns, walking stiffly, clumsily, their heads in the light, but their great stilts knocking aside the little gray men in the shadowed streets. Suddenly exalted, Al found himself walking among them in a town full of men with offices richly clean, their knives and guns registered with their cops, their words registered too, but he himself was up there with the ones on stilts, clumsy, high and in the open. (p. 65)

To Callaghan, then, good reading of fiction, the best kind of reading is by nature heuristic: it must be instrumental in changing the reader, altering perceptions, making the reader more sceptical yet simultaneously more accommodating, compassionate, and loving. In other words, reading Callaghan, for Callaghan, must lead toward metamorphoses, transformations. Reading is here akin to guerrilla activity: subversion from without inspiring subversion within. For the reader who holds on to the text (and does not hurl the book across the room), he or she has the potential to enter the sacral Church of criminality so valued by the elusive Callaghan/Shore.

Callaghan's implicit contrast here of subversive and acceptable forms of criminality is made explicit in the overall structure of the novel. As in *The Many Colored Coat* he here uses a variety of minor structural devices, all of which are subsumed under a general dialectical shape. This shape continues or extrapolates the book's principal themes which, in this case, stress the need for the reader's own dialectical engagement with the text which, in turn, is the starting point for a more aggressive engagement with the larger society.

Put simply, *A Fine and Private Place* deals primarily with the anarchic writings of Eugene Shore and how they affect a number of people, either leading them into the fine and private place of imaginative criminality or frightening them further back into the brutal and public comforts of a state-sanctioned criminality. As in *Luke Baldwin's Vow*, Callaghan here uses as his principal structure the dialectical opposition of opposing realms, one obviously desirable, the other equally repugnant. The first is the imaginative world of Shore himself, magus-like, mysterious, and faintly reminiscent in both appearance and function to Alex Kemp (and Callaghan himself). Shore's imaginative world is a virtually inverted world of social institutions and is portrayed variously as a circus, a renegade law unto itself, a crazy University, and most importantly, as a personal Church, a secular inversion of the all-embracing sacred Mystical Body. Parodic images of each of these institutions abound throughout: Shore is compared to a clown, a judge, a lawyer, a chancellor, and as a subversive founder of his own Church. As Al remarks to Lisa (again disclosing the effects of Shore's fiction on the reader):

"I said to [Shore]: 'What do you think you are? Your own church?' Lisa, I didn't know how right I was." His voice breaking, he want on: "Oh, it's a lovely idea, Lisa. His temperament! His Church! . . . . Yeah. Shore's temple — where his outlaws are all in his light, that baffling light, all free to become aware of the adventurous possibilities of their mysterious personalities. . . . I feel I've been in that temple . . . I've felt the exciting warmth of these strange outlaws. It does something for me. Others bigger than I am in their humanity — their fates. I become a little bigger myself — yet without caring about it. See what I mean? Now I can make my own banquet hall, stand at the door and keep the riffraff out." (pp. 200–01)

Related religious imagery is ever present and Shore appears as a Bishop, a priest, and a "Cardin"-al. Like the Cathedral in *Strange Fugitive*, Shore's imagination — the imagination of the anarchist-creator-clown — is "right in the centre of things," "you can't get away from it" (*SF*, p. 73). Shore's world, then, emerges as the crucial realm offering light, life, and creativity. Into this "temple" the questers of the novel make their personal pilgrimages.

In direct contrast is Callaghan's second realm which, like that of Uncle Henry's in *Luke Baldwin's Vow*, is a world of analysis and breakdown, fragmentation and fact. And to Callaghan this is but a small step away from repression and authoritarianism, non-imagination and dispiritedness. Here is the neo-puritan world of middle-class Canada, replete with stuffy and/or trendy neighbours, staid businessmen (plagued with piles), analytical academics, and most synecdochic, with oppressive "cops": a catch-all term for the Jason Dunsfords of society, the agents of ideology, conventional respectability, and narrow-minded public morality. Significantly enough, Shore's home is separated by a ravine from the "tombstone slabs" (p. 7) of the city; Shore himself first appears (like two of Callaghan's own earlier outlaws, Harry Trotter and Kip Caley) crossing a bridge, suspended precariously between the polar opposites of the anarchic, inverting imagination and the repressive force of social respectability. Around these two realms Callaghan structures his text of *A Fine and Private Place*. The dialectic is then placed before the reader, begging the question, as it were, of redemptive synthesis.

Within this overall pattern of inversion Callaghan uses a number of cohering devices that not only help structure the novel but more importantly, direct the reader toward both critically synthesizing the opposing movements of the text, and critically scrutinizing how this synthesis is affecting his own beliefs and values. Al Delaney, for example, is a fictional analogue of the learning reader, a directional signpost pointing us to the correct ways of reading Callaghan's novel. Not only does he continually read, criticize, and evaluate Shore, but his eventual *correct* way of reading texts leads to a more vitalizing "reading" of life itself. As Al says to Shore, "The more I read you, the more life becomes a mystification" (p. 77).

As Al moves away from an analytical critique towards this mysterious appreciation of the text (a movement suggested by his physical journeys to and from Shore's home), so too does he cease to try to analyze the mysterious qualities of Lisa, learning to love her "holistically," appreciating the wonderment which she, like Shore's texts, can effect in his own mind. (A nice counterpoint occurs where Lisa is "in" Shore's novels but conspicuously absent in Al's journal.) Appropriately enough Al abandons his initial ambition to be one of academia's "cops" —

"Are you a cop?"
"Not quite, not until I'm a professor." (p. 17)

— moving more toward the anarchic freedom offered by Shore's vision. Jake Fulton puts it in a nutshell for Lisa:

But Al . . . now he's found something he can't organize, and Goddamn it, I envy him. What is it, Lisa? Something hidden from him? A way of looking at things? An effect in life? An effect in art that's wonderfully mysterious? . . . Maybe having no sense of mystery means having no real sense of love, eh, Lisa? (p. 140)

Such a discovery is most powerfully evoked in Al and Lisa making love in Al's study — a workplace previously reserved for analytical and passionless criticism (p. 64).

Just as Al comes to prize the anarchic wonderment of Shore's imaginative world, so too, Callaghan implies, should the reader of *A Fine and Private Place*. Like Al, we are encouraged to enter the Church of the Imagination, a church of Dionysian exuberance which not only celebrates the body beautiful, but accepts holistically the darker contours of the whole person. Callaghan's refusal to hunt down Dunsford, his killing off of Shore, and his uncompromising portrayal of Lisa (the novel's working title was "In the Dark and the Light of Lisa")[86] — all confirm the humanistic basis of Callaghan's work, one well contained in Terence's famous epigram: "I am human and nothing human is alien to me." Heuristically, the Callaghan text aims to bring the critical reader to this point of courageous accommodation, this point of visionary realism.

As a critical retrospective of his own work, A Fine and Private Place testifies both to Callaghan's consistency of purpose and diversity of execution. Thematically his work has always dealt with major moral issues; as Callaghan remarked in 1956, "all great writers are really moralists."[87] Of all his concerns — the role of the self in society, the nature of art and its role as a kind of subversive liberator, the need for compassion, the need for autonomy — perhaps the most recurrent is that of justice and the impossibility of achieving its natural form through social institutions. As Eugene Shore remarks to Al, "Why is it . . . that law and order are so often destructive of all natural justice? That cop with his gun is law and order . . . . Nothing must be allowed to happen to weaken our respect for the cop's gun" (p. 172). As an ironic motto the remark may well be applied to Callaghan's entire oeuvre, from the intervention of the "cop" in "A Windy Corner at Yonge-Albert," to the belligerent intrusions of Jason Dunsford.

Structurally, technically, Callaghan must be recognized as one of Canada's few revolutionary writers, placed as he was in the historical context of a milky and escapist romanticism. His tough, ironic style, his blending of myth and realistic detail, his neo-imagistic credo — these alone confirm Callaghan as a stronger Canadian talent, hardly content to idealize, concerned more to appropriate for himself in the construction of his own artistic canon. But more so, Callaghan is distinguished from those historical Canadian contexts most powerfully by his insistence on the important, heuristic nature of fiction; he demanded that the reader not only take an active role in reading, but that he or she use this reading to initiate his or her own agonistic relationship with the social world. Magus-like, niggling, Morley Callaghan is one of Canada's most demanding talents, pushing the reader toward an individual anarchic evolution.

NOTES

[1] Biographical information included in this essay is derived from Robert Weaver, "A Talk with Morley Callaghan," *The Tamarack Review*, No. 7 (Spring 1958), pp. 3–29; Brandon Conron, *Morley Callaghan*, Twayne's World Authors Series, No. 1 (New York: Twayne, 1966); Donald Cameron, "Morley Callaghan: There Are Gurus in the Woodwork," in his *Conversations with Canadian Novelists — 2* (Toronto: Macmillan, 1973), pp. 17–33; and David Latham, "A Callaghan Log," *Journal of Canadian Studies*, 15 (Spring 1980), 18–29.

[2] Edmund Wilson, "Morley Callaghan of Toronto," *The New Yorker*, 26 Nov. 1960, pp. 224, 226, 228, 230, 233–34, 236–37.

[3] Morley Callaghan, *That Summer in Paris: Memories of Tangled Friendships with Hemingway, Fitzgerald and Some Others* (New York: Coward-McCann, 1963), p. 22. All further references to this work (*TSP*) appear in the text.

[4] Weaver, p. 20. All further references to this work (Weaver) appear in the text.

[5] For detailed bibliographical information, see David Latham, "A Callaghan Log," *Journal of Canadian Studies*, 15 (Spring 1980), 18–29; and David Staines, "Morley Callaghan: The Writer and His Writings," in *The Callaghan Symposium*, Re-Appraisals: Canadian Writers, ed. David Staines (Ottawa: Univ. of Ottawa Press, 1981), pp. 111–21. These reference works are now superseded by Judith Kendle, "Morley Callaghan: An Annotated Bibliography," in *The Annotated Bibliography of Canada's Major Authors*, ed. Robert Lecker and Jack David, v (Downsview: ECW, 1984), pp. 13–177.

[6] Weaver, p. 20.

[7] For an account of Callaghan's work for *New World Illustrated*, see Judith Kendle, "Callaghan as Columnist, 1940–48," *Canadian Literature*, No. 82 (Autumn 1979), pp. 6–20.

[8] Harold Bloom, *The Anxiety of Influence: A Theory of Poetry* (New York: Oxford Univ. Press, 1973), p. 5.

[9] Desmond Pacey, "Fiction, 1920–1940," in *Literary History of Canada: Canadian Literature in English*, gen. ed. and introd. Carl F. Klinck (Toronto: Univ. of Toronto Press, 1965), p. 658.

[10] F.W. Watt, "Morley Callaghan as Thinker," *Dalhousie Review*, 39 (1959), 305.

[11] For an analysis of this theme in Callaghan's work, see Judith Kendle, "Spiritual Tiredness and Dryness of the Imagination: Social Criticism in the Novels of Morley Callaghan," *Journal of Canadian Fiction*, No. 16 (1975), pp. 115–30.

[12] Morley Callaghan, Letter to Raymond Knister, Raymond Knister Archives,

William Ready Division of Archives and Research Collections, McMaster Univ. Library.

[13] Morley Callaghan, "An Ocean Away," *Times Literary Supplement*, 4 June 1964, p. 493; rpt. in *Morley Callaghan*, Critical Views on Canadian Writers, No. 10, ed. Brandon Conron (Toronto: McGraw-Hill Ryerson, 1975), p. 19.

[14] "An Ocean Away," in *Morley Callaghan*, ed. Brandon Conron, p. 22.

[15] For discussions of this influence on Callaghan's work, see Judith Kendle, "Callaghan and the Church," *Canadian Literature*, No. 80 (Spring 1979), pp. 13–22; John J. O'Connor, "Fraternal Twins: The Impact of Jacques Maritain on Callaghan and Charbonneau," *Mosaic*, 14 (Spring 1981), 145–63; and Barbara Helen Pell, "Faith and Fiction: The Novels of Callaghan and Hood," *Journal of Canadian Studies*, 18 (Summer 1983), 5–17.

[16] For discussions of Hemingway's influence on Callaghan, see Conron, *Morley Callaghan*, pp. 167–71; Fraser Sutherland, "Hemingway and Callaghan: Friends and Writers," *Canadian Literature*, No. 53 (Spring 1972), pp. 8–17, and his *The Style of Innocence: A Study of Hemingway and Callaghan* (Toronto: Clarke, Irwin, 1972); and Pacey, "Fiction 1920–1940," pp. 688–93.

[17] F.S. Flint, "Imagisme," in *Imagist Poetry*, ed. Peter Jones (Harmondsworth: Penguin, 1972), p. 129; and Ezra Pound, "A Few Don'ts by an Imagiste," in *Imagist Poetry*, ed. Peter Jones (Harmondsworth: Penguin, 1972), p. 131.

[18] "An Ocean Away," in *Morley Callaghan*, ed. Brandon Conron, p. 17.

[19] George Orwell, "Politics and the English Language," in *The Collected Essays, Journalism and Letters of George Orwell: In Front of Your Nose 1945–1950*, ed. Sonia Orwell and Ian Angus, Vol. 4 (London: Secker & Warburg, 1968), pp. 134–37.

[20] Morley Callaghan, "Novelist," in *Writing in Canada: Proceedings of the Canadian Writers' Conference, Queen's University, 28–31 July, 1955*, ed. George Whalley (Toronto: Macmillan, 1956), p. 31.

[21] Malcolm Ross, "Morley Callaghan," *Proceedings and Transactions of the Royal Society of Canada, Third Series*, 54 (1960), 56–57; rpt. in *Morley Callaghan*, ed. Brandon Conron, p. 78.

[22] Cleveland B. Chase, "Morley Callaghan Tells What a Bootlegger Thinks About," *The New York Times Book Review*, 2 Sept. 1928, p. 7; rpt. in *Morley Callaghan*, ed. Brandon Conron, p. 24.

[23] Chase, pp. 24, 25.

[24] Jonathan Daniels, "Night of the Soul," *The Saturday Review of Literature*, 17 Sept. 1932, p. 104; rpt. in *Morley Callaghan*, ed. Brandon Conron, pp. 40–41.

[25] Mary M. Colum, "The Psychopathic Novel," *The Forum and Century*, April 1934, pp. 219–23; rpt. in *Morley Callaghan*, ed. Brandon Conron, p. 53.

[26] J.R. MacGillivray, rev. of *Now That April's Here*, in "Letters in Canada:

1936, Fiction," *University of Toronto Quarterly*, 6 (1937) 363–65.

[27] R.P. Blackmur, "Review of *A Native Argosy*," *The Hound and Horn*, 2, No. 4 (July–Sept. 1929), 439–41; rpt. in *Morley Callaghan*, ed. Brandon Conron, p. 36.

[28] Wyndham Lewis, "What Books for Total War?" *Saturday Night*, 10 Oct. 1942, p. 16; rpt. in *Morley Callaghan*, ed. Brandon Conron, p. 57.

[29] Claude Bissell, quoted in Brandon Conron, Introd., in *Morley Callaghan*, ed. Brandon Conron, p. 16.

[30] See Desmond Pacey, *Creative Writing in Canada: A Short History of English-Canadian Literature* (Toronto: Ryerson, 1952), pp. 179–84; Malcolm Ross, introd., *Such Is My Beloved*, by Morley Callaghan, New Canadian Library, No. 2 (Toronto: McClelland and Stewart, 1957), pp. v–xiii; Hugo McPherson, "The Two Worlds of Morley Callaghan," *Queen's Quarterly*, 64 (Autumn 1957), 350–65; rpt. in *Morley Callaghan*, ed. Brandon Conron, pp. 60–73; F.W. Watt, "Morley Callaghan as Thinker," and introd., *They Shall Inherit the Earth*, by Morley Callaghan, New Canadian Library, No. 33 (Toronto: McClelland and Stewart, 1962), pp. v–x.

[31] McPherson, "The Two Worlds of Morley Callaghan," p. 62.

[32] Edmund Wilson, pp. 224, 237.

[33] Brandon Conron, "Morley Callaghan and His Audience," *Journal of Canadian Studies*, 15 (Spring 1980), 3. Conron makes the same claim in his *Morley Callaghan* (p. 32) and his Introduction to *Morley Callaghan* (p. 3), which he also edited.

[34] Victor Hoar, *Morley Callaghan*, Studies in Canadian Literature (Toronto: Copp Clark, 1969).

[35] Pacey, "Fiction 1920–1940," pp. 688–93.

[36] George Woodcock, "The Callaghan Case," rev. of *A Passion in Rome*, *Canadian Literature*, No. 12 (Spring 1962), p. 63.

[37] George Woodcock, "Lost Eurydice: The Novels of Callaghan," *Canadian Literature*, No. 21 (Summer 1964), pp. 21–35; rpt. in *Morley Callaghan*, ed. Brandon Conron, p. 93.

[38] Woodcock, "Lost Eurydice," p. 99.

[39] William Walsh, *A Manifold Voice: Studies in Commonwealth Literature* (London: Chatto & Windus, 1970), pp. 185–212.

[40] Sutherland, *The Style of Innocence, passim*.

[41] D.J. Dooley, *Moral Vision in the Canadian Novel* (Toronto: Clarke, Irwin, 1979), pp. 61–77.

[42] John Moss, *Patterns of Isolation in English-Canadian Fiction* (Toronto: McClelland and Stewart, 1974), pp. 215–24.

[43] John Orange, "Luke Baldwin's Vow and Morley Callaghan's Vision,"

Canadian Children's Literature, No. 1 (Spring 1975), pp. 9–21.

44 Patricia Morley, *Morley Callaghan*, Canadian Writers, No. 16 (Toronto: McClelland and Stewart, 1978) and "Callaghan's Vision: Wholeness and the Individual," *Journal of Canadian Studies*, 15 (Spring 1980), 8–12.

45 See note 7.

46 See note 5.

47 Ina Ferris, "Morley Callaghan and the Exultant Self," *Journal of Canadian Studies*, 15 (Spring 1980), 13–17.

48 See Leon Edel, "Literature and Journalism: The Visible Boundaries," in *The Callaghan Symposium*, pp. 7–22; Patricia Morley, "Morley Callaghan: Magician and Illusionist," in *The Callaghan Symposium*, pp. 59–65; and Barry Cameron, "Rhetorical Tradition and the Ambiguity of Callaghan's Narrative Rhetoric," in *The Callaghan Symposium*, pp. 67–76.

49 Barbara Godard, "Across Frontiers: Callaghan in French," in *The Callaghan Symposium*, pp. 47–58.

50 Larry McDonald, "The Civilized Ego and Its Discontents: A New Approach to Callaghan," in *The Callaghan Symposium*, Re-Appraisals: Canadian Writers, ed. David Staines (Ottawa: Univ. of Ottawa Press, 1981), pp. 77–94.

51 Graham Carr, "Crucifiction," rev. of *A Time for Judas*, *Essays on Canadian Writing*, No. 30 (Winter 1984–85), p. 309.

52 Mark Abley, "Plain Man's Scripture," rev. of *A Time for Judas*, *Canadian Literature*, No. 103 (Winter 1984), pp. 66–69. For a similar discussion of Callaghan's style, see Carr's review of the novel.

53 Anthony John Harding, "Changing the Story," rev. of *A Time for Judas*, *Canadian Literature*, No. 110 (Fall 1986), pp. 144–47.

54 Morley Callaghan, *Strange Fugitive* (New York: Scribner's, 1928), pp. 68–71. All further references to this work (*SF*) appear in the text.

55 Morley Callaghan, "A Windy Corner at Yonge-Albert," *Toronto Star Weekly* [*Toronto Daily Star*], 6 Aug. 1921, p. 17. All further references to this work appear in the text.

56 Woodcock, "Lost Eurydice," p. 91ff.

57 Conron, *Morley Callaghan*, p. 28.

58 Morley Callaghan, "A Girl with Ambition," in *A Native Argosy* (New York: Scribner's, 1929), p. 84. All further references to this work (*NA*) appear in the text.

59 Donald Cameron, p. 24.

60 McPherson, "The Two Worlds of Morley Callaghan," p. 65.

61 Thomas Schatz, *Hollywood Genres: Formulas, Filmmaking, and the Studio System* (New York: Random House, 1981), pp. 83–84.

62 See, respectively, Conron, *Morley Callaghan*, pp. 24–25; Woodcock, "Lost

Eurydice," p. 92; Hoar, p. 16; and Morley, *Morley Callaghan*, pp. 13–14.

[63] Morley Callaghan, *A Fine and Private Place* (Toronto: Macmillan, 1975), p. 177. All further references to this work appear in the text.

[64] Compare Callaghan's remarks on his own "anarchistic" views: "In some ways it's a quite anarchistic view of the world . . . in the sense that it is fiercely dependent upon the individual view never yielding to another man's sense of rectitude" (Donald Cameron, pp. 29–30).

[65] Morley Callaghan, *They Shall Inherit the Earth* (New York: Random House, 1935), p. 116.

[66] Compare Callaghan's later remarks to Robert Weaver:

Innocence has always fascinated me. There's a very thin borderline between innocence and crime. I'm not talking now about respectability; which is quite a different thing; respectability is simply in its final analysis a kind of an agreement to keep out of jail. But you see the saint and the sinner, or the saint, let us say, and the man guilty of the sin of monstrous pride — there's a very thin line there because the saint in his own way has a kind of monstrous egotism. The saint puts himself against the world, opposes himself in what he stands for to the whole world — which he calls, of course, usually the work of Satan. But the great criminal also puts himself against the world and the laws of society. I haven't thought of this before; it's just that you brought the subject up. But I'm glad you mentioned it. It's a very interesting theme. (Weaver, p. 22)

Also, compare Kip's remarks on Father Butler in *More Joy in Heaven*, pp. 217–18.

[67] Morley Callaghan, *Such Is My Beloved* (New York: Scribner's, 1934), p. 175. All further references to this work (*SMB*) appear in the text.

[68] For a discussion of this subject, see Morley, *Morley Callaghan*, p. 27.

[69] Morley Callaghan, *More Joy in Heaven* (New York: Random House, 1937), pp. 217–18. All further references to this work appear in the text.

[70] Callaghan presents this "magic touch" graphically in *Close to the Sun Again* (Toronto: Macmillan, 1977), pp. 71–72. Horler, in order to resuscitate a half-frozen man (Jethroe Chone), embraces him nakedly, literally saving his life with human warmth.

[71] For discussion of this issue, see Ross, introd., pp. v–xiii; McPherson, "The Two Worlds of Morley Callaghan," pp. 66–68; Conron, *Morley Callaghan*, pp. 84–86; Kendle, "Callaghan and the Church," pp. 15–16; and Ferris, p. 14.

[72] Frank Kermode, *The Sense of an Ending: Studies in the Theory of Fiction* (New York: Oxford Univ. Press, 1967), p. 39.

[73] Morley Callaghan, *Luke Baldwin's Vow* (1948; rpt. Toronto: Macmillan,

1974), p. 65. All further references to this work (*LBV*) appear in the text.

[74] Morley Callaghan, *The Many Colored Coat* (Toronto: Macmillan, 1960), p. 313. All further references to this work appear in the text.

[75] Cf. Morley, "Callaghan's Vision."

[76] For discussion of the implications of this vow, see Morley, *Morley Callaghan*, pp. 39–41.

[77] What a character reads in Callaghan's fiction often reflects the quality of the character's imagination. Harry Trotter in *Strange Fugitive* is fond of mystery and adventure stories; Scotty Bowman in *The Many Colored Coat* sticks to business reports; and Jason Dunsford in *A Fine and Private Place* has no taste for fiction.

[78] Walsh, p. 190.

[79] Morley, *Morley Callaghan*, p. 39.

[80] Callaghan's short story "The Man with the Coat" was first published in *Maclean's*, 16 April 1955, pp. 11–19, 81–94, 100, 102–19.

[81] Woodcock, "Lost Eurydice," p. 101.

[82] Cf. Callaghan's remarks in his interview with Donald Cameron: "I've always felt that women, whatever their obsessions might be, weren't given over to . . . frantic idealism in the way that men were. Remember, the woman looks after the human race — she bears the children, she feeds the children when they're very very young, and she guards them and looks after them. Biologically, her whole intent and purpose is to survive. . . . By and large women have to be on the side of life more than men because of the way they function" (p. 25).

[83] Morley Callaghan, *A Time for Judas* (Toronto: Macmillan, 1983), pp. 159–60.

[84] One of Callaghan's early interests was Chinese Haiku because "it's always completed by the reader inside his own mind. That's what I was doing in my stories" (personal interview with Morley Callaghan, 1984).

[85] Georges Poulet, "Criticism and the Experience of Interiority," in *Reader-Response Criticism: From Formalism to Post-Structuralism*, ed. Jane P. Tompkins (Baltimore and London: Johns Hopkins Univ. Press, 1980), pp. 41–49.

[86] Latham, "A Callaghan Log," p. 25.

[87] Callaghan, "Novelist," p. 31.

SELECTED BIBLIOGRAPHY

Primary Sources

Callaghan, Morley. "A Windy Corner at Yonge-Albert." *Toronto Star Weekly*, 6 Aug. 1921, p. 17.

———. *Strange Fugitive*. New York: Scribner's, 1928.

———. *A Native Argosy*. New York: Scribner's, 1929.

———. *It's Never Over*. New York: Scribner's, 1930.

———. *No Man's Meat*. Paris: Black Manikin Press, 1931.

———. *A Broken Journey*. New York: Scribner's, 1932.

———. *Such Is My Beloved*. New York: Scribner's, 1934.

———. *They Shall Inherit the Earth*. New York: Random House, 1935.

———. *Now That April's Here and Other Stories*. New York: Random House, 1936.

———. *More Joy in Heaven*. New York: Random House, 1937.

———. *Luke Baldwin's Vow*. 1948; rpt. Toronto: Macmillan, 1974.

———. *The Varsity Story*. Toronto: Macmillan, 1948.

———. *The Loved and the Lost*. Toronto: Macmillan, 1951.

———. "The Man with the Coat." *Maclean's*, 16 April 1955, pp. 11–19, 81–94, 100, 102–19.

———. "Novelist." *Writing in Canada: Proceedings of the Canadian Writer's Conference, Queen's University, 28–31 July, 1955*. Ed. George Whalley. Toronto: Macmillan, 1956, pp. 24–32.

———. *Morley Callaghan's Stories*. Toronto: Macmillan, 1959.

———. *The Many Colored Coat*. New York: Coward-McCann, 1960.

———. *A Passion in Rome*. New York: Coward-McCann, 1961.

———. *That Summer in Paris: Memories of Tangled Friendships with Hemingway, Fitzgerald and Some Others*. New York: Coward-McCann, 1963.

———. "An Ocean Away." *Times Literary Supplement*, 4 June 1964, p. 493.

———. "The Meterman, Caliban, and Then Mr. Jones." *Exile*, 1 (1973), 124–57.

———, with photographs by John de Visser. *Winter*. Toronto: McClelland and Stewart, 1974.

———. *A Fine and Private Place*. Toronto: Macmillan, 1975.

———. *Season of the Witch*. Toronto: House of Exile, 1976.

———. *Close to the Sun Again*. Toronto: Macmillan, 1977.

———. *No Man's Meat & The Enchanted Pimp*. Toronto: Macmillan, 1978.

———. "From *The Stepping Stone*." *Exile*, 6 (1979), 216–52.

———. *A Time for Judas*. Toronto: Macmillan, 1983.

———. *Our Lady of the Snows*. Toronto: Macmillan, 1985.

———. *The Lost and Found Stories of Morley Callaghan*. Toronto: Lester & Orpen Dennys, 1985.

———. *A Wild Old Man on the Road*. Toronto: Stoddart, 1988.

Secondary Materials

Aaron, Daniel. "Morley Callaghan and the Great Depression." in *The Callaghan Symposium*. Re-Appraisals: Canadian Writers. Ed. David Staines. Ottawa: Univ. of Ottawa Press, 1981, pp. 23–35.

Abley, Mark. "Plain Man's Scripture." Rev. of *A Time for Judas*. *Canadian Literature*, No. 103 (Winter 1984), pp. 66–69.

"The Achievement of Morley Callaghan (A Panel Discussion)." In *The Callaghan Symposium*. Re-Appraisals: Canadian Writers. Ed. David Staines. Ottawa: Univ. of Ottawa Press, 1981, pp. 95–107.

Avison, Margaret. "Callaghan Revisited." *The Canadian Forum*, March 1960, pp. 276–77.

Bessie, Alvah C. "The Importance of Not Being Ernest." *The Saturday Review of Literature*, 28 Sept. 1935, p. 6.

Bissell, Claude. Rev. of *The Loved and the Lost*. In "Letters in Canada: 1951, Fiction." *University of Toronto Quarterly*, 21 (1952), 260–63.

Blackmur, R.P. "Review of *A Native Argosy*." In *Morley Callaghan*. Critical Views on Canadian Writers, No. 10. Ed. Brandon Conron. Toronto: McGraw-Hill Ryerson, 1975, pp. 34–36.

Bloom, Harold. *The Anxiety of Influence: A Theory of Poetry*. New York: Oxford Univ. Press, 1973.

Brown, E.K. "The Immediate Present in Canadian Literature." *Sewanee Review*, 41 (Oct.–Dec. 1933), 430, 431, 433–35, 442.

Callwood, June. "The Many-Colored Career of Morley Callaghan." *Toronto Star Weekly Magazine*, 17 Dec. 1960, pp. 16–19.

Cameron, Barry. "Rhetorical Tradition and the Ambiguity of Callaghan's Narrative Rhetoric." In *The Callaghan Symposium*. Re-Appraisals: Canadian

Writers. Ed. David Staines. Ottawa: Univ. of Ottawa Press, 1981, pp. 67–76.

Cameron, Donald. "Morley Callaghan: There Are Gurus in the Woodwork." In his *Conversations with Canadian Novelists — 2.* Toronto: Macmillan, 1973, pp. 17–33.

Carr, Graham. "Crucifiction." Rev. of *A Time for Judas. Essays on Canadian Writing*, No. 30 (Winter 1984–85), pp. 309–15.

Carroll, John. Rev. of *That Summer in Paris.* In "Letters in Canada: 1963, Humanities." *University of Toronto Quarterly*, 33 (1964), 424–26.

Chamberlain, John. "Morley Callaghan's Inarticulate People." In *Morley Callaghan.* Critical Views on Canadian Writers, No. 10. Ed. Brandon Conron. Toronto: McGraw-Hill Ryerson, 1975, pp. 37–39.

Chase, Cleveland B. "Morley Callaghan Tells What a Bootlegger Thinks About." In *Morley Callaghan.* Critical Views on Canadian Writers, No. 10. Ed. Brandon Conron. Toronto: McGraw-Hill Ryerson, 1975, pp. 24–26.

Clever, Glenn. "Callaghan's *More Joy in Heaven* as a Tragedy." *Canadian Fiction Magazine*, Nos. 2–3 (1971), pp. 88–93.

Colum, Mary M. "The Psychopathic Novel." In *Morley Callaghan.* Critical Views on Canadian Writers, No. 10. Ed. Brandon Conron. Toronto: McGraw-Hill Ryerson, 1975, pp. 47–54.

Conron, Brandon. *Morley Callaghan.* Twayne's World Authors Series, No. 1. New York: Twayne, 1966.

——— . "Morley Callaghan as a Short Story Writer." *Journal of Commonwealth Literature*, No. 3 (July 1967), pp. 58–75.

——— , ed. *Morley Callaghan.* Critical Views on Canadian Writers, No. 10. Toronto: McGraw-Hill Ryerson, 1975.

——— . "Morley Callaghan and His Audience." *Journal of Canadian Studies*, 15 (Spring 1980), 3–7.

Dahlie, Hallvard. "Destructive Innocence in the Novel [sic] of Morley Callaghan." *Journal of Canadian Fiction*, 1, No. 3 (Summer 1972), 39–42.

——— . "Self-Conscious Canadians." *Canadian Literature*, No. 62 (Autumn 1974), pp. 6–16.

Daniels, Jonathan. "Night of the Soul." In *Morley Callaghan.* Critical Views on Canadian Writers, No. 10. Ed. Brandon Conron. Toronto: McGraw-Hill Ryerson, 1975, pp. 40–41.

Darling, Michael E. "Callaghan and His Critics." *Essays on Canadian Writing*, No. 4 (Spring 1976), pp. 56–60.

Dooley, D.J. *Moral Vision in the Canadian Novel.* Toronto: Clarke, Irwin, 1979.

Dunn, William. "Notes on a Master Novelist." *Lost Generation Journal*, 3, No. 2 (Spring–Summer 1975), 24–25.

Edel, Leon. "Callaghan Cinema." *Canadian Literature*, No. 77 (Summer 1978), pp. 100, 102–03.

———. "Literature and Journalism: The Visible Boundaries." In *The Callaghan Symposium*. Re-Appraisals: Canadian Writers. Ed. David Staines. Ottawa: Univ. of Ottawa Press, 1981, pp. 7–22.

Ellenwood, Ray. "Morley Callaghan, Jacques Ferron, and the Dialectic of Good and Evil." In *The Callaghan Symposium*. Re-Appraisals: Canadian Writers. Ed. David Staines. Ottawa: Univ. of Ottawa Press, 1981, pp. 37–46.

Ellmann, Richard. "A Talent as Big as the Ritz." *New Statesman*, 22 Nov. 1963, p. 746.

Ferris, Ina. "Morley Callaghan and the Exultant Self." *Journal of Canadian Studies*, 15 (Spring 1980), 13–17.

Flint, F.S. "Imagisme." In *Imagist Poetry*. Ed. Peter Jones. Harmondsworth: Penguin, 1972, pp. 129–30.

Frye, Northrop. Rev. of *The Varsity Story*. *The Canadian Forum*, Nov. 1948, p. 189.

Gervais, Marty. "Portrait of the Artist." *Canadian Literature*, No. 73 (Summer 1977), pp. 116–18.

Godard, Barbara. "Across Frontiers: Callaghan in French." In *The Callaghan Symposium*. Re-Appraisals: Canadian Writers. Ed. David Staines. Ottawa: Univ. of Ottawa Press, 1981, pp. 47–58.

Gregory, Horace. "Mr. Callaghan's Medium." In *Morley Callaghan*. Critical Views on Canadian Writers, No. 10. Ed. Brandon Conron. Toronto: McGraw-Hill Ryerson, 1975, pp. 45–46.

Harding, Anthony John. "Changing the Story." Rev. of *Our Lady of the Snows*. *Canadian Literature*, No. 110 (Fall 1986), pp. 144–47.

Hoar, Victor. *Morley Callaghan*. Studies in Canadian Literature. Toronto: Copp Clark, 1969.

Kendle, Judith. "Spiritual Tiredness and Dryness of the Imagination: Social Criticism in the Novels of Morley Callaghan." *Journal of Canadian Fiction*, No. 16 (1976), pp. 115–30.

———. "Callaghan and the Church." *Canadian Literature*, No. 80 (Spring 1979), pp. 13–22.

———. "Callaghan as Columnist, 1940–48." *Canadian Literature*, No. 82 (Autumn 1979), pp. 6–20.

———. "Tragic or Romantic Vision." *Journal of Canadian Fiction*, No. 24 (1979), pp. 141–44.

———. "Morley Callaghan: An Annotated Bibliography." In *The Annotated Bibliography of Canada's Major Authors*. Ed. Robert Lecker and Jack David.

v. Downsview: ECW, 1984, pp. 13–177.

Kermode, Frank. *The Sense of an Ending: Studies in the Theory of Fiction.* New York: Oxford Univ. Press, 1967.

Korte, D.M. "The Christian Dimension of Morley Callaghan's *The Many Colored Coat.*" *English Quarterly*, 8, No. 3 (Fall 1975), 11–15.

Latham, David. "A Callaghan Log." *Journal of Canadian Studies*, 15 (Spring 1980), 18–29.

Lewis, Sinclair. "The American Scene in Fiction." In *Morley Callaghan*. Critical Views on Canadian Writers, No. 10. Ed. Brandon Conron. Toronto: McGraw-Hill Ryerson, 1975, pp. 30–33.

Lewis, Wyndham. "What Books for Total War?" In *Morley Callaghan*. Critical Views on Canadian Writers, No. 10. Ed. Brandon Conron. Toronto: McGraw-Hill Ryerson, 1975, pp. 55–59.

"Literary Fisticuffs." Rev. of *That Summer in Paris*. *Times Literary Supplement*, 1 Nov. 1963, p. 885.

Ludwig, Jack. "Fiction for the Majors." *The Tamarack Review*, No. 17 (Autumn 1960), pp. 65–71.

MacGillivray, J.R. Rev. of *Now That April's Here*. In "Letters in Canada: 1936, Fiction." *University of Toronto Quarterly*, 6 (1937), 363–65.

Mailer, Norman. "Punching Papa: A Review of *That Summer in Paris.*" In *Morley Callaghan*. Critical Views on Canadian Writers, No. 10. Ed. Brandon Conron. Toronto: McGraw-Hill Ryerson, 1975, pp. 120–23.

McDonald, Larry. "The Civilized Ego and Its Discontents: A New Approach to Callaghan." In *The Callaghan Symposium*. Re-Appraisals: Canadian Writers. Ed. David Staines. Ottawa: Univ. of Ottawa Press, 1981, pp. 77–94.

McKenna, Isobel. "Women in Canadian Literature." *Canadian Literature*, No. 62 (Autumn 1974), pp. 69–78.

McPherson, Hugo. "Morley Callaghan's April." *The Tamarack Review*, No. 13 (Autumn 1959), pp. 112–16.

————, Introd. *More Joy in Heaven*. By Morley Callaghan. New Canadian Library, No. 17. Toronto: McClelland and Stewart, 1960, pp. v–x.

————. "A Tale Retold." *Canadian Literature*, No. 7 (Winter 1961), pp. 59–61.

————. "The Two Worlds of Morley Callaghan." In *Morley Callaghan*. Critical Views on Canadian Writers, No. 10. Ed. Brandon Conron. Toronto: McGraw-Hill Ryerson, 1975, pp. 60–73.

Miles, Ron. "A Religious Thing." *Canadian Literature*, No. 84 (Spring 1980), pp. 120–22.

Moon, Barbara. "The Second Coming of Morley Callaghan." *Maclean's*, 3 Dec. 1960, pp. 19, 62–64.

Morley, Patricia. *Morley Callaghan*. Canadian Writers, No. 16. Toronto: McClelland and Stewart, 1978.

———. "Callaghan's Vision: Wholeness and the Individual." *Journal of Canadian Studies*, 15 (Spring 1980), 8–12.

———. Morley Callaghan: Magician and Illusionist." In *The Callaghan Symposium*. Re-Appraisals: Canadian Writers. Ed. David Staines. Ottawa: Univ. of Ottawa Press, 1981, pp. 59–65.

Moss, John. *Patterns of Isolation in English-Canadian Fiction*. Toronto: McClelland and Stewart, 1974.

New, W.H. "Independent Criticism." *Canadian Literature*, No. 44 (Spring 1970), pp. 74–76.

———. "Callaghan Revisited." *Canadian Literature*, No. 49 (Summer 1971), p. 98.

O'Connor, John J. "Fraternal Twins: The Impact of Jacques Maritain on Callaghan and Charbonneau." *Mosaic*, 14 (Spring 1981), 145–63.

Orange, John. "Callaghan and Hemingway." *Journal of Canadian Fiction*, 2 (Autumn 1973), 95–96.

———. "Luke Baldwin's Vow and Morley Callaghan's Vision." *Canadian Children's Literature*, 1 (Spring 1975), 9–21.

———. "Morley on Morley." *Journal of Canadian Fiction*, Nos. 31–32 (1981), pp. 223–26.

Orwell, George. "Politics and the English Language." In *The Collected Essays, Journalism and Letters of George Orwell: In Front of Your Nose 1945–1950*. Ed. Sonia Orwell and Ian Angus. London: Secker & Warburg, 1968, pp. 127–40.

Pacey, Desmond. *Creative Writing in Canada: A Short History of English-Canadian Literature*. Toronto: Ryerson, 1952.

———. "Fiction 1920–1940." In *Literary History of Canada: Canadian Literature in English*. Gen. ed. and introd. Carl F. Klinck. Toronto: Univ. of Toronto Press, 1965, pp. 658–93.

Pell, Barbara Helen. "Faith and Fiction: The Novels of Callaghan and Hood." *Journal of Canadian Studies*, 18 (Summer 1983), 5–17.

Perkins, Max. "To Morley Callaghan." In *Morley Callaghan*. Critical Views on Canadian Writers, No. 10. Ed. Brandon Conron. Toronto: McGraw-Hill Ryerson, 1975, pp. 42–44.

Poulet, Georges. "Criticism and the Experience of Interiority." In *Reader-Response Criticism: From Formalism to Post-Structuralism*. Ed. Jane P. Tompkins. Baltimore: Johns Hopkins Univ. Press, 1980, pp. 41–49.

Pound, Ezra. "A Few Don'ts by an Imagiste." In *Imagist Poetry*. Ed. Peter Jones.

Harmondsworth: Penguin, 1972, pp. 130–34.

Ricks, Christopher. "Murder in the Mtsensk District." *New Statesman*, 17 Aug. 1962, p. 206.

Ross, Malcolm, Introd. *Such Is My Beloved*. By Morley Callaghan. New Canadian Library, No. 2. Toronto: McClelland and Stewart, 1957, pp. v–xiii.

———. "Morley Callaghan." In *Morley Callaghan*. Critical Views on Canadian Writers, No. 10. Ed. Brandon Conron. Toronto: McGraw-Hill Ryerson, 1975, p. 78.

Saroyan, William. "The Adventures of American Writers in Paris in 1929." In *Morley Callaghan*. Critical Views on Canadian Writers, No. 10. Ed. Brandon Conron. Toronto: McGraw-Hill Ryerson, 1975, pp. 124–28.

Schatz, Thomas. *Hollywood Genres: Formulas, Filmmaking, and the Studio System*. New York: Random House, 1981.

Staines, David, ed. *The Callaghan Symposium*. Re-Appraisals: Canadian Writers. Ottawa: Univ. of Ottawa Press, 1981.

———. "Morley Callaghan: The Writer and His Writings." In his *The Callaghan Symposium*. Re-Appraisals: Canadian Writers. Ed. David Staines. Ottawa: Univ. of Ottawa Press, 1981, pp. 111–21.

Sutherland, Fraser. "Hemingway and Callaghan: Friends and Writers." *Canadian Literature*, No. 53 (Spring 1972), pp. 8–17.

———. *The Style of Innocence: A Study of Hemingway and Callaghan*. Toronto: Clarke, Irwin, 1972.

Walsh, William. *A Manifold Voice: Studies in Commonwealth Literature*. London: Chatto & Windus, 1970.

Ward, Anthony. "A Way of Feeling." In *Morley Callaghan*. Critical Views on Canadian Writers, No. 10. Ed. Brandon Conron. Toronto: McGraw-Hill Ryerson, 1975, pp. 104–05.

Ward, Margaret. "The Gift of Grace." *Canadian Literature*, No. 58 (Autumn 1973), pp. 19–25.

Watt, Frank W. "Morley Callaghan as Thinker." *Dalhousie Review*, 39 (1959), 305–13.

———. Rev. of *The Many Colored Coat*. In "Letters in Canada: 1960, Fiction." *University of Toronto Quarterly*, 30 (1961), 402–04.

———. "Morley Callaghan's *A Passion in Rome*." *The Varsity Graduate*, 9, No. 5 (March 1962), 6, 8, 10, 12.

———, Introd. *They Shall Inherit the Earth*. By Morley Callaghan. New Canadian Library, No. 33. Toronto: McClelland and Stewart, 1962, pp. v–x.

Weaver, Robert. "A Talk with Morley Callaghan." *The Tamarack Review*, No. 7 (Spring 1958), pp. 3–29.

————. "Stories by Callaghan." *Canadian Literature*, No. 2 (Autumn 1959), pp. 67–70.

————. "A Golden Year." *Canadian Literature*, No. 16 (Spring 1963), pp. 55–57.

————, Introd. *Strange Fugitive*. By Morley Callaghan. Edmonton: M. Hurtig, 1970.

Wilson, Edmund. "Morley Callaghan of Toronto." *The New Yorker*, 26 Nov. 1960, pp. 224, 226, 228, 230, 233–34, 236–37.

————. "That Summer in Paris." *The New Yorker*, 23 Feb. 1963, pp. 139–48.

————. *O Canada: An American's Notes on Canadian Culture*. New York: Farrar, Straus and Giroux, 1964.

Wilson, Milton. "Callaghan's Caviare." *The Tamarack Review*, No. 22 (Winter 1962), pp. 88–92.

Woodcock, George. "The Callaghan Case." Rev. of *A Passion in Rome. Canadian Literature*, No. 12 (Spring 1962), pp. 60–64.

————. "Lost Eurydice: The Novels of Callaghan." *Canadian Literature*, No. 21 (Summer 1964), pp. 21–35.

————. "Callaghan's Toronto." *Journal of Canadian Studies*, 7 (August 1972), 21–24.

Acknowledgements are due to the University of Auckland Grants Committee for funds that allowed me to conduct long-distance research in 1982–83; Margaret Meyer for her bibliographical research assistance; Pat Graham of the CBC Archives; and the staff at the University of Auckland Library and the National Libraries in Auckland and Wellington. Finally, a special word of thanks to Morley Callaghan for a number of very tough conversations. Acknowledgement is also due to Wilfrid Laurier University for the time and space provided in 1989–90 to write the final revisions.

Hugh MacLennan
and His Works

Hugh MacLennan (1907–1990)

HELEN HOY

Biography

JOHN HUGH MACLENNAN was born on 20 March 1907 at Glace Bay, Cape Breton Island, Nova Scotia. His parents, physician Samuel MacLennan (of Highland Scottish ancestry) and Katherine Mac-Quarrie (Scottish, Welsh, and United Empire Loyalist in background) had one other child, a daughter Frances, four years older. The family moved to Sidney in 1914, then settled in Halifax, Nova Scotia, in 1915, where MacLennan experienced the devastating Halifax explosion of 1917. He demonstrated an unusual independence by sleeping in a backyard tent, summer and frosty Maritime winter, from age twelve to twenty-one. These sleeping arrangements suggest a need to gain distance from his demanding Calvinist father, whereas the thoughtful letters of political analysis which MacLennan continued to address to his father for months after Sam MacLennan's death in 1939 reveal an opposing need for parental approval.[1]

Upon completion of a B.A. in classics at Dalhousie University (1928), MacLennan won a Rhodes Scholarship and began an exacting course of studies in this subject at Oxford (1928–32). Vacations took him to France, Italy, Switzerland, and Germany. For his Ph.D. in classics at Princeton (1932–35), he wrote a dissertation on the decline of an early Roman colony in Egypt, later published as *Oxyrhynchus: An Economic and Social Study* (1935).

During these years, MacLennan was writing poetry and working on his two unpublished novels, "So All Their Praises" (completed in 1933) and "A Man Should Rejoice" (completed in 1937).[2] To support himself, he taught history and classics at Lower Canada College in Montreal from 1935 to 1945; for the following six years, he worked as a freelance writer and broadcaster. He joined the staff of McGill University in 1951, teaching in the English department (part-time for the first thirteen years) until his retirement as full professor in 1979.

In 1936 MacLennan married Chicago writer Dorothy Duncan,

whose rheumatic heart restricted her activity, especially from 1947 on, and led to her death in 1957. Two years after Dorothy's death, MacLennan married Frances (Tota) Walker. He had no children, a biographical note of interest for a writer haunted by father-son relationships.

MacLennan's published novels include *Barometer Rising* (1941), *Two Solitudes* (1945), *The Precipice* (1948), *Each Man's Son* (1951), *The Watch That Ends the Night* (1959), *Return of the Sphinx* (1967), and *Voices in Time* (1980). Interspersed among these are collections of essays — *Cross-Country* (1949), *Thirty & Three* (1954), *Scotchman's Return and Other Essays* (1960), *The Other Side of Hugh MacLennan* (1978) — and several other non-fiction works — *Seven Rivers of Canada* (1961) and *The Colour of Canada* (1967).

MacLennan's correspondence suggests the range of his interests and appeal. He corresponded with Canadian politicians Paul Martin, Leslie Roberts, Lester B. Pearson, and Pierre Elliott Trudeau; with historian A.R.M. Lower; with photographer Yousuf Karsh; and with scientists Wilder Penfield and Hans Selye. Among non-Canadian writers, C.P. Snow, Budd Schulberg, Edmund Wilson, and Bernard DeVoto were significant correspondents.[3]

Acknowledgements of MacLennan's contribution to Canadian literature has taken the form of the Governor General's Award for *Two Solitudes, The Precipice, Cross-Country, Thirty & Three,* and *The Watch That Ends the Night*; a score of honorary degrees; the Lorne Pierce Medal (1952); the Molson Award (1966); the Royal Bank Award (1984); and Princeton University's James Madison Medal (1987). In 1943 MacLennan received a Guggenheim Fellowship in creative writing to assist completion of *Two Solitudes* and, in 1963, while working on *Return of the Sphinx*, a Canada Council award. He was made a Fellow of the Royal Society of Canada (1952), a Fellow (1956) and later a Companion (1967) of the Royal Society of Literature in England, and a Companion of the Order of Canada (1967).

Hugh MacLennan died at his Montreal home on November 7, 1990.

Tradition and Milieu

. . . . it seemed to me that for some years to come the Canadian novelist would have to pay a great deal of attention to the background in which he set his stories. He must describe, and if necessary, define the social values which dominate the Canadian scene . . . . Whether he liked it or not, he must for a time be something of a geographer, an historian and a sociologist . . . . He must therefore do more than write dramas; he must also design and equip the stage on which they were to be played.[4]

Thus Hugh MacLennan describes the tradition of the Canadian novel when he began work on his first published book, *Barometer Rising* (1941). Challenged by the bare stage of Canadian fiction, Hugh MacLennan established his reputation as Canada's first fictional set-builder. He used explicitly Canadian settings, historical events, and social issues not simply as background but as subject for many of his novels. The boldness of MacLennan's approach to the vexatious question of Canadian allusions, the ambition and national significance of his themes, and the impetus he thus provided to a budding native literature helped overshadow the melodramatic plotting, sentimental style, and conservative technique of his novels.

Although he was exposed as a young man to both British and American cultures during the modernist heyday and although he has been immersed through his teaching in the theory and practice of literature, MacLennan is nevertheless a conservative novelist, technically unselfconscious and rather innocent, more influenced by an older tradition than by modernist experimentation. Virginia Woolf and André Gide, Dorothy Richardson and James Joyce, Ernest Hemingway and William Faulkner, Jean-Paul Sartre and Franz Kafka all published their masterpieces during MacLennan's writing apprenticeship. Yet the authors whom critics cite most often as his models are John Galsworthy, Arnold Bennett, and, to a lesser extent, Leo Tolstoy, Honoré Balzac, and Thomas Hardy. MacLennan himself later maintained that in 1930 he had "never heard of James Joyce, T.S. Eliot, Ezra Pound, Marcel Proust, John Dos Passos, or Scott Fitzgerald."[5] Elsewhere he speaks of having cramped his style for two years "by trying to write like James Joyce," undoubtedly a surprise to readers of his stylistically unadventuresome prose.[6] And he praises Hemingway's stylistic skill in capturing sensation, but deplores the American author's inability to convey psychological or intellectual complexity.[7] However, MacLennan's derivative, overwrought, Joycean stream-of-consciousness style and his Hemingwayesque paratactic syntax run their complete course in the two unpublished novels. He ignored such post-modernist novelists as

John Barth, Vladimir Nabokov, and William Gass.

As suggested by his own differentiation between romantic and naturalistic novelists, MacLennan is a realist: "The romantics overlooked the fact that society has an integration and character of its own, the naturalists that the individual is a great deal more than the product of the social and economic conditions which they confidently believed had produced him."[8] Like Galsworthy and Bennett, he works within the tradition of the realist novel, meticulously recording the details of ordinary middle-class life. Like H.G. Wells, Sinclair Lewis, George Orwell, John Steinbeck, Graham Greene, or (authors he has mentioned with admiration) Arthur Koestler and Alan Paton, MacLennan stresses socio-political analysis. His work focuses on that point, as he approvingly quotes D.H. Lawrence, " 'where the soul meets history.' "[9] Accordingly, character is less central in his novels than in many realist works, his attacks on naturalistic reductionism notwithstanding. In MacLennan's praise of modern writers for their characterization, the wording itself — "creating characters of profound and universal validity and . . . weaving them into a pattern of absolute significance"[10] — reveals his allegiance to the wider picture rather than to characterization as an end in itself. Analyzing the trend towards non-fiction, he even suggests that today only powerful national states, not individuals, are capable of the hubris essential to tragic drama. Nations, he suggests, have displaced human beings as the protagonists in much modern literature.[11]

Another modifying influence on MacLennan's realism, one suggested by this reference to hubris, is his training in the classics. Not only do classical myths underlie many of his novels and characters, but Aristotle's theory and Sophocles' practice of drama often direct him towards a tightly structured plot somewhat at odds with the casual ordering of experience typical of realist novels.[12] There is a distinctly lowbrow strain in MacLennan's fiction which further strengthens this emphasis on action and plot, despite a valiant effort in The Watch That Ends the Night to substitute inner life for external action. MacLennan names Ivanhoe and Treasure Island as early influences, and one detects the subsequent influence of shoot-'em-ups, popular thrillers, and sentimental romances as background for the sensational violence and adventure plots seen most baldly in the unpublished work but also sporadically in his published fiction.[13] Documentary, drama, and romance, then, all colour MacLennan's realism.

In an early draft of *The Watch That Ends the Night*, George Stewart's favourite book during the depression of the 1930s is identified as Somerset Maugham's *Of Human Bondage*. The mood of this novel, what would "now be called Existentialism,"[14] appeals to Stewart; MacLennan's protagonists, especially in his unpublished fiction, suffer the *anomie* of existential heroes. Yet the philosophical core of MacLennan's fiction is moral conservatism. Though sympathetic to the modernist reaction against Victorian sentimentalism and response to the social collapse of the 1920s and 30s, MacLennan objected to the waste-land vision of modernist poetry and fiction. With reference to his early reading of the poetry of Eliot, Ezra Pound, and Auden, he noted, with irony: "Dutifully I turned my back on the poets I had loved . . . and joined the column that trudged off into the wasteland."[15] He cited the "precocious decadence" and "self-pitying elegance" of much modernist literature,[16] isolating Eliot as the exemplar of the obscurity and distaste for life fashionable in academic circles.[17] Further, he deplored the spirit of "middle-class *chic*" he found in modern fiction:

> Middle-class sentimentality has been replaced, in our fiction, by a peculiar middle-class *chic* which finds homosexuality more interesting than normal relationships, which is interested in women only if they are bitches, which believes ostensibly in liberal politics, yet views the materialistic society produced by the triumph of liberalism with a fascinated revulsion. . . . Our period, which thinks itself realistic, has adopted in the fiction its critics praise the realism of an alcoholic or a potential suicide.[18]

For MacLennan, the value of the novel lies elsewhere, "in its capacity to entertain," "in its characters," and in "its power to become an active agent within a society."[19]

As a novelist MacLennan is a realist; as a critic he is a pragmatist. His concern is primarily with literature's effect on the reader rather than with literature as an expression of the author or as a self-referential world. Very much in the tradition of Matthew Arnold and of F.R. Leavis, to whose criticism he was introduced in the 1930s, MacLennan's critical touchstone is the moral truth of a work.[20] For example, in 1948 he argued that

> . . . we are now entering . . . a period of reconstruction, both in society and in the arts. Such periods are always hard for the

artist, for it is incumbent on him, not on the Statesman, to discover new values. This he can do only by the process of creating potential values into real symbols.[21]

Influenced by mimetic theories of art and glossing easily over the complex relation between life and art, reality and fiction, which so exercises modernist and postmodernist writers, MacLennan defended his own work, not with aesthetic arguments, but with reference to subsequent historical developments validating his judgements. He has stated, for example, that *Barometer Rising* "was a book with something of a contrived plot, though the plot turned out to be almost dead accurate . . . ."[22] Even when MacLennan's analysis of literature seems to be technical, we find the same thematic and social preoccupations surfacing.[23] Relatively genre-blind as a result of this emphasis on representational truth, MacLennan moves freely in discussion from poetry to fiction to drama as illustrations of the same problems, and remains impervious to the New Critics' formalist emphasis on the technique and autonomy of the literary work.

As a non-fiction writer, Hugh MacLennan is similarly indebted, not to such contemporary developments as the New Journalism, but to an older tradition of the personal or familiar essay. His standards for non-fiction can be inferred from his appraisal of Francis Bacon, Joseph Addison, and Charles Lamb as the three supreme British essayists. He deemed Bacon the greatest because he is "the most intimate."[24] A commonplace of MacLennan criticism is the complaint that his ease and experience with non-fiction have led to unassimilated patches of philosophical, sociological, and historical exposition in his novels which violate their aesthetic integrity. MacLennan's response to this charge — "The literary highbrows . . . seemed to believe that prose should not be taken seriously if it is used to tell a story"[25] — implies that non-fiction is intrinsically a more substantial genre than fiction, or at least one with the same basic aims as fiction, though, as MacLennan indicates elsewhere, lacking fiction's intimacy, emotion, and capacity to entertain.[26] MacLennan's journalistic experience shows its influence, not just in extraneous exposition, but in the general stance of the novels with their emphasis on representative characters, on intellectual illumination, and on a detached understanding rather than an impressionistic involvement.

In the Canadian literary tradition, MacLennan's place is a curious one. Of his predecessors, only Frederick Philip Grove reveals signi-

ficant affinities, with the same strong sense of place, moral ponder-
ousness, and interest in generational conflict and socio-historical
definition. Grove in fact wrote to MacLennan praising the tone and
characterization of *Barometer Rising*, though criticizing the resolution's evasion of the central conflict.[27] Hugh Garner, in a clumsier
fashion than MacLennan, was also attempting sociological documentation in the years following the publication of MacLennan's first
novels. Among contemporary writers, MacLennan has taught and
encouraged Leonard Cohen, Marian Engel, and Robert Kroetsch.[28]
He has privately and publicly supported Gwethalyn Graham and
Colin McDougall (also a former student), both of whom share his
social and moral concerns.[29] He has corresponded with Stephen
Vizinczey concerning a screenplay of *Barometer Rising*.[30] And he has
received expressions of appreciation from writers as diverse as
Robertson Davies, Margaret Laurence, Leo Kennedy, Gratien
Gélinas, Farley Mowat, Roger Lemelin, F.R. Scott, Brian Moore,
Gabrielle Roy, and Earle Birney.[31] Yet, with the possible exception of
Rudy Wiebe, whose work has a similar social scope, historical
emphasis, and moral seriousness but is less conservative in form and
technique, MacLennan has no direct literary descendants. In many
ways, he is the E.J. Pratt of Canadian fiction, a lone Canadian
mythmaker, innovative in his choice of national and "non-literary"
subject matter, distinctive in his documentary and social focus,
conventional, even old-fashioned, in his choice of form. Too individual to be a model for subsequent writers, MacLennan's work is a
turning point in the development of a distinctly national literature.
Not the founder or even member of a Canadian literary movement,
MacLennan has functioned instead in a much more general way, as
what Robert Kroetsch calls the "enabling figure," showing later
writers "how to be a writer in Canada, how to be a Canadian
writer."[32]

Critical Overview and Context

Hugh MacLennan so satisfied the growing need for a fictional
delineation and interpretation of Canadian realities that, for a long
time, critics refused to heed their own strictures on his formal,
technical, and stylistic deficiencies when assessing his stature. So

argue Roger Hyman and Elspeth Cameron in their surveys of critical responses to MacLennan. Hyman suggests that only when Mac-Lennan's social vision turned more pessimistic (and less acceptable) in *Return of the Sphinx* did critics focus critically on the literary weakness of his work.[33] Cameron complains that emphasis on MacLennan's ideas has led to critical neglect of the formal qualities of his work, such as archetypes, imagery, structure, and to critical ignorance of his unpublished novels, manuscript revisions, and underlying literary theories.[34] Although some technical analysis has always been present in MacLennan criticism, it has not always borne sufficient weight in critical assessments of his achievement.

From the first positive reviews of *Barometer Rising*, critics, particularly in Canada, have assumed MacLennan's importance as a major Canadian novelist, often ironically while expressing disappointment over his technical weaknesses or failure to fulfil his putative potential.[35] With *The Watch That Ends the Night*, many reviewers found this potential realized: "The Canadian novel takes a great stride forward," proclaimed Robertson Davies.[36] Sales of the novel have reflected that judgement.[37] The apparent loss of artistic power in *Return of the Sphinx* produced a louder outcry in the book pages than had a similar falling-off in *The Precipice* two decades later. American reviewers have frequently, particularly with "political" novels like *Two Solitudes* and *Return of the Sphinx*, promoted the novels condescendingly and uncritically as short-cuts to a socio-political understanding of their northern neighbour. At its worst, this produces the fatuousness of William du Bois' description of the characters in *Two Solitudes* as having the "hard true brightness that is part of the clean bright land they march through.[38]

Important early criticism of MacLennan includes Roy Daniells' suggestion that MacLennan emphasizes religion and not class struggle as Canada's problem,[39] and George Woodcock's characterization of MacLennan as "a social novelist, using his central myth [the Odyssey] to demonstrate the underlying universality of the personal and national experience he recreates."[40] Warren Tallman provides an iconoclastic reading of "the civilized surface confronting the violent self" in *Each Man's Son*, with MacLennan seen as being of the devil's party without knowing it and as being unable to animate the protagonist's facade because "it has so little to do with the profound naiveté and relative crudity of response in which MacLennan's true force as an artist is rooted."[41] Paul Goetsch identifies three stages in

MacLennan's novels, personal incompleteness, disheartenment, and quiet affirmation, suggesting that ". . . . few modern writers have dared to encompass, in one novel, the movement from violence to such full affirmation . . . ."[42] Edmund Wilson's 1964 appreciation in *O Canada* of MacLennan, whom he characterizes as a "secretary of society," has had an impact simply from the stature and nationality of the critic, although details of Wilson's analysis (his praise for MacLennan's characterization of "decent women") and his selection of novels to celebrate (*The Precipice* along with *The Watch That Ends the Night*) remain curious.[43] Less innocuous commendation comes a few years later from Ronald Sutherland, who describes MacLennan as one of the first writers in the emerging "mainstream" of Canadian literature, a mainstream characterized prescriptively and uncritically by an awareness of the co-existence of the two main ethnic and language groups in Canada (and coincidentally, as a result, by the exclusion of most major English-Canadian novelists).[44]

Along with George Woodcock's early recognition of MacLennan's innovation in taking "the drama of the development and survival of Canada . . . . as the framework for fiction"[45] has gone repeated analysis of the symbolic, even allegorical, significance attached as a result to character and event. Anticipating W.H. New's caution that such allegorizing is most effective where it is most effortless,[46] Hugo McPherson speaks for a score of other critics in arguing that the symbolic structure appropriate for MacLennan's treatment of social conflict frequently "stumbles over the concealed trip-wire of individual uniqueness."[47] This particular criticism points up a general concern with MacLennan's didacticism, notably with the load of exposition his omniscient narrators carry. As Roger Hyman notes, "few contemporary writers have used the [omniscient] technique so bluntly, with so little concern for the characters' intrinsic needs or for the demands on them of plot and situation as has MacLennan."[48] Although critics have praised his skill in creating lively, comic, and eccentric minor characters, they have found fault in MacLennan's characterization of his protagonists, particularly in their dialogue which is seen to be too articulate, undifferentiated, and inappropriate to the occasion.[49] In addition to his sometimes intrusive allegorizing, several critics also perceive an underlying framework of myth in MacLennan's fiction (either Odysseus, Oedipus, or Adam and Eve) giving archetypal significance to the action. Whether or not they attribute MacLennan's recurring character types to the influence of myth, various critics have traced clear lines of descent among the characters of different novels. George Woodcock links the recurring figures of the returning wanderer, waiting woman, fatherless child, wise doctor, and primitive, violent, good giant to the Odysseus myth. Robert Cockburn attributes the similarity of MacLennan's various wholesome heroines, older termagants, sages, businessman villains, and humourless heroes to poverty of the imagination; and Patricia Morley divides the heroes into pairs, one a thinker and the other a doer.[50]

While reflecting over MacLennan's oeuvre as a whole, critics have proposed several patterns of development. Catherine Ross detects a deepening gloom in MacLennan's outlook, a shift from "romance and comedy to irony and tragedy."[51] Alec Lucas senses a tragic vision in the later novels which abruptly reverses the affirmation of the earlier works while W.H. New and I see a consistent progression towards pessimism.[52] Many critics trace a movement away from a focus on social and national issues to psychological or even religious concerns,[53] with Catherine Ross suggesting that in *The Watch That Ends the Night* MacLennan has committed himself to a spiritual, ideal world in preference to the visible one.[54] A third development in MacLennan's career highlighted in the criticism is a shift in the age of his characters from youthful in the early novels to middle-aged in the later works.[55]

Critical recognition of the national significance of MacLennan's subject-matter and themes has been supplemented by praise for his evocatively powerful descriptions of scenes and action, with the dramatization of the Halifax explosion in *Barometer Rising* often used as evidence.[56] However, other critics have cited MacLennan's failure of tone in scenes of strong emotion, producing grandiloquent dialogue, and in descriptions of sexuality, causing embarrassed clumsiness and coy romanticism.[57] With the exception thus far of *Voices in Time*, the ending of each novel has inspired at least scattered complaints. *Barometer Rising* and *Each Man's Son* have been criticized for the fatalistic, arbitrary violence of the ending, which in the case of *Barometer Rising* is seen as an evasion of the main conflict.[58] Alec Lucas has objected to the smug, "almost sermon-like peroration" to *The Watch That Ends the Night*, an ending which suggests a pietistic rejection of this-worldly life incongruous with the rest of the novel.[59] Likewise, *Return of the Sphinx* has been criticized for the facile optimism of an epilogue which is not supported by the action.[60]

A greater structural problem has been detected in *Two Solitudes*: the two halves of the novel are seen as poorly connected, a criticism culminating in Claude Bissell's abridged school edition of the book which simply omits the second half of the novel, Parts III and IV.[61]

Although *Barometer Rising* is occasionally praised as MacLennan's best-sustained though not his most ambitious novel,[62] *The Watch That Ends the Night* is commonly considered to be MacLennan's greatest achievement, with its profound theme and emotional power dwarfing its weaknesses.[63] *Each Man's Son* does have some defenders as MacLennan's strongest novel, and recently *Voices in Time* has been proposed for that accolade.[64] *Return of the Sphinx* arouses largely negative reactions, while *The Precipice* has the distinction of being repeatedly cited as MacLennan's least successful novel.[65] Because of its structural disunity, *Two Solitudes* provokes such dubious tributes as George Woodcock's contention that MacLennan's achievement "rests, apart from his essays, on three good novels, *Each Man's Son*, *Barometer Rising*, and *The Watch That Ends the Night*, and on the earlier half of *Two Solitudes*."[66] Interestingly, W.J. Keith names a non-fiction work, *Seven Rivers of Canada*, as one of the MacLennan works he most admires.[67]

With the exception of Paul Goetsch's 1961 *Das Romanwerk Hugh MacLennans* (not translated and so of limited influence), monographs on MacLennan sprang up almost simultaneously and without the opportunity for profitable cross-pollination.[68] Three monographs by George Woodcock, Peter Buitenhuis, and Robert Cockburn appeared in 1969, with Alec Lucas' study following in 1970. Woodcock's *Hugh MacLennan* provides several chapters on MacLennan's thought, literary and national, and then expands on the archetypal reading of the novels begun in his earlier essay "A Nation's Odyssey: The Novels of Hugh MacLennan" in *Odysseus Ever Returning*. Peter Buitenhuis, while identifying problems created by MacLennan's lack of technical innovation, nevertheless defends the novelist as a "great trail-blazer" in Canadian literature who "has journeyed alone into the Canadian mind."[69] To his analysis of the novels, Buitenhuis appends a chapter on MacLennan's non-fiction (an often overlooked area). Most provocative, original, and persuasive is Robert Cockburn's often blunt critical assessment of MacLennan. Unabashedly evaluative and analytic, Cockburn's book restores balance to MacLennan criticism, while at the same time (with the possible exception of its championing of *Each Man's Son* as MacLennan's best novel and ultimate disparagement of *The Watch That Ends the Night*) serving as a useful compendium of critical judgements about MacLennan. Alec Lucas' *Hugh Mac-Lennan*, the only one of these four monographs to eschew a chapter-by-chapter analysis of the novels, discusses MacLennan's romance plotting, use of the chronicle form, character types, and mythic structures, here expanding on Woodcock's brief mention of the Oedipus myth and proposing it as the controlling framework of several novels.[70] While challenging interpretations of MacLennan as valuing only the personal and abandoning social action, Lucas defines the novels as "parables centred on religious humanism."[71]

Another early publication on MacLennan is Patricia Morley's *The Immoral Moralists: Hugh MacLennan and Leonard Cohen* (1972). Comparing the responses of MacLennan and Leonard Cohen to their Puritan heritage, Morley goes beyond MacLennan's overt attack on Puritan repression in his novels to suggest that "he is marked, to a greater extent than he has yet acknowledged, by the strengths and affirmations of that historic Puritanism."[72] She demonstrates this influence in MacLennan's treatment of work, love, and sex; in his structural method of opposing values of life and death; and in his use of patterns of death and rebirth.

Significant individual articles since 1975 have tended to be specialized, though several are panoramic. Robin Mathews exposes Mac-Lennan's "personalist" evasion of issues of class (with the initial exception of *Barometer Rising*'s anticolonialism),[73] and David Staines classifies the novels into national and character novels, with a much-needed discussion of the two unpublished novels.[74] T.D. MacLulich traces MacLennan's use of the Oedipus and Eve myths to argue that "MacLennan's true subject is the individual in his family setting,"[75] while Laurel Boone examines *Each Man's Son* to demonstrate MacLennan's temperamental affinity with romance, despite an intellectual commitment to realism.[76] More often, though, we have close study of individual texts: for example, Warren Stevenson's argument for the unity of *Two Solitudes*; Elspeth Cameron's study of the overlay theme of *The Precipice*; Roger Hyman's evaluation of the weaknesses of *Return of the Sphinx*; Joseph Zezulka's analysis of the City-of-God theme in *Return of the Sphinx*; and Catherine Kelly's analysis of patterns of imagery in *Two Solitudes*.[77] Other critics have studied the influence of Anthony Tudor's ballet *Pillar of Fire* on *The Precipice*, Yeats's poetry on *Return of the*

Sphinx, and G. Rattray Taylor's *Sex in History* and Sophocles' *Oedipus at Colonus* on the same novel.[78] Others have compared MacLennan with Rainer Maria Rilke and *Barometer Rising* with W.D. Howells' *The Rise of Silas Lapham*.[79]

Several collections of essays on MacLennan have also appeared. *Hugh MacLennan* (1973), edited by Paul Goetsch, includes influential essays by George Woodcock and Hugo McPherson as well as W.H. New's analyses of imagery in *Barometer Rising* and *Return of the Sphinx*.[80] The Winter 1979–80 Hugh MacLennan issue of *Journal of Canadian Studies* includes, among others, my analysis of the paradise-lost motif in the novel; MacLulich's identification of *The Precipice* as a pivotal work, marking MacLennan's shift to a religious viewpoint; Stephen Bonnycastle's structuralist argument that the rendering of a pantheistic vision in *The Watch That Ends the Night* is the source of the novel's power; and Francis Zichy's analysis of problems of point of view and tone in the same work as evidence of the novel's unconscious tendency to "accommodate and celebrate the ills of the protagonists."[81] The proceedings of a conference on MacLennan have been published in *Hugh MacLennan: 1982*, edited by Elspeth Cameron. Largely historical and political in its orientation and so continuing the traditional preoccupation with MacLennan's vision rather than his craft, the collection does include W.J. Keith's proposal that MacLennan's "bold refusal to separate imaginative literature from everyday experience" in *The Watch That Ends the Night* poses a challenge to contemporary critical assumptions, and Eli Mandel's cryptic application of Harold Bloom's anxiety-of-influence thesis (MacLennan's "rewriting" of Frederick Philip Grove) and Freud's *Beyond the Pleasure Principle* to MacLennan's fiction.[82]

Elspeth Cameron's thoroughly researched and documented *Hugh MacLennan: A Writer's Life* (1981) provides essential new information on MacLennan's youth, correspondence, influences, manuscripts, unpublished novels, publishing history, and critical reception. Slightly distorted by an over-emphasis on MacLennan's opportunism in choosing Canadian subject-matter and, conversely, by over-dependence on MacLennan's own view of his life, the biography remains an essential source of information. T.D. MacLulich's *Hugh MacLennan* (1983) includes a sustained examination of the unpublished novels. MacLulich argues that MacLennan's life illuminates "a theme that is at the heart of his fiction — the divided feelings of a dutiful but independent-minded son toward a demanding and undemonstrative father."[83] Insisting that individual, national, and collective psychology in MacLennan's novels is consistently modelled on generational and Oedipal tensions in the patriarchal family, MacLulich concludes that the chronology of MacLennan's work demonstrates an increasingly complex understanding of human nature.

There are three main interviews of MacLennan conducted by Donald Cameron in 1973, Ronald Sutherland in 1976, and Alan Twigg in 1981, respectively. Cameron and Sutherland focus questions on MacLennan's literary career, Twigg on the novelist's political thinking.

MacLennan's Works

A. Unpublished Fiction

MacLennan's two unpublished novels, "So All Their Praises" (1933) and "A Man Should Rejoice" (1937), like his published novels, explore societies on the edge of a precipice and characters on the verge of a breakdown. Both unpublished works express the disillusionment with social structures and fear for civilization which become strong again in MacLennan's last novels; "So All Their Praises" particularly anticipates the emphasis on private solutions over public action amplified later in *The Watch That Ends the Night*. Especially in "So All Their Praises," MacLennan is stylistically more experimental, in a jejune fashion, then he would ever be again. Readers familiar with the conservative MacLennan may well find the manner, if not the matter, of these early writings a revelation. Until the latter part of "A Man Should Rejoice," however, MacLennan does not know how to control his material. In his first unpublished novel, one does not detect much literary talent; in his second, despite continuing problems with focus and organization, one does.

"So All Their Praises" is unwittingly two novels in one, a lost-generation chronicle of disillusioned young men flirting with nihilism against the backdrop of the depression and rising fascism, and a gangster thriller of smuggling, hijackings, danger, and double-crosses. The action of the thriller is contrived to keep the protagonists occupied (and to transport them between the "raucous" vitality of New York and the "undiscovered" tranquility of Nova Scotia, alternatives to the corruption of Europe), while we eavesdrop on their philosophical and emotional crises. Like most MacLennan novels, "So All Their Praises" involves a search for meaning in a disordered social situation. Two possible outcomes of this search are explored here. Adolph Fabricius, a rebellious young German whose character is realized through his actions and family background, finds comfort in his loving relationship with Sarah MacRae, whereas his companion, Michael Carmichael, a rather disembodied, embittered young English writer, is left contemplating his own isolation. As these two work on a road crew in Germany, drift in and out of bed with various women, observe wide-spread unemployment, political unrest, and the rise of Naziism, fall accidentally into the North American bootlegging business aboard the *Martin Swicker*, or attempt suicide (Adolph near the beginning, Michael near the end of the novel), what is at issue is the ability to enjoy and endure, to stay human and not go "dry." Such a description gives the novel more coherence than it possesses, since the lack of focus created by the double protagonist is compounded by a structural aimlessness. Except for the strengthening relationship between Adolph and Sarah MacRae, whom the two men meet in Halifax, the material of the novel is unified only by the presence of one or both protagonists and a mood of overwrought emotionalism.

Somewhat undifferentiated in their thwarted idealism, initial cynicism about love, fear of proving incapable of feeling, and free-floating bitterness, Michael and Adolph provide windows on world events. They permit MacLennan to explore, naturalistically, the individual's impotence amid international upheaval:

> [Adolph] saw .... himself, the individual, subject to accident, but the movements of the mass predetermined.... In everything we see and hear something is struggling to be born.... Until the birth comes the non-creative individual can do nothing of objective importance. Grow inwardly.[84]

Such a philosophy has unfortunate effects for characterization. Michael and Adolph become observing automatons, "hardly thinking at all" (or, more accurately, hardly deciding at all — they do all too much thinking), merely "moving in events" (chap. 29).

Among his experimental methods of capturing social and personal reality, MacLennan uses headlines (reminiscent of Dos Passos' newsreels), an expressionistic barrage of the voices of actual and representative contemporary figures — the Pope, Hitler, a professor, a businessman — and, especially, stream-of-consciousness narrative. The first-person, present-tense, sometimes fragmented passages of inner sensation used for all three major characters (like similar passages in "A Man Should Rejoice") come unintentionally close at times to hysteria. They anticipate the brief patches of florid excess of Daniel Ainslie in *Each Man's Son* and George Stewart in *The Watch That Ends the Night* during moments of personal crisis. Pretentious and gauche even when valid, the ponderings of the characters can produce such dubious philosophizing as the proposition that a man's greatness is proportionate to "the potential energy of his spirit," a potential energy converted perhaps at death into kinetic energy (chaps. 17, 23). The novel does show the beginnings of MacLennan's skill with landscape lyricism. The descriptions are strongly romantic: for example, the pastoral power of the Nova Scotia countryside, the prehistoric "green continent," is contrasted with the destructive power of the "machine of the world and its indifference" (chap. 14). Even here, in the scene in which Adolph and Sarah first spend the night together in a Nova Scotia hollow, MacLennan lapses into purple prose: "Under a tor of the Great Glacier under the Acropolis beside the Lapis Niger our causes were unloosed . . . . back among the Neolithic bones of the earth" (chap. 14). We get hints too in the handling of Sarah's sexuality of a mystical instinctualism reminiscent of D.H. Lawrence — "it is being offered that I may myself be offered" — as well as in later descriptions of a pregnant woman — " 'Her body is her real life . . . . only her body means' " (chaps. 14, 21). With the exception of scenes involving Sarah, who is spared some of the self-conscious intensity of Adolph and Michael, the fragmented, alienated, and undirected experience of these characters, dispassionately recorded, ultimately leaves the reader disengaged.

For those who saw the use of first-person perspective in *The Watch That Ends the Night* as a technical advance and discovery for Hugh MacLennan, the manuscript of "A Man Should Rejoice" may come as a surprise. The first chapter of this novel builds towards the dramatic twist of its conclusion, where the ostensibly omniscient narrator is revealed to be the offspring of the marriage he has just been describing. The book begins much as "So All Their Praises" does with a pair of characters: one the observing artist-loner, here the narrator David Culver, an aspiring painter; and the other the active friend early involved in a healing love affair, here revolutionary Nicholas Eisenhardt. But Nicholas is never as central as Adolph was in "So All Their Praises," dropping rather abruptly from view when the setting shifts from the north-eastern United States to Austria. At the same time, David becomes lover and man of action. The author's problem with focus here is less a question of which character to emphasize — the point of view helps resolve that issue — than a question of which approach to take to David Culver's life.

"A Man Should Rejoice" is primarily a *Bildungsroman*, with elements of a *Künstlerroman*. The novel moves chronologically through David's early ideological conflicts with his millionaire father, a mechanical engineer; his year of art training in Paris; his attempts as a communist to organize Bernard Culver's workers during the depression, culminating in a riot led by company-recruited agitators and counterpointed ironically with the serenity of David's honeymoon with Anne Lovelace; his jail term, which, he reflects, "distilled my perceptions and made me at last what I had desired to become — a painter,"[85] but which also brings him temporarily to the verge of total alienation from humankind, including Anne; and, finally, his participation as a painter in a disastrous but necessary socialist resistance movement in Anne's hometown, Lorbeerstein, Austria. While David's philosophical, emotional, and artistic development lends coherence to the novel, as does his narrative voice, only in the last third, especially in the Austrian scenes, do character and event really coalesce. We finally find ourselves involved with the characters, rather than instructed by the author with the characters as lay figures. The drama here is intrinsic to character development, not merely backdrop against which to unfold an independently conceived characterization. But the strength of these scenes makes them the heart of the novel, with earlier events seeming to belong to another world, another novel. A more dramatic and less linear structure, then, focusing on the Lorbeerstein conflict, might have provided the unity of action still absent here. Although the novel is retrospective, narrated, as we are told in the Preface, from a distant Nova Scotia where a shattered and solitary David has retreated to "freeze a durable form" out of what has happened, only the Preface provides hints, and these oblique ones, of the context into which the early events of the narrative must be fitted. If MacLennan had employed not just the first-person perspective, but also the flashback technique which was to serve him well in *The Watch That Ends the Night*, "A Man Should Rejoice" could have been a stronger novel.

Although publishers' readers complained rightly that this novel was overwritten, "A Man Should Rejoice" is more mature philosophically, less high-strung, and less burdened with theorizing than the first novel.[86] Rather than seeming wilful or forced, David's early frustration is clearly rooted in home life, particularly in father-son tensions (a recurring issue in MacLennan's work). In handling emotionally delicate scenes, such as Nicholas' wife's pregnancy and unwelcome abortion, MacLennan shows he can write with sensitivity, avoiding bathos.

Apart from its artistic potential, "A Man Should Rejoice" is intriguing for the light it sheds on MacLennan the writer. While drafting it, he was also commenting dismissively on the "Hemingway school" of writers.[87] Yet the last part of the novel, set in the snow-covered Austrian hills, with Anne's pregnancy and the protagonists' vulnerable happiness together placed in the context of an approaching civil war, contains distinct echoes of Hemingway's *A Farewell to Arms*, even to the ingenuous tone of some dialogue, for example, Anne's " 'Your wife isn't much good for you these days, is she?' " (chap. 31). D.H. Lawrence's philosophy of male and female principles also makes its influence felt in Anne's wholesome contempt for men "who did not instinctively honor the female in her," and in her simultaneous desire to be mastered and to struggle against mastery (chap. 32).

There are many parallels between this early and later novels. David's destructive American industrialist father provides a prototype for Stephen Lassiter in *The Precipice*; the elder Eisenhardt is the figure of the sage found also in so many later novels; the description of peaceful Nova Scotia's ability to cleanse and cool the mind looks forward to a similar scene in *Return of the Sphinx*; and the question-and-answer format of the trial scene resembles the television interview and Hansard transcript in *Return of the Sphinx*. MacLennan's examination here of "the most rapid transition from one era to another that mankind has ever known" (Preface) and of an entire world undergoing a nervous breakdown (chap. 15) links "A Man Should Rejoice" with MacLennan's last three novels. Most striking and suggestive is the early novel's function as a template for *The*

Watch That Ends the Night. Both novels begin with an observer-narrator and an activist, although, as we have seen, David eventually incorporates into himself the functions divided in the later novel between George Stewart and Jerome Martell. Both novels explore the defeat of the idealism of the 1930s. As David says in the Preface, "We were people who lived hard and tried to change the world by thinking about it, and were beaten from the start by attempting the impossible." Small-scale communist involvement issuing in disastrous riots and temporary defeat for the protagonist (the result of both sabotage and naïveté) leads to more dangerous engagement in a larger leftist struggle and war. There are echoes even in details: in the midst of the unrest, like George after him, David wonders how long it has been since we could accept the assurance of the Psalm that goodness and mercy shall follow us all the days of our lives (chap. 15). Juxtaposed in each case to the political tension is the personal "paradise" of a marriage which, however, cannot remain the island of tranquility the lovers wish it to be. Both novels end with the death of the heroine, the overwhelming loss for a protagonist of what he most values (developed much more fully in *The Watch That Ends the Night*), and an estrangement from the world different in kind from earlier youthful disillusionment. In "A Man Should Rejoice," MacLennan even employs in miniature the narrative strategy of the later novel of anticipating and reflecting upon the final crisis before narrating it in detail. "A Man Should Rejoice" has two endings, the stronger showing David confronting his inescapable solitude. The other, apparently a revision at the behest of publishers, has David directed by the Superior of a monastery towards a perception of the eternal, not to be located within this world, and so anticipates, in a facile way, the religious impulse in the conclusion to *The Watch That Ends the Night*.

Both are novels about disillusionment and defeat, and "A Man Should Rejoice" therefore challenges any simplistic conception of MacLennan's thinking as a steady progression towards pessimism and acquiescence. David proposes, after his imprisonment, one of the central hypotheses tested in *The Watch That Ends the Night*, that twentieth-century society has "vitiated almost everything and made most things except affection between person and person either bad or meaningless" (chap. 28). Nevertheless, links with the more politically engaged and reformist orientation of the early novels can be seen in the unpublished work, because David goes on to fight for socialist Lorbeerstein: "In a dying world here was a spot where workmen and peasants and thinkers were building things" (chap. 32). Although leftist activism is defeated, it is not discredited here.

B. Published Fiction

"The essence of man's fate today," Hugh MacLennan stated in 1970, "is the dying struggle of the brave and able individual against the force of disintegration inherent in technology." In this world, "the modern novel can be trivial and perfect, or utterly imperfect and at least try to tear its bare hands on the barbed wire of the mid-twentieth century."[88] Eschewing perfection and turning in his published novels to Canadian experience, that part of the twentieth century he knows best, MacLennan analyses meaning and meaninglessness, power and powerlessness, through a simultaneous exploration of personal and public worlds. The search for meaning is the focus of middle novels; the study of power is the focus of the early and the later novels. MacLennan has also argued, not inconsistently, that the tragedy occupying modern British and American writers, unlike European writers, has been the gradual "wearing away of the importance of the family."[89] As I have pointed out elsewhere, his oeuvre proceeds with decreasing hopefulness from symbolic depictions of young lovers through descriptions of marriages under stress to portraits of families destroyed.[90]

Structurally, the novels are diverse, comprising three main types. First, MacLennan chooses tight, chronological narratives covering short time periods, such as the nine- and eight-day narratives of *Barometer Rising* and *Return of the Sphinx* (the latter with an epilogue set some months later) for immediate drama, both personal and national. Second, more diffuse chronological narratives, like the twelve-year chronicle of *Two Solitudes* or the seven-year narrative of *The Precipice*, provide more documentary overview, more attention to psychological and social development. *Each Man's Son*, a three-month chronological account, with half the novel devoted to the first and final days of the sequence, falls somewhere between these two types, closer to the former. Third, MacLennan combines the strengths of both forms in his retrospective novels, which survey even longer time periods — fifty years in *The Watch That Ends the*

Night, one hundred and thirty years in *Voices in Time* — but create a focus through present-time sequences developing chronologically over a short period. Significantly, only the retrospective novels abandon omniscient narration for the more subjective, intimate first-person perspective.

In 1937 MacLennan spoke of his desire to create in *Two Solitudes* "a picture of Canada and Canadian life, not a formula-plotted story," thus identifying early on not only a continuing aim but also an underestimated, recurring temptation.[91] The "formula-plotted story" he was attempting to jettison, exemplified in the heroes and villains of *Barometer Rising* and its contrived resolution through fortuitous violence, reappears in the romance complications of the second half of *Two Solitudes*, in the first half of *The Precipice*, and in the sensational climaxes of *Each Man's Son*, *Return of the Sphinx*, and *Voices in Time*. MacLennan alternates between the devices of melodrama — morally coded characters, vignettes of violence, emotionally charged confessions, malevolent intrigue, sentimental clichés, and coincidence — and original explorations of social and psychological complexity. He shows an awareness of these two competing models in his well-known comment on the composition of *The Watch That Ends the Night*:

> Somewhere around 1950, it seems to have occurred to millions of readers that this kind of external action — this drama played as a means of revealing the tragic nature of man — was apt to be both inaccurate and inadequate . . . .
>
> Around this time, it seemed to me, as it seemed to the educated public, that the basic human conflict was 'within' the individual. . . . Somehow I was going to write a book which would not depend on character-in-action, but on spirit-in-action. The conflict here, the essential one, was between the human spirit of Everyman and Everyman's human condition.[92]

In characterizing his first published novel *Barometer Rising* (1941) as an experiment, "more a *tour de force* than a novel," MacLennan has acknowledged its melodramatic plot and improbabilities.[93] Generically, the novel follows the formulas of romantic comedy, with young lovers Penelope Wain and her cousin Neil Macrae reunited despite the machinations of Penny's father, who has unjustly court-martialed his nephew Neil during World War I. As in other romantic comedies, the lovers' triumph marks a shift of social centre from the old to the young, from a Canada still in bondage to Britain to an independent nation coming of age with its own identity. Other conventions of fairy tale and romance also appear: the foster-parent (orphaned Neil has been raised by his uncle); the irrational command and its violation (Neil has disobeyed Wain's contradictory and faulty order in battle); the absent hero (presumed killed in action, Neil is hiding under an assumed name); the quest to win or rescue the princess (before returning to Penny, whose life has become oppressively static, Neil must clear his name); the witness (Alex MacKenzie, one of Wain's employees, can testify to the original military order); feats of heroism (Neil performs valiant rescue work during the Halifax explosion of 1917 and the blizzard which follows); the unmasking of the villain (Wain, a respectable community leader, is found with his mistress, dead and naked, in the aftermath of the explosion); and the concluding revelation and exaltation of the hero (Penny prepares to disclose to Neil the existence of their daughter Jean and travels with him towards *Prince's Lodge*, potentially their new home).

MacLennan employs the formulaic plot, though, in the service of social realism and modifies it in significant ways. For the first time, he uses Canada as the setting of his novel, and, because of his geographical, historical, and political explicitness and the socio-political symbolism of his characters' lives, Canada becomes his subject-matter as well. "I am sure of this," MacLennan commented in 1941, "no artist can possibly write of any society — as a base — than his own."[94] Writing for an American audience but aware that Canadians too had been largely deprived of fictional representations of their experience, he faced the realization attributed to the protagonist of *Two Solitudes*, who is himself a Canadian novelist: ". . . . he realized that his readers' ignorance of the essential Canadian clashes and values presented him with a unique problem. The background would have to be created from scratch if his story was to become intelligible."[95] Accordingly, in *Barometer Rising* Mac-Lennan provides topographical descriptions of Halifax, complete with references to Ice Age glacial activity; celebrates the promise of the sprawling Canadian landscape (in imitation of John of Gaunt's famous panegyric in Shakespeare's *Richard II*); attacks the dangerous stupidity of militarists; reflects on the impact of urban technology upon rural communities and traditional values; and analyses Canada's shift from a British colony to a mediating power in the world community. Furthermore, the course of young love portrayed in this novel, with its earlier simplicity nostalgically remembered, its traumas, and its new hope, carries a weight of meaning absent from the usual love story. The characters and actions parallel in allegorical detail the stages of Canada's development articulated in the novel, with World War I shown as painfully but constructively destroying Canada's subservience to its mother country and catapulting it into independence. (Incidentally, this focusing on Canadian experience may account for the shift towards optimism in MacLennan's early published novels. Although rhetoric about individual impotence does echo the fatalistic philosophizing of the unpublished novels, the Canadian colonialism, anglophone domination of French Canada, and joyless Calvinist heritage which MacLennan attacks in the first four published novels seem more manageable targets than the amorphous, generalized *anomie* and collapse of social order which haunt his earliest and latest writings.)

Part of the realistic orientation of *Barometer Rising* is Penny Wain's transformation from the traditional, passive heroine of romance to the role of protagonist, sharing the action equally with Neil Macrae. Penelope is, moreover, established as a New Woman, working successfully in the male profession of ship design and bearing a child outside marriage.[96] Simultaneously, the conventional false hero or false suitor of romance — here Penny's new suitor, disreputable, war-damaged physician Angus Murray — has been given a more positive function, threatening, as Robert Cockburn suggests, to displace Neil in the readers' sympathies.[97] Neil himself is too tense, hostile, and self-involved to be pure hero. David Arnason has even suggested that there are two incompatible Neil Macraes in the novel: the indecisive, paranoid Neil of the first part and the hero of the second.[98] For all the fortuitousness and arbitrariness of the novel's romance ending, Penny's earlier estrangement from Neil, her frustrations with his obtuseness, and her continuing listlessness and hesitancy all show MacLennan providing psychologically realistic equivalents for the familiar formulaic and chimerical obstacles and misunderstandings between lovers inevitable in romance.

The final comic resolution, too, is a qualified one. On the one hand, romantic optimism is conveyed largely through plot (Murray's physical and psychological recuperation, reunion of the lovers, removal of impediments — Jean's adoptive parents as well as Penny's father) and through symbolism (final departure from the restrictive parental home, end of the storm, imminent revelation of the child, explicit parallels with Odysseus' homecoming, fresh rising wind and bright moonlight). On the other hand, Neil's (and MacLennan's) grandiose dreams of Canada's future as "the central arch which united the new order"[99] and the romance ending itself are edged towards realism and rendered tentative by Murray's noncommittal evaluation of Canada's promise and Neil and Penny's future. Penny's gloomier ruminations on the titanic forces confronting the individual, the inhibiting power of the old guard in Canada, and the uncertain future ahead further qualify romantic optimism.[100] *Barometer Rising*, then, is a romance, but the shading allowed some potentially black or white characters (notably Penny, Murray, and, at times, Neil), the occasional expository qualification of the plot's sunniness, and especially the relatively unprecedented, detailed, and realistic Canadian material help mask this feature.

The structure of *Barometer Rising* is simple and dramatic. A linear narrative spanning nine days from Sunday, 2 December 1917, to Monday of the following week, the novel is classically structured to build towards the climax of the Halifax explosion, coinciding with Neil's vindication and the restoration of Penny's child. Not only is the Thursday of the explosion handled at greater length but that chapter is also subdivided more frequently into the temporal units (i.e., "Seven-thirty A.M.," "Eight-fifteen O'Clock," "Eight-forty O'Clock") which comprise the novel and whose frequency here, like rapid scene shifts in film, contributes to the growing suspense. The subsequent Friday, Saturday, and Sunday, which provide the story's dénouement, are presented more briefly, with merely a single scene for each. The shifts from scene to scene and character to character are mechanical and serve to create a detached overview, offering the reader the distanced excitement of the privileged onlooker, rather than the pleasure of involvement with the characters. But particularly in depicting, one by one, each of the many characters both before and immediately after the explosion which permanently alters the entire configuration of relationships, this method (now the obligatory formula of disaster movies) works to reinforce our sense of the interplay of public and private as well as to intensify the drama. The prominence of plot, division into "acts" and "scenes," clear rising and falling action, and relative unity of time, place, and action all demonstrate MacLennan's predilection for the theatre. The characters, too, with their external conflicts and symbolic significance, though not denuded of inner life, illustrate more clearly than some subsequent characters his propensity, as John Moss points out, for producing *"dramatis personae"* rather than "psychological creations."[101] The conventions of romance, coupled with some of the techniques of drama, however melodramatic and sentimental, provide MacLennan with a firm structure, with a direction and proportion, needed to impose shape on his philosophical and social theorizing. In his unpublished novels, this shaping structure is missing; in his next novel, *Two Solitudes*, structure is again a problem.

Two Solitudes (1945) begins as a realistic internal drama of character set within a chronicle of a family and a society. Only in the last third of the book does MacLennan invoke the formulas of romantic comedy, presumably as a means of bringing the work to a close. Throughout his career, MacLennan alternates uneasily, sometimes within novels, sometimes from one novel to the next, between unpredictable, potentially shapeless inner exploration and well-shaped, potentially superficial melodramatic formulas.

MacLennan's aim in *Two Solitudes* is an ambitious and, for its time, original one. Through the stories of Athanase Tallard, a rural Quebec landowner and member of parliament caught between dreams of social and economic progress for his province and the conservatism of his people, and his son Paul, half-French, half-English, an aspiring writer in the years before World War II, Mac-Lennan is attempting to dramatize relations between French and English Canada within Quebec, a little-explored subject in anglophone Canadian literature of the time. Ironically, MacLennan himself, after ten years in Montreal, was virtually unacquainted with French-Canadian individuals personally and not fluent in French. He was persuaded, however, that "I knew what it was like to be in a minority, because the Celts were."[102] His novel does begin to formulate the previously undramatized racial legends so important in French- and English-Canadians' perceptions of each other. Valuable as this aim is for Canadian self-knowledge, it carries risks for the novelist, as the macrocosm of the novel, the political analysis, threatens to overwhelm the fictional heart of the book, the dilemmas and personalities of individual characters.

Like *Barometer Rising*, *Two Solitudes* develops the theme of power and powerlessness, presenting Canada in the grasp of an aging plutocracy with a vital younger generation restless over its confinement. And it does so in a similarly hopeful manner. While

Athanase Tallard is defeated in his attempt to direct the economic and social change imported into his hometown Saint-Marc by English-Canadian investors, his son Paul more successfully finds ways to become and to express himself amid the cultural conflicts of his family, his province, and his country. In negotiations to build a textile factory on the river at Saint-Marc, Athanase is discarded by his purported partner, English-speaking Huntly McQueen, when Athanase's rupture with the parish leader Father Beaubien threatens Québécois cooperation with the project. Dying, estranged from his community and unsuccessful in providing Saint-Marc with an imaginative alternative to static traditionalism, Athanase exemplifies his own analysis of Québécois innovators:

> In every generation there arose French-Canadians who tried to change the eternal pattern of Quebec by political action, and nearly all of them had been broken, one by one. Indeed, they broke themselves, for while they fought for change with their minds, they opposed it with their emotions. If they went far enough, they were bound to find themselves siding with the English against their own people, and if nothing else broke them, that inevitably did. (p. 69)

Paul, who, like his father, is "the victim of the two racial legends within the country" but who, unlike his father, ensures "that his battle to become himself remained a private one" (p. 270), manages to discover the necessity of cultural authenticity in his writing and to resist efforts by his lover's mother, Janet Methuen, and by Huntly McQueen to prevent his marriage to English-speaking Heather Methuen.

Concerning the structure of the novel, MacLennan has commented, "I concentrated very hard on form in *Two Solitudes* but the book ran away with it and busted it all to pieces, so that I was very unhappy about the form."[103] In planning the book, he originally intended to "introduce the effect of the European and international scene on Canadians and Canadian life by breaking the narrative in four places," with four interludes, "like the chorus of a Greek play," encapsulating the two world wars, the depression, and the international juggling of the 1930s.[104] The novel retains a four-part structure (1917–18, 1919–21, 1934, 1939), but the temporal divisions are shaped less by the dictates of history and more by the exigencies of the narrative and characters. The anticipated choric interludes are absent; political commentary is incorporated, sometimes ponderously, into the action; and moments of lofty, reflective overview dwell more on the Canadian people and their place in the immense Canadian landscape than on international politics.

In part, this change in the shape of *Two Solitudes* was precipitated by the transformation, in MacLennan's mind, of Athanase Tallard from minor figure to a principal character.[105] Parts I and II (almost two-thirds of the novel) trace the classically structured tragedy of Athanase, climaxing in his rupture with his people. Parts III and IV, picking up strands of Paul's childhood from the earlier sections, shift to the more casually plotted realist tradition of the *Bildungsroman* or *Künstlerroman*. Unified neither by place (the setting moves away from Saint-Marc as the novel continues), nor by time, nor by point of view (first-person perspective might have helped as it did in "A Man Should Rejoice"), nor by protagonist, nor even by focus on the fortunes of a single family (in the latter sections, Heather Methuen shares with Paul the role of major protagonist), the novel suffers structurally. In its failure of focus, *Two Solitudes* harks back to the unpublished novels, while its doubling or multiplying of protagonists proclaims a consistent MacLennan characteristic, the product of his historical and social imagination. The conclusion of the novel underscores MacLennan's difficulties here. With neither retrospection nor a tight temporal framework (like that of *Barometer Rising*) to assist him, MacLennan acknowledges encountering "great difficulty finishing the novel. It seemed to keep on going forever."[106] The manuscripts bear this out, containing episodes of Heather's pregnancy, Daphne Methuen's death beside Huntly McQueen in a London blitz, and Paul's injuries in action, extending two years beyond the eventual end of the novel.

In attempting to find a shape for his amorphous material, MacLennan turns to fictional formulas and, as elsewhere, historical landmarks. Paul's artistic and personal struggle is defined as private and contrasted with his father's embroiling of an entire community in his personal crisis of allegiances. Yet in fictional terms, with Paul's development, we are given not inner, psychological exploration but rather the intrigue and external conflict between polarized characters of romantic comedy. Paul and Heather are the young lovers challenging the older order represented by Heather's neurotically cold, manipulative mother and Huntly McQueen (whose magisterial meddling in the lives of both father and son provides one unifying thread in the novel). The triumph of the lovers over the stratagems of a rigid older generation (a triumph symbolic of a new understanding between French and English Canada undeterred by "ancient enmities") furnishes MacLennan with a tidy conclusion for his story. Affinities with romance are reflected in the action and characterization — in the power of Athanase's guilty secret, retrospectively revealed, of consoling himself, the night of his first wife's death, with another woman; in the stereotyping of heroes and villains — in Heather's wise, weatherbeaten grandfather, Captain Yardley, and her angular, repressive mother, for example; and in details and language borrowed from pulp fiction — "Her slim, lissom body, golden in the shaded light, moved gracefully as she threw her silk underclothes on to a chair" (p. 255). History supplies MacLennan's other structure. Just as the novel opens with the conscription crisis of World War I, which touches off Athanase's conflict with Father Beaubien and, nationally, intensifies French- and English-Canadian tensions, so it concludes symbolically with the declaration of World War II, which forces familial and racial cooperation, however reluctant: "And almost grudgingly . . . . the country took the first irrevocable steps toward becoming herself . . . ." (p. 370).

Whereas *Barometer Rising* uses the framework of romantic comedy to support realistic analysis and *Two Solitudes* turns belatedly to such formulas to control an unwieldy story, *The Precipice* (1948) opens with a Harlequin romance or Cinderella plot only to subvert it, at least temporarily. It also marks the beginning of the shift in MacLennan's middle novels from youthful to mature protagonists, from themes of powerlessness to themes of meaninglessness, and from conflict embodied externally in repressive antagonists to conflict manifested inwardly.

MacLennan has acknowledged that the form of *The Precipice* "is not in any way original."[107] The novel is built around an unexpected romance between inexperienced, twenty-seven-year-old Lucy Cameron from small-town Grenville, Ontario, and sophisticated, physically powerful American engineer and efficiency expert Stephen Lassiter. As an exploration of the wasteful effects of a repressive Canadian Puritanism which stifles risk taking and of a demanding American Puritanism which drives people restlessly, guiltily, and competitively forward towards the personal and national precipice of endless material endeavour, the book uses this romance allegorically. Lucy and Stephen's relationship represents the stimulation and energy which the United States can offer a conservative but vital Canada, and the moral stability and good sense which Canada can offer a frenetic and self-destructive America. By contrast, Lucy's dour older sister Jane and Stephen's ruthless friend Bratian illustrate the sterile extremes of these national traits. In "The Canadian Character," published the following year, MacLennan explicitly develops the analogy between Canadian-American relations and the marriage of a good, modest, adaptable, peace-loving, and morally inspiring wife to a flamboyant, robust husband.[108]

The plot of *The Precipice*, in which an "unmarriageable" woman has her attractiveness revealed and rewarded to the surprise of her sisters and community, is indeed a familiar one. Elspeth Cameron has identified a specific source for this plot in Anthony Tudor's ballet *Pillars of Fire*, which places its heroine, under the eyes of a domineering "Eldest Sister" and flirtatious "Youngest Sister," in a romantic-emotional triangle involving a "Young Man from the House Opposite" and a "Friend."[109] But while marriage and vague expectations for happiness ever after form the natural resolution for these traditional plots, MacLennan, as part of a movement towards the anatomizing of marriage in his middle novels, structures *The Precipice* differently. The love affair culminating in Lucy's elopement occupies only the first half of the novel. The remainder details realistically the deterioration and eventual restoration of her relationship with Stephen.

As in *Two Solitudes* and in keeping with his broader social interest, MacLennan uses historical events as structural markers. The ending of Part i coincides with Chamberlain's averting of World War ii. Part ii, in which Lucy's Ontario neighbour Bruce Fraser finally begins to appreciate her, is tied to larger world affairs by being placed in the context of his 1940 leave from wartime training. Part iii, a transitional interlude summarizing five years of development for a number of characters, spans at the same time the war years from 1940 to 1945. Lucy's decision in Part iv to leave a marriage to which Stephen has become indifferent and to return with her children to Grenville coincides with American celebrations of V.E. Day, while Stephen's emotional nadir and Lucy's redemptive return to him in Part v coincide symbolically with the American bombing of Hiroshima and the beginning of a new era. Although MacLennan has called it a "chronicle novel" and although it covers seven years,[110] *The Precipice* escapes some of *Two Solitudes'* desultoriness by devoting most of its attention to the two opening and closing periods of 1938 and late 1945, the moments of interpersonal crisis and decision, choice and consequence, and, at the same time, the periods immediately preceding and following the war.

The plot and language of pulp romance dominate the first half of *The Precipice*. Like the Regency rake or the man of the world of contemporary pulps, Stephen, whose past experience with other women is repeatedly cited,[111] has his curiosity piqued by the heroine's sexual inexperience, her unappreciated merit, and her provocative forthrightness and independence. Their union, complicated by the familiar gulf in background and by familial opposition, is predictably hindered further by an unresolved misperception (Lucy's discovery of Stephen's wife, whom he is in the process of divorcing). Lucy, a latter-day Jane Eyre, is physically awakened — "He had invaded her solitude and taught her finally that she was passionate, probably more passionate than the average woman . . . ." (p. 154) — and experiences the classic conflict between her desire and her sense of self-worth — "She struggled, helpless against his strength, loving the sense of his physical power. . . . 'Don't touch me!' she whispered. 'Don't ever touch me again!' " (p. 156). As these quotations reveal, MacLennan's style here is frequently mawkish and evasive: Lucy's "quiver of ecstasy" grows into "a jet of unbelievable flame flaring out of primeval darkness" (pp. 137–38); after her wedding night, "her hands passed slowly and wonderingly over her breasts and loins" (p. 181); she is contrasted with decadent "long-thighed women who could have handled any three of them [modern men] the same night and cried for more" (p. 73). MacLennan also exploits the easy ironies of the genre: "Tomorrow would be just another summer day," Lucy tells herself on the eve of her first encounter with Stephen (p. 54).

For all its formulaic derivativeness and lapses into bathos, though, this is the more successful half of the book, as George Woodcock has pointed out.[112] Because MacLennan is describing a world for which he has more sympathetic understanding (as opposed to the New York degeneracy pictured later), because the allegorical significance of character and event is not yet dominant, and because he allows himself more leisure here, he can look in careful detail at the psychology of Grenville life. An example of such perceptive characterization appears in Lucy's equivocal claim (to her sister Nina) that she has been formally introduced to Stephen during a previous meeting, her agonized embarrassment when this claim is threatened with exposure, and her simultaneous awareness of the triviality of the entire matter.

MacLennan's decision to challenge the novel's romance structure in its second half, to scrutinize marriage, the symbolic resolution of earlier novels, is a bold one, though not ultimately successful. With Part II, the development of *The Precipice* becomes considerably less predictable. MacLennan begins to explore more directly the break-down of the family which he has defined as the subject haunting British and American writers of this century. Ironically, the forces of Puritanism from which Lucy is fleeing in her marriage are shown to be embodied, in different form, in her deliverer, Stephen, tormented by guilt and relentless expectations of achievement. But MacLennan's undertaking in the last half of *The Precipice* suffers from too sketchy an overview and insufficient detail, from facile, moralistic judgements — for example, the disdainful equation of New York "chrome and steel and blue glass" with "cocktail parties, hangovers, childlessness, psychoanalysis, and divorce" (p. 366) — and from the submerging of individual psychology in national identity and poli-tical symbolism. The reconciliation between Stephen and Lucy grows as much from MacLennan's sense of what an eager, post-war Canada can offer the jaded, guilt-ridden United States (as articulated by Bruce Fraser in the novel) as from the couple's personal needs. A further weakness, cited by several critics, is that MacLennan's central thematic distinction between Canadian and American values and their respective Puritan traditions might as validly be formulated simply as a contrast between small-town and city experiences.[13]

Interestingly, in the last section of the novel, MacLennan returns unabashedly to the romance formula he had apparently jettisoned. Stephen's anagnorisis, his recognition of Lucy's value, is realistically qualified. The novel ends hopefully but unassumingly: "Once again it's a beginning" (p. 372). And love is described as no final answer to Stephen's need: "She learned then that there are moments when human love is no more help to a man than the sight of friends beckoning across a bottomless chasm" (p. 370). The reconciliation comes after years of ordinary domestic tensions and is associated with marital maturity rather than with initial raptures. It is, never-theless, that implicit acknowledgement by the hero of the precedence of the heroine's world which has been identified by critics of popular culture as so gratifying an element in pulp fictions.[14] In Lucy's arms,

Stephen is able to reject punitive, self-imposed isolation issuing from a "useless, ancient guilt" (p. 371).

Each Man's Son (1951) similarly investigates the personal struggle with and victory over the "ancient curse" of Calvinism,[115] although its scope is limited to the psychology of Cape Breton Highlanders rather than extending to the national psyches of two countries. Unlike the earlier published novels, *Each Man's Son* presents Mac-Lennan's familiar and hopeful theme of rebellion against an older tradition (British colonialism, English-Canadian exploitation of Quebec, or Calvinist repression) without recourse to the genre of romantic comedy and its triumphant lovers. Cape Breton Doctor Dan Ainslie's search for meaning — for a God, as his friend Dougald MacKenzie tells him, but a God of loving-kindness not of damnation — expresses itself in the quest for a son. Ainslie attempts to adopt eight-year-old Alan MacNeil, son of gentle Mollie MacNeil and her absent prize-fighter husband, Archie. In form, *Each Man's Son*, with its sensational conclusion sweeping away complications and with its persistent reminders of the return of Archie, fate's unwitting agent, shows the influence of Greek drama rather than romance. Disconcertingly, though, the tragic direction of MacLennan's classic models is inverted in the conclusion to accommodate his optimistic theme and partiality for his protagonist.

In structure, *Each Man's Son* lies between MacLennan's compact dramas, like *Barometer Rising* and *Return of the Sphinx*, which detail a few days only, and his more comprehensive chronicles, like *Two Solitudes* and *The Precipice*. Chronological, like all of these, it quickens its pace as it unfolds, with the first eleven chapters devoted to two days, the next ten to two weeks, and the last ten to three months. There is little sweeping overview or broad historical and political context, for that matter, except for a passing reminder of the imminence of World War I. Even in the later sections of the novel, the focus is a close one, with the last three chapters, for instance, devoted to a single evening.

MacLennan has structured this work tightly in other ways as well. Ainslie's medical practice is punctuated by three operations of increasing significance: on a terrified, illiterate Newfoundlander with crushed hands; on a Louisburg longshoreman with a fractured skull; and, most emotionally taxing for Ainslie, on Alan MacNeil with a ruptured appendix. The first and third operations are accompanied by scenes in which Ainslie's friend MacKenzie (who will also offer a final benediction) challenges and counsels him, first on Ainslie's wife Margaret's concerns over an earlier sterilization, and second on the reality behind what Ainslie has dismissed as weakness in his mother. The same two operations are followed by misdirected aggression against the doctor by brawling miners (part of MacLennan's ongoing, condescending characterization of the Highlanders as endearingly childlike primitives). The appendix operation also precipitates the first of two parallel crises in which Ainslie, in a natural setting, loses physical and emotional self-possession and rages at the barrenness of his life. In the first instance, he fixes desperately on Alan as his salvation; in the second, in what is presented as a true purging, he finds that, having relinquished both Alan and the Calvinist God who has given a twisted purpose to his life, he nevertheless "was ready to go on with life" (p. 220). Similar parallel scenes in Chapters vi and xix of Alan awake in bed prepare for the conclusion in which Alan becomes the silent, horrified witness of his father's return home and the killing of Mollie and her lover, Louis Camire. Throughout the novel, too, Archie's course, though treated more briefly, has served as a counterpoint to developments in Broughton, with his defeat in the ring at Trenton juxtaposed with Ainslie's surgical coup at Louisburg, his abortive visit to a Montreal boxing promoter juxtaposed with Mollie's consultation with Margaret about future plans, and his return to Broughton juxtaposed with Mollie's preparations for departure. The setting of scenes involving Archie, in ever closer proximity to Cape Breton — first in Trenton, New Jersey, then in Montreal, and then on the train from Moncton — further shapes the novel towards its climax.

Despite the omniscient perspective and the periodic shifts in focus away from Ainslie, his inner conflict dominates *Each Man's Son*, providing a central protagonist and a unifying focus absent in earlier novels which apportion psychological or moral crises among several actors. As in *The Precipice*, the conflict is increasingly personal, a struggle with internalized forces, aspects of the protagonist's psyche, rather than with social institutions embodied in inflexible antagonists. Nor is Ainslie's tussle with Puritan grimness, however representative, an allegory of a larger national or historical development. Still, MacLennan is an intellectual and analytical, not a psychological, novelist. Ainslie is the illustration of an *idea* about the pernicious effects of loveless religion upon an entire people. Given Ainslie's centrality, MacLennan might have been wiser to choose the unifying perspective of first-person narration. Deviations from Ainslie's centre of consciousness, particularly to Archie's, jar slightly. More important, a first-person point of view might have helped alleviate the unintentional insufferability which weakens Ainslie's characterization. Although MacLennan recognizes and explains Ainslie's aloof superiority and impatience with the people of Broughton, he encourages a greater sympathy, even reverence at times, for the character — through authorial judgements like Alan's fictionally unjustified conclusion, "He knew that Dr. Ainslie had come to give, as Mr. Camire had come to take" (p. 231) — than Ainslie's curt arrogance warrants. With Ainslie as a subjective narrator, his smugness would not receive authorial endorsement.

With its exploration of inner turmoil, the plot of *Each Man's Son* is less predictable than the romantic conflicts between morally typed characters in the earlier, published novels. Old Mrs. MacCuish, attempting to inculcate a sense of sin upon Alan, is an exception to the general, and uncharacteristic, absence of heroes and villains here. Where inevitability enters is in the Greek fatalism of the final catastrophe, triggered by the well-meaning but presumptuous Ainslie. But the inexorability of the converging plot lines of Ainslie's and Archie's stories is curiously skewed when Ainslie becomes the beneficiary, rather than tragic victim, of MacLennan's formulaic resolution through violence. From a figure of nemesis, Archie becomes a much more arbitrary *deus ex machina*, removing Alan's inconvenient mother with a blow intended for Camire and then opportunely dying of a cerebral embolism himself. Neither the childlike Mollie and Archie, nor the constantly belittled Camire — even Alan refers to him as "the little Frenchman" (p. 230) — has the moral stature to sustain tragedy. So, the bloody climax comes as a fortuitous reward for Ainslie's difficult renunciation of a life-denying philosophy and of his impertinent claims to Alan. Although Ainslie accuses himself of responsibility for Mollie's death, MacKenzie and, by implication, the author reject this analysis. Instead, the novel's conclusion emphasizes Ainslie's transfiguring discovery of the value of a loving human being. MacLennan has commented that he could not write his next novel until he shed the intellectual assumptions of his generation, which decreed optimism in the face of his own contrary intuitions.[116] *Each Man's Son* demonstrates the power of this need for affirmation, even when it is at odds with his literary model.

As early as 1952, MacLennan was talking of the need for a new approach to the novel on the part of its practitioners,[117] and his often-quoted declaration in "The Story of a Novel" of having "spent more than six years learning how to shape a new bottle for a new kind of wine" reflects his sense of having achieved such a technical revolution with *The Watch That Ends the Night* (1959).[118] Even more emphatically than in *Two Solitudes*, with its attempted abandonment of the "formula-plotted story," MacLennan saw himself, in his new novel, as challenging his own recourse to violent action and external conflict between opposing characters in favour of conflict within the mind of the character.[119] In reality, the techniques of *The Watch That Ends the Night* are far from original, as critics have not hesitated to announce.[120] Nevertheless, retrospective narrative, with flashbacks sometimes nested one within another, and a first-person narrator were new for MacLennan in his published fiction and, as such, marked a fruitful technical breakthrough for him.

The Watch That Ends the Night is, with *Voices in Time*, one of MacLennan's most ambitious novels in the grandeur of its theme — the accommodation of the human being to an apparently indifferent or unjust universe — and in its fusion of microcosm and macrocosm — the personal life of George Stewart and the international drama of the depression, the unrest of the 1930s, the Spanish Civil War, World War II, and the apolitical rebound of the postwar period. Ironically and inconsistently, MacLennan's careful attention to social conditions and his delineation of the psychological devastation caused by political collapse become arguments for political acquiescence and for inner self-transformation. By the end of the novel, politics have become unreal for George and the world itself a shadow; the novel's resolution is a retreat from social and political issues to philosophical, specifically existential, ones.

More directly than his other published novels, *The Watch That Ends the Night* focuses on the aimlessness and solitude of an individual severed from sources of meaning. George Stewart, an unassuming family man, has belatedly been able to make his adolescent sweetheart, Catherine, his rock and his salvation, after her first marriage to pre-eminent surgeon and political idealist Jerome Martell is destroyed by the Spanish Civil War. Catherine's rheumatic heart, however, reveals this refuge to be impermanent, illusory. Other characters, seeking to belong to something larger than themselves, similarly discover the insubstantiality of religious faith, involvement in career, or political dedication. When God, the loving father, proves unresponsive, and substitutes fail, then, says George, "comes the Great Fear. For if a man cannot believe that he serves more than himself, if he cannot believe there is meaning in the human struggle, what are his chances of emotional survival?"[121] MacLennan has described this novel as a lament for the worldwide failure of the idealism of the 1930s and as a tragedy.[122] Its conclusion is a stirring repudiation of George's earlier despair, an acceptance of the beauty of the passing moment as a gift in itself: ". . . . to be able to love the mystery surrounding us is the final and only sanction of human existence" (p. 372). George defines his own story as the conflict between the human spirit and the human condition of mortality (pp. 25, 34).[123] By learning, like Jerome and Catherine before him, to imaginatively experience his own death and so to transcend it, he can accept without fear the contingency of life. But the other-worldly nature of this resolution and the very real losses it encompasses strictly limit the magnitude of the final affirmation. The optimism introduced into MacLennan's early published novels, as he turned to the more manageable issues of Canadian life and threats to personal and national self-determination, begins to evaporate here as his field widens again.

MacLennan's new retrospective structure in *The Watch That Ends the Night* enables him to combine the immediacy of his short dramas with the breadth of his protracted chronicles. The frame story (Parts I, III, and VII, set in February 1951) and the Epilogue (set in 1951) develop the crisis caused by Jerome's return to Canada years after his presumed death, specifically his threat to the marital tranquility of George and Catherine, his impact on Catherine's health (as another embolism endangers her life), and, most significantly, his challenge to George's precariously based peace of mind. The flashbacks (Parts II, IV, and VI) provide a chronological counterpoint, covering three earlier decades, from George's adolescence through his late marriage. Interrupting this symmetry is Part V, the unexpected narrative of Jerome's life, as told to George in the late 1930s. This interpolation is a bold one, not only because it introduces an anomalous time period, but also because it employs a second narrative perspective within a first-person account. The unity, suspense, and emotional power of Jerome's story — of his flight down a New Brunswick river from his mother's killer and of his rescue by a kindly, childless Halifax couple — with its archetypal patterns and fairy-tale framework, has the potential to shatter MacLennan's larger narrative. The section has, indeed, been anthologized as a self-contained narrative, and commentators have been outspoken in their praise of MacLennan's skill here.[124] This narrative is nevertheless well-integrated into the novel, particularly through MacLennan's adroit shift from Jerome's reported voice to George's own reconstruction and narration of the experience, and through the function of this section in introducing vital social and psychological symbolism. The image of a small boy in a canoe at the mercy of a vast watercourse becomes a repeated metaphor for the political vulnerability of modern civilization and for the threat to personal identity posed by anarchic primal emotions.

Part of MacLennan's aim in *The Watch That Ends the Night* is to provide a multilayered depiction of a single, universal experience. George repeatedly refers to himself as "Everyman." Each character's life story is presented as an individual version of a basic human dilemma. The political developments of the novel appear as manifestations of a collapse of old certainties. And the stages of Catherine's marriages and illness serve as an allegory of the historical events reported in the novel.[125] Just as George can appropriate the story of Jerome's childhood, claiming that it "wove itself into me later on" (p. 170), so distinctions between time periods within one's own life lose significance. George declares: "The past seemed part of the present, today. Time had lost its shape." Then he questions: "When was I living, now or twenty-five years ago, or in all those periods of my life simultaneously?" (p. 90). The novel's structure, with its shifts from story to story and, especially, from present to past, superimposes experiences in an approximation of simultaneity. In this respect, Catherine's embolisms may be emblematic, providing a commentary on the work's structure. The term "embolism," in addition to its medical significance, denotes something inserted, particularly the intercalation of a day or days in a calendar to complete a period.[126] Catherine's embolisms, invasive and unjust as they are, are essential to the spiritual growth she is ultimately able to share with George. So, too, the interpolated flashbacks which interrupt the drama of the present (and, in the case of Part v, interrupt even the orderly disclosure of George's past) are required to round out the later sequences.

Technically, *The Watch That Ends the Night* also marks an advance in the appropriateness of the point of view chosen. First-person perspective creates a new psychological richness and intimacy with the reader, while potentially exempting MacLennan from responsibility for the failures of tone and judgement which often mar his narrative voice. Although a vehicle for MacLennan's historical and philosophical ideas, George exists more fully on the personal level, with intrinsic individual and psychological interest, than some earlier protagonists. In part, this may be an accidental by-product of the narrative perspective, for unsuitable attributes of earlier omniscient narrators, such as sententiousness, sentimentality, and primness, can be interpreted here as evidence for complex characterization. Manuscript evidence, however, substantiates MacLennan's self-conscious use of such traits. In the manuscript draft of the novel, even more explicitly than in the final text, George admits his "prosaic nature," his fear of impotence with other women, his lack of Jerome's kind of vitality, and, with regards to the human capacity to transform grit into pearls, his limitations as "a middle-aged oyster." In this earlier draft, George appears as a deliberately weaker, less attractive, more defeated protagonist. He admits that he doesn't have the character to conceal Jerome's return from Catherine. He calls a doctor out of his own need, not Catherine's. He betrays his unprepossessing stoutness while attempting to gloss over it as no greater than that of some football players. And Jerome overtly challenges his courage to undertake the responsibilities of being Catherine's husband.[127] While less insistent in the novel itself, George's unheroic self-deprecation is an engaging change from the fictionally unsubstantiated authorial admiration which diminishes our sympathy for such characters in previous novels as Neil Macrae, Stephen Lassiter, Lucy Cameron (at times), and Daniel Ainslie. MacLennan, unfortunately, fails to exploit the potential of his subjective point of view fully, so that awe before Jerome's brusque egotism and Catherine's tiresomely inspirational pluckiness acquires fictional authority rather than simply reflecting George's susceptible nature.

In *The Watch That Ends the Night*, MacLennan's focus on inner conflict does allow him to transcend formulas, despite the sensational plot complication of a spouse's disruptive return from the grave and a lovers' triangle. The issues in the novel and their resolution are unpredictable, complex, and emotionally powerful. The sometimes inflated style, however, links MacLennan more closely with sentimental fiction. In addition to biblical allusions and the creation of stylized biblical rhythms through parallelism and repetition (a stylistic affinity which, no doubt, explains some of MacLennan's admiration for Alan Paton[128]), George indulges, from time to time, in ludicrously hard-boiled, hysterical, or portentous language. Nor, given the retrospective insight informing George's reassessment of earlier events, can such lapses be explained away as the inadvertent self-revelation of an unreliable narrator. Nevertheless, despite this continued difficulty with tone, *The Watch That Ends the Night* achieves a psychological subtlety unmatched elsewhere in MacLennan's oeuvre.

After MacLennan's technical ventures in *The Watch That Ends the Night*, *Return of the Sphinx* (1967) reverts to earlier structures and concerns. It returns to the subject-matter of *Two Solitudes* — Quebec's place within confederation; revives a character from *Each Man's Son* — Dan Ainslie's adopted son, Alan, now an adult and the protagonist of *Return of the Sphinx*; and reworks the theme and form of *Barometer Rising* — tension between generations expressed through the juxtaposed lives of characters narrated omnisciently over a short, linear time span. Once again, the action develops through external conflict between characters and is resolved through violence or, in this case, through violence narrowly averted. Like *Each Man's Son*, *Return of the Sphinx* seems modelled on Greek tragedy (in a note written during the composition of the novel, MacLennan associates it with Sophocles' *Oedipus at Colonus*[129]) but fails to sustain a tragic climax.

In telling the story of Alan Ainslie, whose career as federal Minister for Cultural Affairs is destroyed by his son Daniel's separatist activities, beginning with a seditious television program and culminating in an attempted bombing, MacLennan presents Quebec as "the psychic center of the world," representative of a world crisis precipitated by loss of faith in human nature.[130] Ainslie's happy marriage to a French-Canadian functions as an allegory for the cultural marriage of English and French Canada. " 'No wonder,' " one character remarks to Daniel, " 'with a marriage like that, your father should think that this country could have a wonderful future' " (p. 152). For all its references to Canadian and international political instability, MacLennan insists that the novel is actually about fathers and sons, not about separatism or politics, because of its persistent reduction of political activism to psychological neurosis.[131] "Young men never plunge into movements like this without some kind of personal reason," says Marielle, Daniel's mature lover, with her Old World wisdom (p. 141). Oedipal conflicts pervade the novel. The subplot of Ainslie's daughter Chantal's restorative affair with his best friend Gabriel Fleury provides a positive counterpoint to sexually repressed Daniel's furtive involvement with Marielle. Ainslie's near duplication of his own father's murderous assault on guilty lovers, sparked by his discovery of the latter couple in the parental bedroom, is what provokes Daniel's wild, sexually symbolic flight with a bomb. Heavy-handedly evoked, these Oedipal conflicts provide simplistic explanations for larger world problems. "All the politics of the world originated in the nurseries of large families," MacLennan has argued.[132]

Daniel, says Ainslie, has " 'destroyed any meaning my work might have had' " (p. 287). With his despair over the emptiness of all work, love, and hope, and with his vision of the country no longer as a nation but as a wilderness containing a few, presumptuous human ant hills, Ainslie reveals himself to be very much the son of his adoptive father Dan Ainslie, confounded by life's apparent meaninglessness and fortuitousness. Although MacLennan has cited Ainslie's hubris in thinking that he can succeed with his political ideals,[133] the real hubris here, as in *The Watch That Ends the Night*, has shifted from individuals to nations, the only modern forces, according to MacLennan, capable of the control over their own fates necessary for tragic drama.[134] Endorsing Gabriel Fleury's sombre diagnosis that " 'when a man tries to do something positive in the world . . . . he's safe so long as he can believe the shadows are real' " (p. 299), *Return of the Sphinx* mines more thoroughly the vein of pessimism running through *The Watch That Ends the Night*. Marriage and families, with their symbolic promise in the early novels and manifestations of difficulty in the middle novels, are fractured here, destroyed even before the novel's opening. The consolation injected into the Epilogue that the Canadian landscape is "too vast even for fools to ruin all of it" (p. 303), like Ainslie's final expression of thankfulness for the opportunity to share in this enduring loveliness, is, in addition to being beside the point, limited by a concluding fatalism. Even the apparently invulnerable stars are, like humanity, "trapped in equations" (p. 303).

MacLennan has called *Return of the Sphinx* "the best book I ever wrote, formally."[135] Manuscript drafts of the novel show that he initially attempted to employ the same first-person technique as in *The Watch That Ends the Night*, with Gabriel Fleury acting as the observer, Ainslie as the more active protagonist.[136] While maintaining this familiar use of the doubled protagonist in the published version of the book, MacLennan employs the third-person point of view and constructs the novel as a series of separate scenes, temporally simultaneous or consecutive, shifting repeatedly between Fleury (often with Chantal), Ainslie, and Daniel. The novel begins slowly, with Book I (over half the novel) detailing at length the events of a single Saturday, apparently in June, and with the Intermezzo treating the events of next day briefly. Book II covers the succeeding week intermittently. The Epilogue synoptically recapitulates the several days after the climactic father-son confrontation, then the succeeding weeks, leaving us finally in early September with Ainslie's forced serenity. After the elaborate and portentous opening, the novel's resolution at the end of Book II has an anticlimactic abruptness: Daniel's destructive defiance peters out in an unexploded bomb and the expectation of judicial leniency; Ainslie's resignation from politics and his breakdown, though simultaneous with news of Daniel's arrest and Chantal's romance, seem somehow inevitable in any case. The disjointed structure of the novel (Book I, for example, is composed of ten chapters, many of them further interrupted by flashbacks) seems a deliberate counterpoint to its theme — "Things are falling apart. . . . The center cannot hold" (p. 51). This Yeatsian sense of disjointedness is intensified by the fruitless game of musical chairs Ainslie and Daniel play throughout Book I and the Intermezzo, moving from Ottawa to the family's Montreal home and then to its Laurentian cottage, each unwittingly following and missing the other, sometimes by a matter of hours. The juxtaposition of scenes — same time, different places; same place, different times — underscores the failures of communication.

MacLennan's conviction of the tightness of the novel's structure arises presumably from the insistent contrasts and parallels created by the juxtaposition of lives and of memories. Unfortunately, this is where *Return of the Sphinx* becomes most formulaic and contrived. In particular, vignettes from the past, most often of trauma and violence, act as substitutes for character development. Precocious seductions (Ainslie's wife Constance and Marielle), war wounds (Ainslie, Fleury's father), grisly deaths (Constance, Ainslie's natural parents, Marielle's father), often presented as dramatic confessions like the obligatory secrets of popular romance, function simplistically and automatically to code the characters as profound and experienced. Ainslie displays many of the classic motifs of the hero, in the secret of his birth, his foster-parents, his father-king, his future kingdom, his reign, his loss of favour, and his banishment from the throne. The traumas of his childhood and his marriage thus confirm his place in a long line of romantic heroes in MacLennan from Neil Macrae and Stephen Lassister to Dan Ainslie and Jerome Martell, heroes who have endured superhuman physical or psychological torment.

But MacLennan fails to convey to us the anguish of his characters, so that the novel's overall impression is not of profundity and passion but of hysteria. The characters all seem to be in a funk before their individual crises: Ainslie before Daniel's rebellion, Fleury before his turmoil over Chantal, businessman Tarnley before his son's suicide. So the crises appear as excuses for self-indulgence. Each character's overwrought emotion is linked to the brooding sense of imminent social collapse in the novel, reinforced by lurid and hyperbolic jungle and hurricane imagery, but that collapse is still hovering unrealized at the conclusion. In place of adequate motivation for and dramatization of individual moments of high emotion, MacLennan simply insists on their presence, often in trite, melodramatic, or incongruous images. Daniel as a character suffers most severely from this technique. As a result of this failure, the narrator, not merely his characters, seems on the verge of nervous collapse. A different problem of tone plagues MacLennan's characterization of Chantal, his most unpleasantly smug and superior heroine, whose supercilious condescension, particularly towards her own generation, receives unquestioning narrative approval, and whose merit is conveyed through exasperatingly sentimental passages reporting Fleury's febrile response to her. Despite all the self-conscious structural symmetries of *Return of the Sphinx* and the potential significance of its psychological and social themes, MacLennan's failure to render successfully the experiences he has selected makes it his least satisfactory novel.

With *Voices in Time* (1980), MacLennan continues the ambitiousness of *The Watch That Ends the Night*, in the scope of its themes, the breadth of its time frame, and the novelty, for the author, of its form. Contrasting it with the *Return of the Sphinx*, MacLennan has described this novel as diffuse and tempestuous, in keeping with the contemporary age:

> Now I'm writing a new book, and the concision I used in *The Sphinx* will probably be absent from it. Concision is not appro-

priate to an age as diffuse as ours. Now I find I'm writing a very tempestuous prose compared to what I wrote in the past.[137]

Constructed of ten parts which shift forward sixty years into the future and backward seventy years into the past, which recount the lives of three separate protagonists, and which employ one omniscient and three first-person perspectives, *Voices in Time* is indeed sweeping in its range. To avoid the disunity of a loose chronicle, MacLennan, as in *The Watch That Ends the Night*, uses the drama of a present-tense frame story and the focus of one central narrator. In this novel, as in his earlier work, the influence of the well-plotted story prevails over theories of inner conflict or simple verisimilitude. Crises of history (including MacLennan's fictional future history), familiar coincidences, disclosures of personal secrets, and violent confrontations shape the form of the novel.

Still, *Voices in Time* surprises us, accustomed as we are to MacLennan's conservative and meticulously documentary fiction, by beginning as science fiction. It opens in the fourth decade of the twenty-first century, after the "Great Fear" and the "Destructions," with the world in ruins and the "Diagram of the Third Bureaucracy" successful in destroying most memories of the past. However apparently different from his other work, this novel is in fact the logical sequel to MacLennan's earlier fictional warnings about the vulnerability of civilization, the moral bankruptcy of technology and commerce, and the impotence of intellectual and political leaders to avert social collapse. The novel concentrates, not on the imagined future world (wisely, in view of the perfunctoriness of its creation), but on two voices from the past, two men whose documents have unexpectedly been preserved. The main narrator, John Wellfleet, an elderly and apathetic survivor of worldwide destruction, finds new vitality in piecing together the stories of Timothy Wellfleet, an older cousin who is a controversial Montreal television host during the volatile days of the 1960s and the October Crisis in Quebec, and Conrad Dehmel, John's stepfather, a history professor who naïvely allows himself to be trapped in Hitler's Germany. The two narratives intersect when Timothy misguidedly attempts to expose Conrad as a former Nazi and so unintentionally brings about his violent death. Through the juxtaposition of three periods of social disorder and political collapse — Timothy's, Conrad's, and Wellfleet's — and the explicit connections made between the fatal obliviousness of the

participants of each crisis, MacLennan issues an urgent caution to
the contemporary world. In so doing, he betrays, in yet another way,
the fundamental hopefulness he is incapable of expunging from even
his gloomiest work.

Like the startling reappearances from the dead of Neil Macrae and
Jerome Martell in earlier novels, the voices from the dead contained
in the iron box which young André Gervais presents to John Wellfleet
at the opening of *Voices in Time* provoke a crisis in the present-time
sequences of the novel. Wellfleet's emotional growth and intellectual
questioning over the five years, from about 2038 to 2042, in which
he re-creates the others' stories, provide an essential, recurring
reference point in a novel which ranges as far back in time as
Conrad's conception before World War I. Wellfleet's present life,
though, is far less interesting than George Stewart's in *The Watch
That Ends the Night*. Ironically, for a Canadian novelist renowned
for being a nationalist and for treating contemporary problems and
future dangers, MacLennan writes most memorably in *Voices in
Time* about Conrad Dehmel's fortunes in war-time Germany. These
are reconstructed in Wellfleet's voice in Parts I, V, and VII of the novel
(just as George mediates Jerome Martell's story in *The Watch That
Ends the Night*) and narrated directly by Conrad in Parts IV and VIII.
Timothy Wellfleet, by comparison, never narrates his own story,
though his blunt, colloquial idiom appears repeatedly in quotations
used by Wellfleet to flesh out Timothy's story in Parts II and IX. What
we have is a much more complicated version of the nesting of voice
within voice and flashback within flashback first used in *The Watch
That Ends the Night*. Each narrative prepares for and comments
afterwards on an earlier and more important one. As in *The Watch
That Ends the Night*, the sequence of flashbacks — here moving
further and further into the past and then progressively forward
again — is not a totally consistent one, interrupted as it is by
Wellfleet's present voice or experiences from the more recent past.
MacLennan seems to be aiming for what he has described, in a 1971
letter to Robertson Davies, as a kind of continuity which is more
interesting because it is temporally relative rather than linear, a kind
of dramatic continuity exemplified in Sophocles' plays or in Yeats's
poetry. As he explained to Davies, "a great novel is likely to contain,
over an immense canvas, the same kind of internal counterpoint of
vision that Yeats crammed into The Second Coming."[138] For the most
part, the effect of this structure is one of gratifying complexity,

although occasionally, as in the references to Conrad's, Timothy's, and Wellfleet's grandfathers, the proliferation of points of view and stories can be confusing.

Despite the number of narrators employed, MacLennan does not particularly exploit the potential ambiguities and ironies inherent in multiple, subjective perspectives. Deviations from authorial judgements are signalled clearly, being filtered, in Timothy's case for example, through a more reliable spokesman. Nor does the first-person point of view function mainly to give prominence to the intimate, individual, inner experience of a character. Even with Conrad, whose hazardous work within the Nazi bureaucracy to save his Jewish lover forms the core of the novel, personal life is used illustratively to exemplify larger issues and make them more immediate. After George Stewart, John Wellfleet is a disappointingly grey narrator, whose own story is deliberately downplayed, whose permissive youth with its indulgence in easy sex and drugs does not ring true to character, and whose centrality as narrator contributes less than might be expected to indirect character development. Still, the scrupulousness, conservatism, and righteousness of his voice do individualize him somewhat, while freeing the novel from authorial pontificating. Overall, though, in his late novels, as in his earliest ones, MacLennan demonstrates most clearly that his imagination is fundamentally historical and social rather than psychological.

As a result of MacLennan's concern with external action and suspense, *Voices in Time*, like earlier novels, shows traces of melodramatic plotting. There are wise or noble characters — Conrad, his lover Hanna Erlich, her father, Timothy's Jewish lover Esther Stahr, Wellfleet's mother Stephanie, and Admiral Canaris — and decadent or evil ones — Wellfleet's sister Charlotte, and Conrad's ex-wife Eva Schmidt. As Jews, Hanna and Esther suffer added stereotyping, being attributed, automatically, a preternatural racial sagacity and conscience, the instinctive understanding of barbarism genetically transmitted within an ancient, civilized race. There is malevolent intrigue, though responsibility for it has largely moved away from individuals who embody social ills (like Colonel Wain or Huntly McQueen of earlier novels) to the social order itself. Powerful secrets, trauma, violence, and coincidence — Esther's rape as a child; Stephanie's innocent, illegitimate pregnancy; Conrad's father's anguish as a German naval officer; Conrad's calamitous encounter with his ex-wife while fleeing the Nazis and his subsequent torture by the ss; the deaths of Hanna and her father; and Conrad's murder by a holocaust survivor misled by Conrad's resemblance to Eva Schmidt's Gestapo husband — provide the building blocks of character and plot. The climactic revelation of Conrad's murder and its circumstances, capstone of the novel's tragic structure, suffers, in particular, from improbabilities: Conrad's role as inadvertent stand-in, a score of years later and thousands of miles away, for his former wife's cold husband; Timothy's ignorance of the marriage of his favourite cousin, Stephanie, to Conrad Dehmel; and Wellfleet's ignorance of Timothy's contribution to Wellfleet's own stepfather's death. Such contrivances, fortunately, are relatively submerged in the vigorous action and documentation which wash the novel. Formulas are less obtrusive in a work providing the range of character, incident, and historical colour which this one does.

The novel carries the reader along successfully. It works as a lively thriller, if not always as the profound social document MacLennan intends. However, when he tries to create atmosphere, convey emotion, or pass judgement, style and tone fail. Theories about the perils of a shift from a "patrist" or authoritative social order to a "matrist" or indulgent one, which underlie this novel as they did *Return of the Sphinx*, contribute to a tone of righteous moralism and prudish repugnance, especially in descriptions of the frenzy of the 1960s and the license preceding the "Destructions."[139] Discussions of impending social disintegration, so crucial to the novel's theme, have an inadvertent edge of hysteria, as in *Return of the Sphinx*: " 'And how could anyone do that [capture the news] unless he opened his lungs and veins to the full, intoxicating brew of poisons, to all the dreads, lusts, ambitions, greeds, and inner terrors churning like microbes in the belly of the technological loneliness?' "[140] What MacLennan intends as a diagnosis of our current malaise appears instead as his personal Puritan distaste for modern manners. He goes so far, for example, as to link a new understanding of Timothy's deficiencies with André Gervais' pained introduction to rock music. This characteristic MacLennan weakness does not, however, overwhelm this novel as it did *Return of the Sphinx*. Adept in its manipulation of point of view, well-structured, thematically weighty (even if sometimes not persuasive), and dramatic in its action sequences, *Voices in Time*, though not as rich psychologically, shows the same technical sophistication as *The Watch That Ends the Night*.

C. Non-fiction

Critical pieties to the contrary, MacLennan's non-fiction is read largely for the light it sheds on his fiction, rather than for its own sake. Only *Seven Rivers of Canada* (1961) is a sustained, unified work of prose. *The Colour of Canada* (1967) is an occasional piece, a coffee-table book, providing MacLennan's reflections on the Canadian nation, in its centennial year, as accompaniment to a series of photographs. The other four non-fiction works — *Cross-Country* (1949), *Thirty & Three* (1954), *Scotchman's Return and Other Essays* (1960), and *The Other Side of Hugh MacLennan* (1978) — are eclectic selections of essays from among the approximately four hundred MacLennan has written.[141] Of these, *The Other Side of Hugh MacLennan*, which contains essays from the earlier collections, uncollected material, and a few previously unpublished pieces, displays MacLennan at his most engaging, while providing the best proportion of substantial to ephemeral material.

The heterogeneous essays in MacLennan's published collections include autobiographical reminiscences; reflections on places (Oxford, New York, Cape Breton, Scotland); light, occasional pieces (on rose gardening, hockey, eccentrics, fiftieth birthdays); literary theory; historical and political analyses (on bilingualism, Canadian cultural sovereignty, Mackenzie King, the Suez crisis); and thoughts on current issues (religion and science, education, the Canadian and American character, youth, male and female psyches). Personal, familiar, sometimes even chatty, they illustrate well MacLennan's conviction that the success of non-fiction depends upon the intimacy created between writer and reader. As he explains, non-fiction

> depends more than any other form of writing on a relationship between author and reader so close that at times the author at his desk has the illusion that he is lounging in his library late in the evening on a well-spent day, a glass of beer at his elbow and a personal friend in the opposite chair.[142]

Those essays which are not merely whimsical and entertaining show MacLennan as a teacher, with anecdote and dialogue enlivening the thoughtful, assured reflections of a cultivated speaker sharing concerns with a like-minded audience. Here MacLennan functions as a social conscience, challenging the reader with moral and spiritual issues, defending the humanities, education, decency, intelligence, heroism, and civilization, warning against bureaucracies, consumerism, materialism, cynicism, and ideologies of many kinds, including rationalism. In so doing, he reveals himself as an idealist, an elitist, and a conservative, a man of strong religious impulses caught without an orthodox faith. For all the urgency of conviction in these essays, MacLennan here demonstrates a better command of tone than in the least successful passages in the novels, being less sententious and heavy-handed in his assertions, more capable of moving us subtly without sentimentality in his appeals to emotion.

MacLennan's *Seven Rivers of Canada: The MacKenzie, the St. Lawrence, the Ottawa, the Red, the Saskatchewan, the Fraser, and the St. John* is a celebration of human courage and endurance. The book also shows a profound reverence for the vast and powerful Canadian landscape which inspires lyricism in MacLennan's novels and there repeatedly provides abiding consolation in the face of human folly. As a non-fiction account of human beings in elemental nature, it may owe something to Frederick Philip Grove's *Along Prairie Trails*, which MacLennan explicitly praises here.[143] What interests the author are the natural and human, not the technological and commercial, dimensions of the rivers' histories, so that he omits discussion, for example, of the St. Lawrence Seaway. His profiles of the rivers reveal his fascination with history and with heroism; his skill with landscape description and dramatic action (in the powerful verbs describing the Fraser or the St. John at Grand Falls, for example); his tendency towards humanistic philosophizing (and the same unabashed confidence in broad generalization found in the essays); his pastoral values; his inclination for uplifting sentiment; his ability to make facts and statistics speak eloquently (in evidence about the voyageurs' accomplishments or the force of the Fraser, for instance); and his awe before the land. Faced with the difficulty of maintaining variety and interest with a basically static subject and repetitive structure, MacLennan creates dramas of river versus land, river versus river, river versus people; anthropomorphizes without embarrassment; and at times lapses into superlatives. He refers in this work to what he calls "a *bravura* passage" in *Two Solitudes* describing the extravagance of the St. Lawrence,[144] and his prose here sometimes shows an even greater rhetorical straining for effect. What works more effectively are the familiar manner, the personal asides, the confiding tone found also in the essays.

As critics have observed, the prose writer and the novelist are less distinct in MacLennan than in many other writers. His fictional moral dramas of self-determination and quest for meaning — even when focused, as in his early and late novels, on individual power-lessness and, in the late novels, on the consequent breakdown of community — take place in an historical and social context. Given MacLennan's historical imagination, it is not surprising that the novels consistently operate on both a personal and a broader social level, that characters are representative rather than gloriously origi-nal. The difficulty enters, as we have seen, in the discrepancy between the gravity of MacLennan's themes and the value of his national documentation, on the one hand, and the means he sometimes employs to delineate these, on the other. He has demonstrated a facility with a variety of techniques for handling both time — linear and retrospective, compressed and expansive — and narrative per-spective — omniscient, first-person, and multiple. Yet tyrannical imperatives of plot (augmented, perhaps, by awareness of his con-trasting weakness for rambling discursiveness) and his own awk-wardness at times with style and tone lead him to dramatize his narratives through sensational action and overblown language more suited to popular fiction than to the serious material he is handling. Nevertheless, his contribution, historically, to the development of a distinctively Canadian literature is unquestioned, and, at his best, he engages us in a fiction that is both discerning and moving.

NOTES

[1] Letters to Sam MacLennan, Hugh MacLennan Papers, Special Collections Division, Univ. of Calgary Library (HMP, Calgary), 14.2.42 ff.

[2] "So All Their Praises" was accepted for publication by the New York publisher Robert O. Ballou, but the firm closed before the novel was published. See Elspeth Cameron, *Hugh MacLennan: A Writer's Life* (Toronto: Univ. of Toronto Press, 1981), p. 87.

[3] See HMP, Calgary, 14.2.70, 14.3.31, 14.3.43; and Hugh MacLennan Papers, Department of Rare Books and Special Collections, McGill Univ. Library (HMP, McGill), Box 1, Part 1, Files 2, 3, 5 and Part 2, Files 5–6.

[4] Hugh MacLennan, "My First Book," *Canadian Author and Bookman*, 28, No. 2 (Summer 1952), 4.

[5] Hugh MacLennan, "Fiction in Canada — 1930 to 1980," *University of Toronto Quarterly*, 50 (Fall 1980), 35.

[6] Hugh MacLennan, "The Future of the Novel as an Art Form," in his *Scotchman's Return and Other Essays* (Toronto: Macmillan, 1960), p. 143.

[7] Hugh MacLennan, "Homage to Hemingway," in his *Thirty & Three*, ed. Dorothy Duncan (Toronto: Macmillan, 1954), pp. 85–96.

[8] Hugh MacLennan, "The Future Trend in the Novel," *Canadian Author and Bookman*, 24, No. 3 (Sept. 1948), 4.

[9] Hugh MacLennan, "The Writer Engagé," in his *The Other Side of Hugh MacLennan*, ed. Elspeth Cameron (Toronto: Macmillan, 1978), p. 270.

[10] Hugh MacLennan, "Fiction in the Age of Science," *Western Humanities Review*, 6 (Autumn 1952), 332.

[11] Hugh MacLennan, "The Changed Functions of Fiction and Non-Fiction," in *The Other Side of Hugh MacLennan*, p. 243.

[12] Ronald Sutherland, "Hugh MacLennan" [interview], *Canadian Literature*, Nos. 68–69 (Spring–Summer 1976), p. 47.

[13] Alan Twigg, "Patricius: Hugh MacLennan," in *For Openers: Conversations with 24 Canadian Writers* (Madeira Park, B.C.: Harbour, 1981), p. 92.

[14] Hugh MacLennan, "Requiem," Hugh MacLennan Papers, Thomas Fisher Rare Book Library, Univ. of Toronto (HMP, Toronto), Box 1, l.118.

[15] Hugh MacLennan, "Sunset and Evening Star," in *Scotchman's Return and Other Essays*, p. 239.

[16] Hugh MacLennan, "Where Is My Potted Palm?" in *Thirty & Three*, p. 54.

[17] Hugh MacLennan, Letter to Leonard Cohen, 13 Feb. 1955, Leonard Cohen Papers, Thomas Fisher Rare Book Library, Univ. of Toronto, Box 10, Ms. 127.

[18] MacLennan, "Where Is My Potted Palm?" p. 50. See also his "The Future of the Novel as an Art Form," p. 156.

[19] MacLennan, "The Future of the Novel as an Art Form," pp. 145–46.

[20] MacLennan acknowledges Leavis' influence in his "Sunset and Evening Star," p. 239.

[21] MacLennan, "The Future Trend in the Novel," p. 5.

[22] Sutherland, p. 46. See also Hugh MacLennan, Letter to Sam MacLennan, 16 Sept. 1939, HMP, Calgary, 14.2.42.7a; and Roy MacGregor, "A Voice out of Time," *Maclean's*, 22 Sept. 1980, p. 46.

[23] See, for example, MacLennan's comments on Rebecca West's style in Donald Cameron, "Hugh MacLennan: The Tennis Racket Is an Antelope Bone," in *Conversations with Canadian Novelists – 1* (Toronto: Macmillan, 1973), p. 132. See also MacLennan's comments on the introspective technique of Alan Paton and Boris Pasternak in his "The Changed Functions of Fiction and Non-Fiction," p. 246.

[24] Hugh MacLennan, "The Writer and His Audience," in *The Other Side of Hugh MacLennan*, p. 4.

[25] MacLennan, "The Changed Functions of Fiction and Non-Fiction," p. 241.

[26] See MacLennan, "The Future of the Novel as an Art Form," pp. 145, 153; and "Fiction in the Age of Science," p. 333.

[27] Frederick Philip Grove, Letter to Hugh MacLennan, 20 Nov. 1941, HMP, Calgary, 14.1.57.1. This letter is included in *The Letters of Frederick Philip Grove*, ed. Desmond Pacey (Toronto: Univ. of Toronto Press, 1976), pp. 415–16.

[28] See Leonard Cohen Papers, Thomas Fisher Rare Book Library, Univ. of Toronto, Box 10, Ms. 127; Marian Engel, "The Office on the Landing," in *Hugh MacLennan: 1982: Proceedings of the MacLennan Conference at University College*, ed. Elspeth Cameron (Toronto: Canadian Studies Program, University College, Univ. of Toronto, 1982), pp. 147–52; and Robert Kroetsch, "Hugh MacLennan: An Appreciation," in *Hugh MacLennan: 1982*, pp. 135–39.

[29] See, for instance, Solange Chaput-Rolland, "Two Solitudes and Two Certitudes," in *Hugh MacLennan: 1982*, p. 140. For MacLennan's correspondence with McDougall and Graham, see HMP, McGill, Box 1, Part 1, File 2 and Box 1, Part 2, File 6.

[30] For MacLennan's correspondence with Vizinczey, see HMP, Calgary, 14.1.35

[31] For MacLennan's correspondence with these Canadian literary figures, see HMP, Calgary, 14.1.36, 14.1.50, 14.2.19; HMP, McGill, Box 1, Part 1, Files 1–2 and Part 2, Files 5–6; and the Earle Birney Collection, Thomas Fisher Rare Book Library, Univ. of Toronto, Ms. 49, Mac Box.

[32] Kroetsch, pp. 136–37.

[33] Roger Leslie Hyman, "Hugh MacLennan: His Art, His Society and His Critics," *Queen's Quarterly*, 82 (Winter 1975), 526.

[34] Elspeth Cameron, " 'A Late Germination in a Cold Climate': The Growth of MacLennan Criticism," *Journal of Canadian Studies*, 14, No. 4 (Winter 1979–80), 3–19.

[35] For a summary of reviews of *Barometer Rising*, see Elspeth Cameron, *Hugh MacLennan*, pp. 143–47. See also MacLennan's scrapbooks of reviews, HMP, Calgary, 14.8–12. For this mixed critical reaction to MacLennan's novels, see, for example, J.R. MacGillivray, "Letters in Canada 1945: Fiction," rev. of *Two Solitudes*, *University of Toronto Quarterly*, 15 (April 1946), 282–83; Patricia Owen, rev. of *The Precipice*, *The Canadian Forum*, Nov. 1948, p. 190; Claude T. Bissell, "Letters in Canada 1948: Fiction," rev. of *The Precipice*, *University of Toronto Quarterly*, 18 (July 1949), 263–66; and Michael Dalt, "Fiction Chronicle," rev. of *Return of the Sphinx*, *The Tamarack Review*, No. 45 (Autumn 1967), pp. 114–22.

[36] Robertson Davies, "MacLennan's Rising Star," rev. of *The Watch That*

Ends the Night, *Saturday Night*, 28 March 1959, p. 29.

[37] For sales figures, see Elspeth Cameron, *Hugh MacLennan*, pp. 298–99.

[38] William Du Bois, "Novel of Quebec, Between Two Wars," rev. of *Two Solitudes*, *The New York Times Book Review*, 21 Jan. 1945, p. 5.

[39] Roy Daniells, "Literature: 1: Poetry and the Novel," in *The Culture of Contemporary Canada*, ed. Julian Park (Toronto: Ryerson, 1957), p. 29.

[40] George Woodcock, "A Nation's Odyssey: The Novels of Hugh Mac-Lennan," in his *Odysseus Ever Returning: Essays on Canadian Writers and Writing*, New Canadian Library, No. 71 (Toronto: McClelland and Stewart, 1970), p. 23.

[41] Warren Tallman, "Wolf in the Snow, Part One: Four Windows on to Landscapes," *Canadian Literature*, No. 5 (Summer 1960), pp. 20, 18.

[42] Paul Goetsch, "Too Long to the Courtly Muses: Hugh MacLennan as a Contemporary Writer," *Canadian Literature*, No. 10 (Autumn 1961), p. 29.

[43] Edmund O. Wilson, *O Canada: An American's Notes on Canadian Culture* (New York: Farrar, Straus and Giroux, 1964), pp. 59–82.

[44] Ronald Sutherland, "Fourth Separatism," *Canadian Literature*, No. 45 (Summer 1970), p. 20.

[45] George Woodcock, *Hugh MacLennan*, Studies in Canadian Literature, No. 5 (Toronto: Copp Clark, 1969), p. 34.

[46] W.H. New, "Winter and the Night-People," in *Hugh MacLennan*, ed. Paul Goetsch (Toronto: McGraw-Hill Ryerson, 1973), pp. 165–66.

[47] Hugo McPherson, "The Novels of Hugh MacLennan," in *Hugh Mac-Lennan*, ed. Paul Goetsch, p. 24. See also Robert H. Cockburn, *The Novels of Hugh MacLennan* (Montreal: Harvest House, 1969), pp. 77–79; and Woodcock, *Hugh MacLennan*, pp. 87–89.

[48] Hyman, "Hugh MacLennan: His Art, His Society and His Critics," p. 517.

[49] For commentary on MacLennan's minor characters, see Cockburn, pp. 38–39, 121–23, 151; Alec Lucas, *Hugh MacLennan*, New Canadian Library, Canadian Writers No. 8 (Toronto: McClelland and Stewart, 1970), pp. 38–39; and David Arnason, "Canadian Nationalism in Search of Form: Hugh Mac-Lennan's *Barometer Rising*," *Journal of Canadian Fiction*, 1, No. 4 (Fall 1972), 71.

[50] Woodcock, "A Nation's Odyssey," p. 14; Cockburn, pp. 21, 146–47; and Patricia A. Morley, *The Immoral Moralists: Hugh MacLennan and Leonard Cohen* (Toronto: Clarke, Irwin, 1972), p. 60.

[51] Catherine Sheldrick Ross, "Hugh MacLennan's Two Worlds," *Canadian Literature*, No. 80 (Spring 1979), pp. 5–12.

[52] Lucas, pp. 56–57; New, "Winter and the Night-People," pp. 163, 165; and Helen Hoy, " 'The Gates Closed on Us Then': The Paradise-Lost Motif in Hugh

MacLennan's Fiction," *Journal of Canadian Studies*, 14, No. 4 (Winter 1979–80), 30–31, 34, 38–39, 42.

[53] See, for example, Naïm Kattan, "Le roman canadien anglais," *Les Lettres nouvelles*, déc. 1966-jan. 1967, pp. 26–27; Paul Goetsch, "Introduction," *Hugh MacLennan*, ed. Paul Goetsch, p. 7; T.D. MacLulich, "*The Precipice*: Mac-Lennan's Anatomy of Failure," *Journal of Canadian Studies*, 14, No. 4 (Winter 1979–80), 64; and McPherson, p. 30.

[54] Ross, pp. 11–12.

[55] See, for example, Lucas, p. 47; Hoy, pp. 30–31, 44; T.D. MacLulich, "Oedipus and Eve: The Novels of Hugh MacLennan," *Dalhousie Review*, 59 (Autumn 1979), 517; and T.D. MacLulich, *Hugh MacLennan*, Twayne's World Authors, No. 708 (Boston: Twayne, 1983), p. 122.

[56] See, for example, G.C. Andrew, "The Great Explosion," rev. of *Barometer Rising*, *The Canadian Forum*, Dec. 1941, p. 282; rev. of *Barometer Rising*, *Saturday Review*, 25 Oct. 1941, p. 21; and Wilson, p. 77.

[57] See, for example, Cockburn, pp. 35, 150; Woodcock, *Hugh MacLennan*, p. 105, and "A Nation's Odyssey," p. 15; Arnason, p. 71; and Lucas, p. 17.

[58] See, for example, F.T. Marsh, rev. of *Barometer Rising*, *Books*, 12 Oct. 1941, p. 8; Peter Buitenhuis, *Hugh MacLennan*, Canadian Writers and Their Works (Toronto: Forum House, 1969), p. 24; Woodcock, *Hugh MacLennan*, pp. 67, 99; Arnason, p. 70; Elspeth Cameron, *Hugh MacLennan*, pp. 153–54; MacLulich, *Hugh MacLennan*, pp. 76–77; and McPherson, p. 32.

[59] Lucas, p. 42. See also Paul West, "New Novels," rev. of *The Watch That Ends the Night*, *New Statesman*, 19 Dec. 1959, p. 888; Goetsch, "Too Long to the Courtly Muses," p. 28; Buitenhuis, p. 64; and Morley, p. 108. For defences of the ending of this novel, see David J. Dooley, *Moral Vision in the Canadian Novel* (Toronto: Clarke, Irwin, 1979), pp. 87–92; and W.J. Keith, "Novelist or Essayist? Hugh MacLennan and *The Watch That Ends the Night*," in *Hugh MacLennan: 1982*, pp. 55–63.

[60] See, for example, Cockburn, p. 144; Buitenhuis, pp. 71–72; Woodcock, *Hugh MacLennan*, p. 118; Roger Leslie Hyman, "Return to *Return of the Sphinx*," *English Studies in Canada*, 1 (Winter 1975), 456; Joseph Zezulka, "MacLennan's Defeated Pilgrim: A Perspective on *Return of the Sphinx*," *Journal of Canadian Fiction*, 4, No. 1 (1975), 130; and MacLulich, *Hugh MacLennan*, pp. 102–03.

[61] Hugh MacLennan, *Two Solitudes*, abrid. ed., ed. Claude T. Bissell (Toronto: Macmillan, 1951). See also MacGillivray, pp. 282–83; Desmond Pacey, *Creative Writing in Canada: A Short History of English-Canadian Literature* (Toronto: Ryerson, 1952), p. 188; Woodcock, *Hugh MacLennan*, pp. 76–80; Cockburn, pp. 62–69; Buitenhuis, pp. 35–38; Lucas, pp. 32–35; Elspeth Cameron,

Hugh MacLennan, pp. 189–90; and MacLulich, *Hugh MacLennan*, p. 48.

[62] See, for example, Wilson, p. 77; and Woodcock, *Hugh MacLennan*, p. 56.

[63] See, for example, Kattan, p. 27; Buitenhuis, p. 64; Dooley, p. 80; Keith, p. 55; and MacLulich, *Hugh MacLennan*, pp. 82, 120.

[64] For such defences of *Each Man's Son*, see Cockburn, p. 89; Lucas, p. 3; John Moss, "MacLennan, Hugh," in his *A Reader's Guide to the Canadian Novel* (Toronto: McClelland and Stewart, 1981), p. 179; and Roger Leslie Hyman, "Too Many Voices, Too Many Times: Hugh MacLennan's Unfulfilled Ambitions," rev. of *Voices in Time*, *Queen's Quarterly*, 89 (Summer 1982), 317. For this defence of *Voices in Time*, see Elspeth Cameron, *Hugh MacLennan*, p. 370.

[65] For critical evaluation of *Return of the Sphinx*, see New, "Winter and the Night-People," p. 163; Cockburn, p. 128; Woodcock, *Hugh MacLennan*, pp. 117–18; Hyman, "Return to *Return of the Sphinx*," p. 450; and MacLulich, *Hugh MacLennan*, p. 99. For negative reaction to *The Precipice*, see Pacey, pp. 188–89; Cockburn, p. 88; Buitenhuis, pp. 40, 44; and Woodcock, *Hugh MacLennan*, p. 81. For defences of this novel, see Wilson, pp. 71–74; and William Arthur Deacon, "The Literary Scene," rev. of *The Precipice*, *Canadian Author and Bookman*, 25, No. 3 (Autumn 1949), 36.

[66] Woodcock, *Hugh MacLennan*, p. 118.

[67] Keith, p. 55.

[68] Paul Goetsch, *Das Romanwerk Hugh MacLennans: Eine Studie zum Literarischen Nationalismus in Kanada* (Hamburg: Cram, de Gruyter, 1961).

[69] Buitenhuis, p. 19.

[70] Woodcock, *Hugh MacLennan*, p. 115.

[71] Lucas, p. 57.

[72] Morley, p. 2.

[73] Robin Mathews, "Hugh MacLennan: The Nationalist Dilemma," *Studies in Canadian Literature*, 1 (Winter 1976), 49–63.

[74] David Staines, "Mapping the Terrain," *Mosaic*, 11, No. 3 (Spring 1978), 137–51.

[75] T.D. MacLulich, "Oedipus and Eve," p. 501.

[76] Laurel Boone, "*Each Man's Son*: Romance in Disguise," *Journal of Canadian Fiction*, Nos. 28–29 (1980), pp. 147–56.

[77] Warren Stevenson, "A Neglected Theme in *Two Solitudes*," *Canadian Literature*, No. 75 (Winter 1977), pp. 53–60; Elspeth Cameron, "The Overlay Theme in MacLennan's *The Precipice*," *Journal of Canadian Fiction*, No. 20 (1977), pp. 117–24; Hyman, "Return to *Return of the Sphinx*," pp. 450–65; Zezulka, pp. 121–31; and Catherine Kelly, "The Unity of *Two Solitudes*," *Ariel*, 6, No. 2 (April 1975), 38–61.

[78] See, respectively, Elspeth Cameron, "Ordeal by Fire: The Genesis of

MacLennan's *The Precipice,*" *Canadian Literature,* No. 82 (Autumn 1979), pp. 35–46; Donald R. Bartlett, "MacLennan and Yeats," *Canadian Literature,* No. 89 (Summer 1981), pp. 74–84; and Elspeth Cameron, "MacLennan's *Sphinx*: Critical Reception and Oedipal Origins," *Journal of Canadian Fiction,* No. 30 (1980), pp. 141–59.

[79] See, respectively, E.D. Blodgett, "Intertextual Designs in Hugh Mac-Lennan's *The Watch That Ends the Night,*" *Canadian Review of Comparative Literature,* 5 (Fall 1978), 280–88; and Rosalie Murphy, "A Comparison of *The Rise of Silas Lapham* and *Barometer Rising,*" *American Review of Canadian Studies,* 9, No. 2 (Autumn 1979), 125–29.

[80] See Woodcock, "Hugh MacLennan," in *Hugh MacLennan,* ed. Paul Goetsch, pp. 11–21; McPherson, pp. 23–33; W.H. New, "The Storm and After: Imagery and Symbolism in Hugh MacLennan's *Barometer Rising,*" in *Hugh MacLennan,* ed. Paul Goetsch, pp. 75–87, and "Winter and the Night-People," pp. 163–72.

[81] Hoy, pp. 29–45; MacLulich, "*The Precipice*: MacLennan's Anatomy of Failure," pp. 54–65; Stephen Bonnycastle, "The Power of *The Watch That Ends the Night,*" *Journal of Canadian Studies,* 14, No. 4 (Winter 1979–80), 76–89; and Francis Zichy, " 'Shocked and Startled into Utter Banality': Characters and Circumstances in *The Watch That Ends the Night,*" *Journal of Canadian Studies,* 14, No. 4 (Winter 1979–80), 105.

[82] Keith, pp. 59, 62; and Eli Mandel, "Hugh MacLennan and the Tradition of Canadian Fiction," in *Hugh MacLennan: 1982,* pp. 93–108.

[83] MacLulich, *Hugh MacLennan,* p. 2.

[84] Hugh MacLennan, "So All Their Praises," HMP, McGill, Box 3, Part 1, Files 1–2, chap. 17. All further references to this work appear in the text with chapter numbers within parentheses.

[85] Hugh MacLennan, "A Man Should Rejoice," HMP, McGill, Box 3, Part 2, Files 3–9, chap. 25. All further references to this work appear in the text with chapter numbers within parentheses.

[86] For editorial responses to "A Man Should Rejoice," see Longman's & Co., Letter to Hugh MacLennan, 4 May 1939, HMP, McGill, Box 2, Part 1, File 12; and Letter to Hugh MacLennan, 6 Nov. 1937, HMP, McGill, Box 3, Part 2, File 3.

[87] Hugh MacLennan, quoted in Elspeth Cameron, *Hugh MacLennan,* p. 107.

[88] Hugh MacLennan, Letter to Robert Cockburn, 1 May 1970, HMP, Calgary, 14.1.32.2b.

[89] Hugh MacLennan, "Youth and the Modern Literature," in his *Scotchman's Return and Other Essays,* p. 244.

[90] Hoy, pp. 30–31.

[91] Hugh MacLennan, Fellowship Application, 29 June 1937, HMP, McGill, Box

I, Part I, File I.

[92] Hugh MacLennan, "The Story of a Novel," *Canadian Literature*, No. 3 (Winter 1960), pp. 38–39.

[93] MacLennan, "My First Book," p. 4.

[94] Hugh MacLennan, Letter to George Barrett, 20 Oct. 1941, quoted in Elspeth Cameron, *Hugh MacLennan*, p. 156.

[95] Hugh MacLennan, *Two Solitudes* (New York: Duell, Sloan and Pearce, 1945), p. 329. All further references to this work appear in the text.

[96] For MacLennan's response to the reaction many readers had against his apparent approval of Penelope's unconventional behaviour, see Donald Cameron, p. 135.

[97] Cockburn, p. 36.

[98] Arnason, p. 71.

[99] Hugh MacLennan, *Barometer Rising* (New York: Duell, Sloan and Pearce, 1941), p. 218.

[100] On the publisher's suggestion, MacLennan tried to reduce the "saccharinity" of the "happy ending" by anticipating, rather than delineating, the couple's first discussion of their child. See Sam Sloan, Memo, enclosed in Charles Duell, Letter to Hugh MacLennan, 28 May 1941, HMP, McGill, Box I, Part I, File 4.

[101] Moss, p. 183.

[102] Sutherland, p. 43.

[103] Donald Cameron, p. 139.

[104] MacLennan, Fellowship Application.

[105] Hugh MacLennan, Note, 16 May 1966, HMP, McGill, Box 2, Part 2, File 4–7. See also Hugh MacLennan, "How Do I Write?" *Canadian Author and Bookman*, 21, No. 4 (Dec. 1945), 6.

[106] MacLennan, Note, 16 May 1966.

[107] Hugh MacLennan, Letter to Marian Engel, 19 June 1956, quoted in Elspeth Cameron, *Hugh MacLennan*, p. 217.

[108] Hugh MacLennan, "The Canadian Character," in his *Cross-Country* (Toronto: Collins, 1949), pp. 5–6, 16.

[109] Elspeth Cameron, "Ordeal by Fire," pp. 35–46. See also her *Hugh MacLennan*, pp. 203–08.

[110] Donald Cameron, p. 139.

[111] Hugh MacLennan, *The Precipice* (Toronto: Collins, 1948), pp. 116, 133, 135, 142–43. All further references to this work appear in the text.

[112] Woodcock, "A Nation's Odyssey," p. 19.

[113] See, for example, William H. Magee, "Trends in the Recent English-Canadian Novel," *Culture*, 10 (March 1949), 29–42; and R.E. Watters, "Hugh MacLennan and the Canadian Character," in *As a Man Thinks . . . .* , ed.

Edmund Morrison and William Robbins (Toronto: Gage, 1953), pp. 228–43.

[114] See, for example, Ann Barr Snitow, "Mass Market Romance: Pornography for Women Is Different," in *Powers of Desire: The Politics of Sexuality*, ed. Ann Barr Snitow and others (New York: Monthly Review, 1983), pp. 245–63.

[115] Hugh MacLennan, *Each Man's Son* (Toronto: Macmillan, 1951), p. 219. All further references to this work appear in the text.

[116] Hugh MacLennan, "Reflections on Two Decades," *Canadian Literature*, No. 41 (Summer 1969), p. 31.

[117] Hugh MacLennan, Postcard to Earle Birney, 26 Jan. 1952, Earle Birney Collection, Thomas Fisher Rare Book Library, Univ. of Toronto, Ms. 49, Mac. Box.

[118] MacLennan, "The Story of a Novel," p. 39.

[119] MacLennan, "The Story of a Novel," pp. 38–39.

[120] See, for example, F.W. Watt, "Letters in Canada 1959: Fiction," rev. of *The Watch That Ends the Night*, *University of Toronto Quarterly*, 29 (July 1960), 461–63; Tom Marshall, "Some Working Notes on *The Watch That Ends the Night*," *Quarry*, 17, No. 2 (Winter 1968), 16; Wilson, p. 75; Buitenhuis, p. 56; and Woodcock, *Hugh MacLennan*, p. 49.

[121] Hugh MacLennan, *The Watch That Ends the Night* (Toronto: Macmillan, 1959), p. 342. All further references to this work appear in the text.

[122] MacLennan, "Reflections on Two Decades," p. 31.

[123] For MacLennan's parallel description of George Stewart's story, see his "The Story of a Novel," p. 39.

[124] See, for example, Cockburn, p. 120; Morley, p. 100; and Hermann Boeschenstein, "Hugh MacLennan, a Canadian Novelist," in *Hugh MacLennan*, ed. Paul Goetsch, p. 52.

[125] For a discussion of this allegory, see Hoy, pp. 40–42.

[126] For this reading of the significance of "embolism," I am indebted to Bonnie Kennedy, University of Lethbridge.

[127] Hugh MacLennan, "Requiem," HMP, Toronto.

[128] For MacLennan's comments on Paton's style, see Twigg, p. 88. See also Hugh MacLennan, Letter to Robert Cockburn, 1 May 1970.

[129] Hugh MacLennan, Note, HMP, Calgary, 14.5.26. For MacLennan's further comments on this structural parallel, see Twigg, p. 86.

[130] Hugh MacLennan, *Return of the Sphinx* (Toronto: Macmillan, 1967), p. 300. All further references to this work appear in the text.

[131] See MacLennan, "Reflections on Two Decades," pp. 36–37; Twigg, p. 86; and Donald Cameron, p. 131.

[132] Twigg, p. 86.

[133] MacLennan, Letter to Robert Cockburn, 1 May 1970.

[134] See MacLennan, "The Changed Functions of Fiction and Non-Fiction," pp. 243, 245.

[135] Donald Cameron, p. 140.

[136] Hugh MacLennan, "Return of the Sphinx," HMP, Calgary, 14.5.

[137] Donald Cameron, p. 141.

[138] Hugh MacLennan, Letter to Robertson Davies, 14 Jan. 1971, HMP, Calgary, 14.1.36.3a-b.

[139] For MacLennan's distinction here between "patrist" and "matrist" social orders, see also his "Reflections on Two Decades," pp. 31–39; and Elspeth Cameron, *Hugh MacLennan*, pp. 314–16, 322–25, 337.

[140] Hugh MacLennan, *Voices in Time* (Toronto: Macmillan, 1980), p. 97.

[141] See Elspeth Cameron, Introd., *The Other Side of Hugh MacLennan*, p.x. See also her bibliography of MacLennan's writings, "Hugh MacLennan: An Annotated Bibliography," in *The Annotated Bibliography of Canada's Major Authors*, ed. Robert Lecker and Jack David (Downsview, Ont.: ECW, 1979), I, 103–53; and her "A MacLennan Log," *Journal of Canadian Studies*, 14, No. 4 (Winter 1979–80), 106–21.

[142] MacLennan, "A Writer and His Audience," p. 3.

[143] Hugh MacLennan, *Seven Rivers of Canada: The Mackenzie, the St. Lawrence, the Ottawa, the Red, the Saskatchewan, the Fraser, the St. John* (Toronto: Macmillan, 1961), p. 106.

[144] MacLennan, *Seven Rivers of Canada*, p. 74.

SELECTED BIBLIOGRAPHY

Primary Sources

Books

MacLennan, Hugh. *Oxyrhynchus: An Economic and Social Study*. Princeton, N.J.: Princeton Univ. Press, 1935.
———. *Barometer Rising*. New York: Duell, Sloan, and Pearce, 1941.
———. *Two Solitudes*. New York: Duell, Sloan, and Pearce, 1945.
———. *The Precipice*. Toronto: Collins, 1948.
———. *Cross-Country*. Toronto: Collins, 1949.
———. *Each Man's Son*. Toronto: Macmillan, 1951.
———. *Thirty & Three*. Ed. Dorothy Duncan. Toronto: Macmillan, 1954.
———. *The Watch That Ends the Night*. Toronto: Macmillan, 1959.
———. *Scotchman's Return and Other Essays*. Toronto: Macmillan, 1960.
———. *Seven Rivers of Canada: The Mackenzie, the St. Lawrence, the Ottawa, the Red, the Saskatchewan, the Fraser, the St. John*. Toronto: Macmillan, 1961.
———. *The Colour of Canada*. Toronto: McClelland and Stewart, 1967.
———. *Return of the Sphinx*. Toronto: Macmillan, 1967.
———. *The Other Side of Hugh MacLennan: Selected Essays Old and New*. Ed. Elspeth Cameron. Toronto: Macmillan, 1978.
———. *Voices in Time*. Toronto: Macmillan, 1980.

Contributions to Periodicals

MacLennan, Hugh. "How Do I Write." *Canadian Author and Bookman*, 21, No. 4 (Dec. 1945), 6–7.
———. "My First Book." *Canadian Author and Bookman*, 28, No. 2 (Summer 1952), 3–4.

———. "Fiction in the Age of Science." *Western Humanities Review*, 6 (Autumn 1952), 325–34.

———. "The Story of a Novel." *Canadian Literature*, No. 3 (Winter 1960), pp. 35–39.

———. "Reflections on Two Decades." *Canadian Literature*, No. 41 (Summer 1969), pp. 28–39.

———. "Fiction in Canada — 1930 to 1980." *University of Toronto Quarterly*, 50 (Fall 1980), 29–42.

Manuscripts and Typescripts

Hugh MacLennan Papers. Department of Rare Books and Special Collections. McGill Univ. Library.

Hugh MacLennan Papers. Special Collections Division. Univ. of Calgary Library.

Hugh MacLennan Papers. Thomas Fisher Rare Book Library. Univ. of Toronto.

Secondary Sources

Andrew, G.C. "The Great Explosion." Rev. of *Barometer Rising*. *The Canadian Forum*, Dec. 1941, p. 282.

Arnason, David. "Canadian Nationalism in Search of a Form: Hugh Mac-Lennan's *Barometer Rising*." *Journal of Canadian Fiction*, 1, No. 4 (Fall 1972), 68–71.

Bartlett, Donald R. "MacLennan and Yeats." *Canadian Literature*, No. 89 (Summer 1981), pp. 74–84.

Bissell, Claude T. "Letters in Canada 1948: Fiction." Rev. of *The Precipice*. *University of Toronto Quarterly*, 18 (July 1949), 263–66.

———. "Letters in Canada 1951: Fiction." Rev. of *Each Man's Son*. *University of Toronto Quarterly*, 21 (April 1952), 263–64.

Blodgett, E.D. "Intertextual Designs in Hugh MacLennan's *The Watch That Ends the Night*." *Canadian Review of Comparative Literature*, 5 (Fall 1978), 280–88.

Boeschenstein, Hermann. "Hugh MacLennan, a Canadian Novelist." In *Hugh MacLennan*. Critical Views on Canadian Writers, No. 8. Ed. Paul Goetsch. Toronto: McGraw-Hill Ryerson, 1973, pp. 35–57.

Bonnycastle, Stephen. "The Power of *The Watch That Ends the Night*." *Journal of Canadian Studies*, 14, No. 4 (Winter 1979–80), 76–89.

Boone, Laurel. "*Each Man's Son*: Romance in Disguise." *Journal of Canadian Fiction*, Nos. 28–29 (1980), pp. 147–56.

Buitenhuis, Peter. *Hugh MacLennan*. Canadian Writers and Their Works. Toronto: Forum House, 1969.

Cameron, Donald A. "Hugh MacLennan: The Tennis Racket Is an Antelope Bone." In his *Conversations with Canadian Novelists*. Toronto: Macmillan, 1973. Part II, pp. 130–48.

Chambers, Robert D. "Hugh MacLennan and Religion: *The Precipice* Revisited." *Journal of Canadian Studies*, 14, No. 4 (Winter 1979–80), 46–53.

———. "The Novels of Hugh MacLennan." In *Hugh MacLennan*. Critical Views on Canadian Writers, No. 8. Ed. Paul Goetsch. Toronto: McGraw-Hill Ryerson, 1973, pp. 59–74.

Chaput-Rolland, Solange. "Two Solitudes and Two Certitudes." In *Hugh MacLennan: 1982: Proceedings of the MacLennan Conference at University College*. Ed. Elspeth Cameron. Toronto: Canadian Studies Program, University College, Univ. of Toronto, 1982, pp. 140–46.

Cockburn, Robert. *The Novels of Hugh MacLennan*. Montreal: Harvest House, 1969.

Dalt, Michael. "Fiction Chronicle." Rev. of *Return of the Sphinx*. *The Tamarack Review*, No. 45 (Autumn 1967), pp. 114–22.

Daniells, Roy. "Literature: I: Poetry and the Novel." In *The Culture of Canada*. Ed. Julian Park. Toronto: Ryerson, 1957, pp. 1–80.

Davies, Robertson. "MacLennan's Rising Sun." Rev. of *The Watch That Ends the Night*. *Saturday Night*, 28 March 1959, pp. 29–31.

Davis, Marilyn J. "Fathers and Sons." *Canadian Literature*, No. 58 (Autumn 1973), pp. 39–50.

Deacon, William Arthur. "The Literary Scene." Rev. of *The Precipice*. *Canadian Author and Bookman*, 25, No. 3 (Autumn 1949), pp. 34, 36–38, 39–44.

Dooley, D.J. "*Each Man's Son*: The Daemon of Hope and Imagination." *Journal of Canadian Studies*, 14 (Winter 1979–80), 66–75.

———. *Moral Vision in the Canadian Novel*. Toronto: Clarke, Irwin, 1979, pp. 79–92.

Du Bois, William. "Novel of Quebec, Between Two Wars." Rev. of *Two Solitudes*. *The New York Times Book Review*, 21 Jan. 1945, p. 5.

Engel, Marian. "The Office on the Landing." In *Hugh MacLennan: 1982: Proceedings of the MacLennan Conference at University College*. Ed. Elspeth Cameron. Toronto: Canadian Studies Program, University College, Univ. of Toronto, 1982, pp. 147–52.

Goetsch, Paul. *Das Romanwerk Hugh MacLennans: Eine Studie zum Literarischen Nationalismus in Kanada.* Hamburg: Cram, de Gruyter, 1961.

———. "Too Long to the Courtly Muses: Hugh MacLennan as a Contemporary Writer." *Canadian Literature*, No. 10 (Autumn 1961), pp. 19–31.

———, ed. *Hugh MacLennan.* Critical Views on Canadian Writers, No. 8. Toronto: McGraw-Hill Ryerson, 1973.

Hoy, Helen. " 'The Gates Closed on Us Then': The Paradise-Lost Motif in Hugh MacLennan's Fiction." *Journal of Canadian Studies*, 14, No. 4 (Winter 1979–80), 29–45.

Hyman, Roger Leslie. "Hugh MacLennan: His Art, His Society and His Critics." *Queen's Quarterly*, 82 (Winter 1975), 515–27.

———. "Return to *Return of the Sphinx*." *English Studies in Canada*, 1 (Winter 1975), 450–65.

———. "Too Many Voices, Too Many Times: Hugh MacLennan's Unfulfilled Ambitions." Rev. of *Voices in Time. Queen's Quarterly*, 89 (Summer 1982), 313–24.

Kattan, Naïm. "Le roman canadien anglais." *Les Lettres nouvelles*, déc. 1966–jan. 1967, pp. 21–30.

Keith, W.J. "Novelist or Essayist? Hugh MacLennan and *The Watch That Ends the Night*." In *Hugh MacLennan: 1982: Proceedings of the MacLennan Conference at University College.* Ed. Elspeth Cameron. Toronto: Canadian Studies Program, University College, Univ. of Toronto, 1982, pp. 55–63.

Kelly, Catherine. "The Unity of *Two Solitudes*." *Ariel*, 6, No. 2 (April 1975), 38–61.

Kroetsch, Robert. "Hugh MacLennan: An Appreciation." In *Hugh MacLennan: 1982: Proceedings of the MacLennan Conference at University College.* Ed. Elspeth Cameron. Toronto: Canadian Studies Program, University College, Univ. of Toronto, 1982, pp. 135–39.

Lucas, Alec. *Hugh MacLennan.* New Canadian Library. Canadian Writers, No. 8. Toronto: McClelland and Stewart, 1970.

MacGillivray, J.R. "Letters in Canada 1945: Fiction." Rev. of *Two Solitudes. University of Toronto Quarterly*, 15 (April 1946), 281–83.

MacGregor, Roy. "A Voice Out of Time." Rev. of *Voices in Time. Maclean's*, 22 Sept. 1980, pp. 45–48, 50.

MacLulich, T.D. "Oedipus and Eve: The Novels of Hugh MacLennan." *Dalhousie Review*, 59 (Autumn 1979), 500–18.

———. "*The Precipice*: MacLennan's Anatomy of Failure." *Journal of Canadian Studies*, 14, No. 4 (Winter 1979–80), 54–65.

———. *Hugh MacLennan.* Twayne's World Authors, No. 708. Boston:

Twayne, 1983.

McPherson, Hugo. "The Novels of Hugh MacLennan." In *Hugh MacLennan. Critical Views on Canadian Writers*, No. 8. Ed. Paul Goetsch. Toronto: McGraw-Hill Ryerson, 1973, pp. 23–33.

Magee, William H. "Trends in the Recent English-Canadian Novel." *Culture*, 10 (March 1949), 29–42.

Mandel, Eli. "Hugh MacLennan and the Tradition of Canadian Fiction." In *Hugh MacLennan: 1982: Proceedings of the MacLennan Conference at University College.* Ed. Elspeth Cameron. Toronto: Canadian Studies Program, University College, Univ. of Toronto, 1982, pp. 93–108.

Marsh, F.T. Rev. of *Barometer Rising. Books*, 12 Oct. 1941, p. 8.

Marshall, Tom. "Some Working Notes on *The Watch That Ends the Night*." *Quarry*, 17, No. 2 (Winter 1968), 13–16.

Mathews, Robin. "Hugh MacLennan: The Nationalist Dilemma in Canada." *Studies in Canadian Literature*, 1 (Winter 1976), 49–63.

Morley, Patricia A. *The Immoral Moralists: Hugh MacLennan and Leonard Cohen.* Toronto: Clarke, Irwin, 1972.

Moss, John. "MacLennan, Hugh." In his *A Reader's Guide to the Canadian Novel.* Toronto: McClelland and Stewart, 1981, pp. 175–83.

Murphy, Rosalie. "A Comparison of *The Rise of Silas Lapham* and *Barometer Rising*." *American Review of Canadian Studies*, 9, No. 2 (Autumn 1979), 125–29.

New, W.H. "The Storm and After: Imagery and Symbolism in Hugh MacLennan's *Barometer Rising*." In *Hugh MacLennan. Critical Views on Canadian Writers*, No. 8. Ed. Paul Goetsch. Toronto: McGraw-Hill Ryerson, 1973, pp. 75–87.

———. "Winter and the Night-People." In *Hugh MacLennan. Critical Views on Canadian Writers*, No. 8. Ed. Paul Goetsch. Toronto: McGraw-Hill Ryerson, 1973, pp. 163–72.

Owen, Patricia. Rev. of *The Precipice. The Canadian Forum*, Nov. 1948, p. 190.

Pacey, Desmond. *Creative Writing in Canada: A Short History of English-Canadian Literature.* Toronto: Ryerson, 1952, pp. 187–90.

Ross, Catherine Sheldrick. "Hugh MacLennan's Two Worlds." *Canadian Literature*, No. 80 (Spring 1979), pp. 5–12.

Staines, David. "Mapping the Terrain." *Mosaic*, 11 (Spring 1978), 137–51.

Stevenson, Warren. "A Neglected Theme in *Two Solitudes*." *Canadian Literature*, No. 75 (Winter 1977), pp. 53–60.

Sutherland, Ronald. "Fourth Separatism." *Canadian Literature*, No. 45 (Summer 1970), pp. 7–23.

————. "Hugh MacLennan" [Interview]. *Canadian Literature*, Nos. 68–69 (Spring–Summer 1976), pp. 40–48.

Tallman, Warren. "Wolf in the Snow, Part One: Four Windows on to Landscapes." *Canadian Literature*, No. 5 (Summer 1960), pp. 7–20.

Twigg, Alan. "Patricius: Hugh MacLennan." In his *For Openers: Conversations with 24 Canadian Writers*. Madeira Park, B.C.: Harbour, 1981, pp. 83–96.

Watt, F.W. "Letters in Canada 1959: Fiction." Rev. of *The Watch That Ends the Night*. *University of Toronto Quarterly*, 29 (July 1960), 461–63.

Watters, R.E. "Hugh MacLennan and the Canadian Character." In *As A Man Thinks . . . .* Ed. Edmund Morrison and William Robbins. Toronto: W.J. Gage, 1953, pp. 228–43.

West, Paul. "New Novels." Rev. of *The Watch That Ends the Night*. *New Statesman*, 19 Dec. 1959, pp. 888–89.

Wilson, Edmund. *O Canada: An American's Notes on Canadian Culture*. New York: Farrar, Straus and Giroux, 1964, pp. 59–82.

Woodcock, George. "Hugh MacLennan." *Northern Review*, 3 (April–May 1950), 2–10. Rpt. in *Hugh MacLennan*. Critical Views on Canadian Writers, No. 8. Ed. Paul Goetsch. Toronto: McGraw-Hill Ryerson, 1973, pp. 11–21.

————. "A Nation's Odyssey: The Novels of Hugh MacLennan." *Canadian Literature*, No. 10 (Autumn 1961), pp. 7–18. Rpt. in his *Odysseus Ever Returning: Essays on Canadian Writers and Writing*. New Canadian Library, No. 71. Toronto: McClelland and Stewart, 1970, pp. 12–23.

————. *Hugh MacLennan*. Studies in Canadian Literature, No. 5. Toronto: Copp Clark, 1969.

Zezulka, Joseph. "MacLennan's Defeated Pilgrim: A Perspective on *Return of the Sphinx*." *Journal of Canadian Fiction*, 4, No. 1 (1975), 121–31.

Zichy, Francis. " 'Shocked and Startled into Utter Banality': Characters and Circumstance in *The Watch That Ends the Night*." *Journal of Canadian Studies*, 14, No. 4 (Winter 1979–80), 90–105.

*Thomas H. Raddall
and His Works*

Thomas H. Raddall (1903–   )

ALAN R. YOUNG

Biography

Thomas Head Raddall was born on 13 November 1903, in Hythe, England, a small town on the southeast coast and the location of the British Army School of Musketry where his father was an instructor. Ten years later, on the eve of the First World War, Raddall's father was transferred to the Canadian army and posted to Halifax, Nova Scotia. During the war two events occurred that deeply influenced the future writer. In December 1917, while Raddall's father was away at the front in Europe, a disastrous explosion occurred in Halifax Harbour as a result of a collision involving a French munitions ship. It was the largest man-made explosion prior to the atomic bomb, and, according to the official records, it killed almost 2,000 people, injured 9,000, and blinded 199. In addition, hundreds of people simply vanished. One of the postcards issued shortly after shows "The Morgue at Chebucto Road School." This was the young Raddall's neighbourhood school where he had been when the explosion blew out the windows. Here, too, later in the day he assisted in a minor way in setting up the temporary morgue. Raddall's mother and sisters, at home at the time of the explosion, escaped serious injury, but along with hundreds of other survivors, all in a state of shock, they and Thomas were forced to flee in the snow when warning was given of a second possible explosion. In his memoirs and in other writings, most notably his short story, "Winter's Tale,"[1] Raddall was to describe in telling detail the trauma and horror of these events. The immediate effect on the fourteen-year-old boy, the only son, was an increasing restlessness: "The truth was that enforced lessons of any kind now gave me a spirit of revolt, and school had become an ordeal . . . the difficulty of home study in our battered and poorly lit house, the lasting effect of the stunning explosion and the macabre scenes that followed all gave me a desperate longing to get away and do something new somewhere else."[2]

Eight months later a second event, the death of his father, added to an already abundant experience of tragedy and suffering, and it is at this time that Raddall seems to have begun to develop his characteristic faith in self-reliance since prayer seemed merely "like shouting down a drainpipe in the dark" and God was "invisible and aloof." It would be far better, he decided, "to face things on your feet and with eyes wide open, watchful for trouble and maybe a bit of luck here and there along the way" (*IMT*, p. 44). Here in essence, one suspects, is the origin of the kind of attitude that was later to be typical of a number of the protagonists in Raddall's fiction. However simply expressed, here too is the philosophical basis for Raddall's own later life.

Recognizing the need to become self-supporting, Raddall left school and began training in September 1918 as a radio telegrapher for the merchant marine service, pretending that he was eighteen, three years more than his actual age. From the spring of 1919 he served in coastal stations and a succession of small ships, rapidly acquiring a knowledge and love of the sea and a rapid, if sometimes painful, education in the ways of the world. In April 1921, he worked for a year at the radio station on Sable Island, the desolate and notorious "Graveyard of the Atlantic," some 175 miles east of Halifax, an experience that later provided the background for his novel, *The Nymph and the Lamp*.

Raddall then quit radio work to take a course in bookkeeping, and in 1923 found employment with a small wood-pulp firm in Milton, on the south shore of Nova Scotia, not far from the town of Liverpool. In this area, which became his permanent home, Raddall began to develop interests in local history, the local Indians, woodlore, hunting, and, with increasing seriousness, the craft of writing. While on Sable Island, Raddall had published a short story, "The Singing Frenchman," in a Halifax newspaper,[3] and earlier at sea he had become an assiduous journal-keeper. Now in Milton, to supplement an income somewhat meagre for a newly married man, Raddall began writing stories for magazines. After an initial success with *Maclean's*, he found a regular outlet in the prestigious British *Blackwood's*, which brought his work to the notice of Rudyard Kipling, John Buchan, Kenneth Roberts, and others whose subsequent praise and encouragement led him to resign his job with the mill in 1938 to work full-time at writing.[4] With the success of his first published novel, *His Majesty's Yankees*, in 1942, Raddall's vocation was finally settled.[5] During a career that he deliberately brought to a close in 1976 with the publication of his memoirs, *In My Time: A Memoir*, he had published some eighty or so short stories; eight historical novels (best-known among these being *His Majesty's Yankees, Roger Sudden, Pride's Fancy, The Governor's Lady,* and *Hangman's Beach*); three novels with modern settings (*The Nymph and the Lamp, Tidefall,* and *The Wings of Night*); seven histories (best-known among these being *Halifax, Warden of the North* and *The Path of Destiny: Canada from the British Conquest to Home Rule, 1763–1850*); five collections of short stories; and numerous articles, many on historical topics.

Appreciation of Raddall's talents, which first came from the United States and Britain, in Canada came only slowly. To date those who have sought to delineate the main traditions of Canadian literature have provided him with only minor and often almost grudging notice, but, as already suggested, recognition of a sort has been his. Three of his books earned Governor-General's Awards, the most coveted of Canadian annual literary prizes. In 1949 he was elected to the Royal Society of Canada and in 1956 was presented with the Lorne Pierce Medal in recognition of his achievement as both novelist and historian; and four Canadian universities have awarded him honourary degrees. In 1968 Raddall was offered the Lieutenant-Governorship of Nova Scotia, an honour he declined, and in 1971 he was made a Companion of the Order of Canada. For one with so unpretentious a beginning in life, with so minimal a formal education, and with such considerable obstacles to face before establishing himself as a professional author, Raddall's achievements must be seen as something of a triumph.

Tradition and Milieu

During his childhood in Hythe, and then in Halifax, Raddall's reading was typical of someone his age — *Robinson Crusoe, Treasure Island, Westward Ho, Masterman Ready,* and plenty of Henty. As Raddall once remarked in an address to the Canadian Authors Association, "To a boy, naturally, the tale of adventure comes to life first, and for me the first real people in print were Buffalo Bill and Jim Hawkins."[6] Much of Raddall's fiction descends from the traditions of such writing, principally the adventure romance, best-represented in the works of a group of writers for whom he has often expressed deep admiration: James Fenimore Cooper, Rudyard Kipling, Robert Louis Stevenson, Arthur Conan Doyle, and Joseph Conrad. This last writer he discovered appropriately enough, when he himself went to sea at fifteen, and Raddall from that time savoured the thought that Pent Farm, Conrad's home between 1898 and 1907, was very close to Hythe,[7] so that "Sometimes when Father wheeled through the little hamlet of Postling with his small passenger we must have passed the man" (*IMT*, p. 17). His admiration for Conrad, however, was no mere sentimental foible. What Raddall chiefly found in his works, and in those of the other authors just mentioned, was an ideal he himself came to emulate, the ability to tell a tale, "unique and good in itself," and to tell it "with style and craftsmanship" (*IMT*, p. 291). This too explains his admiration for Guy de Maupassant and Somerset Maugham, both consummate masters of narrative, though very different in other respects from Conrad and company. Of Somerset Maugham, Raddall once said, "Maugham I think probably influenced me as much as anyone, not that I tried to imitate him at all, but it seemed to me that his approach was the one that I wanted. He always wrote a story as if he were sitting down telling it to somebody in a quiet corner of a hotel."[8]

If Conrad, Kipling, and Stevenson provided Raddall with models for style and narrative technique in fiction, Francis Parkman, G.M. Trevelyan, and, to a lesser extent, Winston Churchill provided models for Raddall the historian. As Raddall has often commented, his own energies as a writer have been divided, not always by preference, between fiction and history, but he has always felt that not only could the subject-matter of the two disciplines overlap (as it frequently does in his works), but that there was a more fundamental kinship: "The art of history, the art of telling a story, the art of narrative — [are] one and the same, all three. And because few historians have possessed this art, few are read, except by other historians."[9] Raddall made this statement while praising the work of Parkman and Trevelyan, and it is the similar gift for narrative and for a vivid and vigorous prose style that has attracted him to Churchill's writings.

Among historians, Parkman has been Raddall's principal model, and his influence has derived not merely from his skills as a writer and his ability to communicate with a wide popular readership. What also influenced Raddall was Parkman's research technique with its combination of vivid detail and precise historical method, and its attempt to recreate the life and spirit of a past age, something in which the use of primary documents and of visits to the scenes of the incidents described plays a major role. For Raddall, Parkman was a historian who "alone got out into the scenes he wrote about ... and so brought to his study of documents a profound knowledge of the realities."[10] Visits to such places as Fort Beauséjour, Louisbourg, Portsmouth (New Hampshire), and McNabb's Island, his friendship with some local Indians, and his own familiarity with both the sea and the backwoods of Nova Scotia, all provided the kind of "Parkman-like" immersion in direct experience that Raddall drew upon so effectively wherever possible in the creation of both fictional and historical works.

In addition to the influences of direct experience, whether deliberately sought in Parkman's way or otherwise, a further influence upon Raddall's writings requires noting. Of relevance to his short stories in particular, but to some extent his three novels set in his own time, is material acquired from the mouths of others. In the messrooms of ships, in the isolation of coastal radio stations, in the woods behind Liverpool, and wherever he travelled, Raddall had an ear for the tales of seamen, lumbermen, Indians, and others. This explains the style and nature of a good number of his short stories which often have the flavour of oral tradition. Indeed, as often as not the source for a story will be found to have come from an orally transmitted yarn.[11] In many instances, Raddall's diary seems to have played an important intermediary role in recording material that he used much later in his writings, (cf. *IMT*, p. 54) but for the period during which his diary must remain "closed" to researchers at Dalhousie University to protect the privacy of living persons, this must remain a matter for speculation.

From the above few paragraphs it must be obvious that Raddall is something of an anomaly among contemporary Canadian writers. Fiercely independent, and proud of his status as a professional writer and of his never having sought after a Canada Council grant, he is independent in another sense in that he does not appear to be part of any contemporary Canadian literary movement where, so far as fiction is concerned, the psychological, the realistic, and the symbolic reign supreme. For the romance, whether historical or otherwise, there seems no place within the current literary mosaic beyond brief acknowledgements in literary histories and literary anthologies of

Raddall's special talents for narrative and colourful detail. Yet Raddall does clearly belong to a literary tradition — one that is very recognizable within world literature and familiar too within the development of Canadian literature. John Buchan, in his laudatory Preface to Raddall's first collection of short stories (*The Pied Piper of Dipper Creek and Other Tales*, 1939), had no doubts about Raddall's literary ancestors. Not only did he praise Raddall's "gift of swift, spare, clean-limbed narrative," and his ability to create "a story which has something of a plot and which issues in a dramatic climax," but he recognized the tradition to which Raddall belonged when he claimed that Raddall's writing was of "a type which has had many distinguished exponents from Sir Walter Scott through Stevenson and Maupassant to Kipling and Conrad. To this school Mr. Raddall belongs, and he is worthy of a great succession."[12] Thirty-five years later, in his Introduction to a new edition of Raddall's *Pride's Fancy*, a prominent Canadian literary critic, vigorously defending Raddall's choice of the mode of romance, again recognized the kinship with Scott: "what such a novelist as Scott did in the nineteenth century for Scotland, his follower, Thomas H. Raddall, might conceivably be attempting with respect to the Nova Scotia of the twentieth century."[13]

As for Canadian literary ancestors, Raddall's work follows the path critics have associated with John Richardson and Rosanna Mullins, mainly known in fiction as Rosanna Leprohon, in the early nineteenth century and with William Kirby, Gilbert Parker, Charles G.D. Roberts, Theodore Roberts, and others somewhat later.[14] However, there is no real evidence that Raddall consciously looked back to any Canadian writer for a model. As for contemporaries, the only figures that Raddall mentions with any consistency are the American Kenneth Roberts, Thomas Costain, a Canadian writer of both fiction and history who had taken up residence in the United States, and Charles Bruce.[15] Kenneth Roberts' historical fiction, both in subject matter and style, has certain affinities with that of Raddall, and Raddall certainly knew Roberts' work, but it would be hard to argue that Roberts provided any major influence. As for Costain, his importance to Raddall's career was that of a skilled and experienced author-editor who gave Raddall considerable guidance and advice during the writing of *His Majesty's Yankees* and *Roger Sudden*. Though Raddall rejected many of Costain's suggestions (such as a happy ending for *Roger Sudden*), his early debt to Costain's common sense and editorial abilities was considerable, as a reading of Costain's letters and a glance at the revisions Raddall subsequently made in his draft manuscripts reveal.[16]

One additional influence in Raddall's literary development now requires brief mention. When the Raddall family first arrived in Halifax, Raddall's father bought several volumes of the Nova Scotian nineteenth-century humorist, Thomas Haliburton. Raddall admits having peeped into the books and finding them very dull, but some years later he again encountered Haliburton's Yankee clockmaker, Sam Slick, in a school reader containing "How Many Fins Has a Cod?": "To me that tale opened a door. . . . I have never yielded the impression which came to me then for the first time, that books could be fun, and that a good tale could involve scenes and characters from my own familiar habitat and not necessarily from half across the world."[17] Raddall also came to admire Haliburton's "ear for an idiom or a word used in an unusual sense," a gift that the two writers clearly share,[18] but Haliburton's example, however, had no specific influence upon his writing beyond these rather general matters, and the impression remains that Raddall, like a number of other Canadian writers of his generation, is a largely self-taught craftsman, who worked during the formative years of his writing career in virtual isolation from his literary compatriots, finding his models, his reputation, and his financial rewards principally in the United States and Britain, despite (in Raddall's case at least) a passionate loyalty to his homeland and its heritage that pervades much of his writing. As Robert Cockburn suggested in his review of *In My Time*, "there can be no doubt — which is ironic, considering his [Raddall's] reputation among the *literati* — that his passage has been less conventional, more truly independent than have been the careers of all but a very few Canadian writers in this century."[19]

Critical Overview and Context

The first detailed consideration of Raddall's work was a 1954 M.A. thesis by Edith Rogers which surveyed Raddall's short stories and novels to date and offered a considerable amount of detail concerning his biography and the composition and publication of his writings.[20] Though it offered little by way of critical analysis, it did include lengthy quotations from several letters received from Raddall. Much of this material was to surface again in Raddall's interviews and talks, and most recently in *In My Time*, but Rogers' "The Life and Works of Dr. Thomas H. Raddall" will remain important for its early recognition of Raddall and for presentation of Raddall's own views on his craft and information about the background to a number of his works.

Prior to 1954, almost all critical discussion of Raddall is to be found in book reviews of his first three historical novels (*His Majesty's Yankees*, *Roger Sudden*, and *Pride's Fancy*), his collections of short stories (*The Pied Piper of Dipper Creek and Other Tales*, *Tambour and Other Stories*, and *The Wedding Gift and Other Stories*), his history of Halifax (*Halifax, Warden of the North*), and his first two full-length fictions with modern settings (*The Nymph and the Lamp* and *Tidefall*). In general these reviews tend to applaud the "ripsnorting," "rousing," "virile," "dramatic" character of the historical novels; they praise Raddall's gift in both fiction and history for creating colour, vivid detail, and a sense of the past; and, like Buchan in his 1939 Preface to *The Pied Piper of Dipper Creek*, they praise Raddall for his narrative skill.[21]

There is, however, a dissenting voice amid the dominant chorus of praise. Desmond Pacey, who recognized the romance tradition to which Raddall belonged, never gave Raddall more than minimal acknowledgement, chiefly because of his belief that romance was not the proper path for a contemporary Canadian author to follow. Thus, after stating in 1947 that Raddall was "the leading present-day exponent of the romantic tradition in Canadian fiction," he gave his somewhat grudging assessment: "Raddall has neither the psychological subtlety nor the rich style of Conrad and Stevenson, but he has his share of vividness and vigour. Perhaps his chief strength is a painstaking concern for factual detail, which gives to his work a certain documentary interest."[22] (For a counter-view, one may turn to Arthur L. Phelps, who in 1951 complained about the neglect of Raddall by Canadians who have been "ignorant, grudging or apathetic," the result, he felt, of "the nemesis of our colonialism at work once again."[23])

In surveying the criticism of Pacey and others prior to 1954, one becomes aware of a turning point in Raddall's critical reputation with the appearance of *The Nymph and the Lamp* in 1950. No longer imbued with the remoteness and colour of the distant past, this work seemed to require a different kind of critical response. *Public Affairs*, attempting to define the new character, discussed the emphasis on sex;[24] the *San Francisco Chronicle* stressed the manner in which the characters are mere puppets alongside the physical forces of nature;[25] and Claude Bissell in the *University of Toronto Quarterly* remarked: "One of Raddall's most admirable qualities as an historical novelist was the easy and confident way with which he assimilated background and mood. Now that, presumably, he is drawing upon his own experience, this quality is even more apparent."[26] Bissell went on to praise Raddall's handling of sexual relationships, "something rare in the Canadian novel," but also drew attention to what he considered a weakness:

> The power to convey a sense of place is a precious asset to a novelist. But it must be accompanied by a like power to create character and to devise a series of situations that will display the moving logic of human motives and emotions. In these last two respects, there is a falling-off in Raddall's achievement, although it still remains a notable one.[27]

This, however, was a judgement with which not every reviewer agreed. John Cournos, for example, went out of his way to praise the handling of character, particularly that of the heroine, whose self-sacrifice he found altogether convincing, "lovely and authentic."[28]

The critical reception of *Tidefall* (1953) also brought its share of compliments. W.A. Deacon, book reviewer for *The Globe and Mail*, called it "the most powerful novel ever written by a Canadian" (*IMT*, p. 306),[29] and Raddall's Toronto publisher wrote him a letter calling him "Canada's most outstanding author" (*IMT*, p. 306). Even after allowing for a degree of over-enthusiasm, there is no doubt that by this stage in his career Raddall was considered to have earned a significant place in Canadian letters, C.L. Bennet suggesting, for example, that this latest novel would "unquestionably increase Mr. Raddall's large and discerning body of readers."[30] However, in the later 1950s and early 1960s Raddall's reputation seems to have evaporated. Robert Cockburn has suggested that this was due to "a transformation in the country's sensibility, changing tastes among the reading audience, and the rise to prominence of a pride of new, fashionable, less conventional novelists," so that by the mid-1960s "West of the Maritimes, . . . when not a forgotten man, he [Raddall] was regarded as a minor talent, as a mere 'popular' historical novelist."³¹ Henceforth Raddall continued to elicit the warmest critical praise from some critics, most of whom have themselves had some connection with Atlantic Canada (Allan Bevan, Donald Cameron, Robert Cockburn, Fred Cogswell, James Gray, Malcolm Ross), but from others his treatment has been lukewarm, negative, or even hostile.³² In fairness, however, it should be noted that after *The Nymph and the Lamp* several of Raddall's books (*The Wings of Night, The Path of Destiny, The Governor's Lady*) fall disappointingly behind the merits he had achieved earlier.

When *At the Tide's Turn and Other Stories*, a collection of Raddall's historical stories, appeared in the New Canadian Library series in 1959, two clear critical attitudes towards Raddall became clear. On the one hand there was that represented by Allan Bevan's sympathetic and laudatory analysis of Raddall's gifts for the special genre of historical fiction and for the fashioning of an effective narrative.³³ On the other hand were the reviews by George Woodcock and Desmond Pacey which took a very different view. Woodcock, in *Canadian Literature*, stated bluntly of the short stories: "apart from their money-earning possibilities, there is very little to be said for them."³⁴ Pacey, who, as shown above, had already made some rather cool remarks about Raddall, modified his point of view somewhat in 1952 in his influential *Creative Writing in Canada*, in which he referred to Raddall as a conscientious craftsman and stylist and as "undoubtedly the most distinguished present day exponent of the historical romance in Canada."³⁵ Now, however, in his review of *At the Tide's Turn*, he revealed what he actually thought about historical fiction. After saying that "Raddall's short stories . . . and Professor Bevan's introduction to them, leave me quite cold," he remarked: "Why, I keep asking myself, would anyone turn his back on the contemporary life of Nova Scotia to write of these fancy-dress personages? . . . Mere prejudice against historical fiction? Precisely!"³⁶

In *Creative Writing in Canada*, Pacey had suggested that the best Canadian novels were those that had transcended the classification of historical romance (or the regional idyll), but he had not directly castigated Raddall for failure to break away from tradition. However, in the revised version of his book, published in 1961, Pacey followed his comments on Raddall, who with *The Governor's Lady* in 1960 had returned to historical fiction, with the following statement, clearly revealing a major reason for his critical bias against historical fiction, however craftsmanlike practitioners like Raddall might be:

> The continuing popular demand for historical romance will no doubt guarantee the survival of this form in Canadian letters, but it is likely to survive merely as a form of popular entertainment rather than as a serious literary enterprise. It is difficult to avoid the conclusion that the long popularity of this form of fiction among Canadian writers arose from a failure of nerve, from a fear of attempting to cope with the complexity and amorphousness of contemporary Canadian society. As that society increasingly takes form, and thus becomes more manageable, it is likely to draw writers away from the past.[37]

Pacey's point of view, with its down-playing of romance and belief that literary greatness can only be found in other genres, seems to be tacitly shared by many subsequent critics, so that, although Raddall has been given a place in Canadian letters in surveys such as Pacey's *Creative Writing in Canada*, Klinck's *Literary History of Canada: Canadian Literature in English*, and *The Oxford Companion to Canadian History and Literature*, there is only one published, full-length assessment of Raddall's achievement,[38] whereas monographs abound on a number of Raddall's contemporaries and on many writers who only began to publish in the 1960s and 1970s. Much of the reason for this, as already suggested, may be the general disappointment with *The Wings of Night*, *The Path of Destiny*, and in particular with *The Governor's Lady*. Perhaps such disappointment is justified, but one senses that the recent lack of enthusiasm for Raddall's work has a deeper origin than a possible falling off in the quality of his later work. The problem seems to be that Raddall is not now part of what rightly or wrongly has been defined as the mainstream of Canadian intellectual life, and that all of his work, however competent and skilful, belongs outside what have been defined as significant and current literary modes of expression. Two remarks in 1976 by George Woodcock in a not totally unsympathetic review of Raddall's memoirs imply an awareness of these two points. First is his suggestion that Raddall is "a man who has gained his experience and insights by adapting to his conditions, by accepting the standards of his neighbours rather than by reacting against them. He is a great amateur scholar [. . .] but in the broader sense he does not fit into the Canadian intelligentsia . . . ." Then there is Wood-cock's view of the novels:

> . . . Raddall's novels have always read as if they were written before rather than after the Great War, their particular style and the very excellence of their storytelling placing them far nearer to writers like Conrad and Robert Louis Stevenson than to Canadian writers of the present generation.[39]

Such is the predominant critical view of Raddall in Canada today. Raddall, it seems generally agreed, is a fine craftsman and stylist but his literary work is simply not as important or interesting as that of other Canadian writers. However, as already pointed out, there is a small but ardent body of apologists who have vigorously defended Raddall. In addition to praising the various positive attributes already referred to above (principally style and narrative skill), such critics have maintained that Raddall's historical fiction has a special place in Canadian literature because it "has given us an imaginative hold on our beginnings as a people, an insight into the first fashioning of an identity, an insight which may do much to sustain us now that our identity is being put severely to the test."[40] Others, like Allan Bevan in his introduction to At the Tide's Turn, have briefly discussed the nature of historical fiction itself and tried to judge Raddall according to the special characteristics of that form rather than seeing him as a literary anachronism in a world where the "good" or "great" novel is expected to be a psychological or realistic work. Then there are others, like Donald Cameron, who have blamed the critical neglect of Raddall upon the narrow vision of current academic criticism,[41] and finally there are those apologies which have concentrated upon some particular aspect of Raddall's art or upon a single work. Belonging to this first category are the M.A. theses of John Leitold and David West, while to the second belong the introductions to the New Canadian Library series editions of His Majesty's Yankees, Roger Sudden, Pride's Fancy, and The Nymph and the Lamp, together with analyses by John Moss of The Nymph and the Lamp, by Arthur Phelps of "Before the Snow Flies," and by Andrew Seaman of Hangman's Beach and The Nymph and the Lamp.[42]

What follows here is a critical assessment of Raddall that largely sides with these apologists. The implication throughout is that

Raddall's contribution to Canadian literature has been misjudged because questionable criteria have all-too-frequently been applied to his work due to a bias against historical fiction and romance by the academic establishment.

Raddall's Works

The bulk of Raddall's fiction belongs to that broad category known as "historical." Though Raddall has denied that he ever consciously followed any specific literary model in his historical fiction, the name that inevitably comes to mind is that of Walter Scott. Georg Lukács in his *The Historical Novel* has done more than any other critic to define the essential features of historical fiction, arguing that Scott was the inventor of its classic form.[43] What has led to the linking, by John Buchan and various subsequent critics, of Raddall's name with that of Scott is the recognition that frequently Raddall's fiction follows the classic model first established by Scott.

Raddall's first full-length work, *Saga of the Rover* (later expanded into a version for adolescent readers entitled *The Rover*), illustrates how, from the beginning, Raddall took as his own one of the key recurring patterns of historical fiction — the placing of the narration within a broad context of historical events through the creation of a drama concerned with the impact of world events upon the lives of ordinary people. These men and women are shown being forced into action because they are caught amid conflicting forces over which they have no control. Such a pattern results in the reader (the living representative of the common person) being brought into a close relationship with the forces of history through vicarious identification with the fictional hero who is also a common person. Though the unsought adventures of such heroes once they are embroiled in the drama of historical events may be extraordinary, their predicament, their responses, and above all their moral and social values all attract the empathy of the reader. Alexander Godfrey in *Saga of the Rover* is just such a figure. Associated initially with the citizens of Liverpool, Nova Scotia, at the time of the Napoleonic Wars, he suffers with them the side-effects of war, and, like them, is gradually forced towards the decision to take up privateering. Although the heroic type in terms of physique, experience, and bravery, he is also representative of the virtually nameless figures of the past who, unlike the Nelsons, the Washingtons, or the Bonapartes, more truly typify the common person. Godfrey's decision to allow himself to be drawn into armed conflict is also that of his community, of those in it who signed on as his crew, and of those who bought shares in his ship the *Rover*. Eventually privateering declined; the *Rover*, after some spectacular successes, was sold, and Godfrey died at sea from a fever. In his final paragraph Raddall, perhaps a little over-insistently, stresses one last time his concern with the common person called upon by history to play a part no less heroic than that of the supposed makers of history:

> Within the grey walls of old Fort Charles, looking southward from Kingston to the dancing Caribbean is a simple tablet reading thus: —
>
> "IN THIS PLACE DWELT HORATIO NELSON. YE WHO TREAD HIS FOOTSTEPS REMEMBER HIS GLORY."
>
> Not far from that tablet — perhaps within a stone's throw — lies the forgotten grave of Alexander Godfrey. Forgotten?
>
> To those who tread his footsteps in the peaceful streets of Herring Cove and Liverpool, the saga of the "Rover" will always recall the glory of this man who, though a simple Nova Scotia trader captain, was not less a hero than the victor of Trafalgar.[44]

Saga of the Rover established for Raddall certain fictional patterns that were to recur with varying degrees of subtlety and effectiveness in his subsequent historical novels. All pervasive is a sense of the intrusiveness of world events upon the life of the common person. In *His Majesty's Yankees*, for example, which depicts the situation of Nova Scotians at the time of the American Revolution, history intrudes early in the novel in a dramatic scene set in the Strang family kitchen. William Smith, a member of the assembly in Halifax where he represents the Liverpool community, has called a meeting where he reminds all present of the past injustices of the colonial regime and goes on to announce that he has just been stripped of all his public offices. One of the Liverpool men then poses the question at the heart of the drama: "What are Mr. Smith's freeborn electors goin' to do about it?"[45] Here is that decisive moment when choice seems forced upon even the most passive of people. In this instance the moment is divisive, something that Lukács has suggested is typical of historical fiction (see, for example, his discussion of Walter Scott, pp. 30–63). Matthew, the head of the Strang family, a man who has experienced the worst excesses of man's inhumanity to man, is for doing nothing and avoiding involvement at all costs, but his sons do not all accept this. Luke is for fighting in the rebel cause, while John declares that such thoughts are treasonous "and hanging's the right remedy" (p. 26). However, it is with David Strang, the hero of the novel, that the reader's prime interest lies. In the kitchen scene David is presented as too young and inexperienced to have a defined political view, but later in the novel he sees first-hand some of the evils of colonialism and is then forced into action when he rescues his brother Mark's wife from an assault by a British seaman whom he kills. Once "on the run," David espouses the rebel cause, and much of the remainder of the novel concerns his growth to adulthood and political maturity, both of which are ultimately achieved, it is implied, when he returns to Liverpool and declares:

> I'm done with fighting for a word, . . . I'm for myself — and Mark and Father and all the rest of us who want to live in some kind of peace on this coast. I'm for fighting whoever interferes with us, whether it's king or Congress or only a bloody Salem pirate flying the Congress colors. (pp. 358–59)

In effect, David comes full circle to a political attitude identical to that of his father.

This final position is middle-of-the-road, conservative, and typical of the classical Scott historical novel, which, according to Lukács, seeks the middle way between extremes and endeavours to demonstrate artistically the historical reality of this way (p. 32). David's final point of view marks the reconciliation of the conflict that was first set in motion in the scene in the Strangs' kitchen. Historically David's point of view is also that adopted by Nova Scotia (and to some extent Canada as a whole) so that David, like Alexander Godfrey in *Saga of the Rover*, is properly to be taken as representative not only of the common person, but of a people. This latter fact adds a special dimension to the novel for the Canadian reader since David then functions as a link between the historical past and the present identity of that reader:

> . . . someday we shall make a nation in this northern wilderness where now is only a scatter of poor British colonies. What form it will take I cannot see, but one thing I know — that nation will

rule itself. For out of our struggle here by the sea has emerged a notion of self-government that cannot die and will not be denied. . . . (p. 368)

Equally typical of historical fiction is Raddall's depiction of part of a momentous historical transition, in this instance the birth of the American republic, and the disassociation of Nova Scotia from its familial and commercial ties with New England and its simultaneous though reluctant shift from neutrality towards loyalty to the crown. Here Raddall is employing a pattern familiar to readers of Scott's works where similar transitions from old to new provide the occasion for dramatic conflicts between family members, generations, societies, and civilizations. In all such conflicts, Lukács has argued, the middle way triumphs and extremism perishes. That middle way is represented primarily by the hero who embodies not only the sufferings and aspirations of a people but their eventual historical destiny. Significantly in *His Majesty's Yankees* David's extremist brothers, Luke the rebel and John the king's man, both perish.

As may be inferred from the above, the political and moral values of the hero are of key importance. In the case of David they are obviously conservative. David's final choice is for peace, stability, and above all domestic love. His love for Fear Bingay, his childhood sweetheart, which provides a romantic sub-plot to *His Majesty's Yankees*, is essential in this respect. Significantly she is the daughter of a prominent local Tory and marries a British officer. The gulf between Fear and David is initially very wide. However, when her husband dies and both she and David return to Liverpool, the way is open for marriage, itself symbolic of the new political and social contract that is established between the Liverpool people and the crown. More than this, however, Fear represents the values of domestic peace, marital love, and the land:

> . . . between these walls if nowhere else he could have peace — the peace that a man finds in the arms of his love, easing his taut nerves in her supple warmth, drawing strength from her eager yielding as lean rivers lie in our green Nova Scotia valleys, drawing strength from the round loveliness of the hills. (p. 374)

Subsequent historical novels by Raddall all make use to some degree of these fictional patterns. *Roger Sudden* is set against the historical transition involving the demise of the French imperial presence in North America and the simultaneous growth of the British, with the hint of the future emergence of Canada. *Pride's Fancy* depicts the conflict created by four differing eighteenth-century societies — the traditional Planter élite of the West Indies, the supposedly egalitarian society of post-revolution Haiti, the aggressive merchant barons of Nova Scotia who were hardly particular where and how they made money from the licensed piracy of privateering, and the very different society and way of life ultimately represented by Nathan Cain, the hero of the novel, who develops values that are non-materialistic and who at the end of the novel opts for domesticity, the creative craftsmanship of shipbuilding, and love for his native province of Nova Scotia. *Hangman's Beach* depicts the interacting forces that transformed the war between Britain and France into something else — the 1812 conflict between Britain and the United States — and *The Governor's Lady* depicts, though only in part and far less effectively than *His Majesty's Yankees*, the American Revolution and the demise of British rule in the rebellious North American colonies.

The protagonists of these works can be classed as reluctant participants in the historical conflicts that intrude upon their private lives and ambitions. Having renounced both the Jacobite cause and his own country, for example, Roger Sudden comes to Nova Scotia, along with the more than two and a half thousand settlers transported for the founding of Halifax in 1749, in quest of a fortune. After exploiting both English and French for his own financial benefit, Roger eventually finds himself present at the British siege of the French fortress of Louisbourg. Here his latent patriotism asserts itself when he aids the British, and his materialism is laid aside and supplanted by other values. Before Roger is executed by the French in the closing moments of the siege, he makes the following confession:

I offer no defence. I tell you simply there must come a time when the soil of his birthplace means more to a man than all the world. I ask you to believe that my love, my fortune, all my new hopes and old struggles were forgotten then. I ask you to believe that Coromandière — Louisbourg — all new France in that moment ceased to exist for me. It was Kent I saw, and the men of Kent in arms to defend her — and I on the wrong side of the Channel![46]

The extremes of colonialism, the object of which is to extract the maximum wealth for reinvestment in Europe (Roger hopes to recoup his family's fortunes and save the family seat in England), are thus discredited. The proffered alternative in *Roger Sudden* is the growth of a new society and nation representative of the triumph of the middle way and the common man. Roger's death prevents him from being a full participant but sufficient hints are given in the novel to imply that had he survived, he would have taken his place in the emerging nation.

Nathan Cain in *Pride's Fancy* initially finds himself following in the footsteps of his step-father, Amos Pride, who is the very embodiment of dehumanized materialism. Nathan then becomes involved in a choice between alternatives. In Haiti he witnesses the end of the reign of privilege, but Republicanism seems little better since chaos and egalitarianism appear to have led to slaughter and destruction and "the richest colony in the West Indies is a desert in five years."[47] Caught amid the conflict of these three forces, Nathan opts for love of homeland, joy in domesticity, the exercise of craftsmanship, and the renunciation of the pursuit of wealth. Like both David Strang and Roger Sudden, his initial state is one of youth and comparative inexperience. His final decision, however, is that of the mature hero who has in the course of his adventures attained wisdom through experience. As with David and Roger, there is also a woman involved, Lia-Marie Dolainde in this instance. Nathan's final union with her is symbolic of his choice of love over materialism, a love both for her and for Nova Scotia, a land now equated with home, a place more suited to their new relationship than the violent world of Haiti:

> Lia, where we are going the sun is a lover, not an enemy. It is a pleasure to be outdoors, to walk about in the full shine of it, to feel it on the skin. Even the earth is greedy for our sun — there is no monstrous mass of green to shut it out, the trees stand tall and clean, and there is a pleasant smell under the branches. Do you remember the smell of the pines? And there is the rocky shore and the cool smell of the sea, and the brown sails of the sailing boats, and the sound of the calkers making music in the shipyards —. (pp. 307–08)

Whereas the influences which draw Roger and Nathan into their respective and unsought confrontations with history are implied rather than explicit, in *Hangman's Beach* Raddall created a specific dramatic incident as in *His Majesty's Yankees* to demonstrate the manner in which history may seize upon the most ordinary of persons for its purposes and so irrevocably change forever the destiny of individual lives. Michel Cascamond, a midshipman in the French navy, is the man, it is eventually revealed, whom fate chooses to be Nelson's killer:

> Smoke and flame and thunder. And we up there in the top like a nest of rooks in a hurricane. All of a sudden the smoke parted below and there was the English admiral, as near as the toss of a hat. A moment in the history of France, of England, of the world! And in that moment our brave *aspirant* here aimed his musket and fired. Without hesitation. As if he had been waiting for that moment all his life.[48]

The point is, however, that it is not a moment of Cascamond's choosing, and as a result he is perpetually in fear for his life once he becomes a prisoner of the English in Halifax. Should his earlier act ever become known, he would be a dead man. In time and with the progression of events, there is a resolution to Cascamond's near outlaw existence. At the end of the novel he and the lover he has found in Nova Scotia, Ellen Dewar, are offered sanctuary among the Acadian French, a home, domesticity, and a vocation, like that of Nathan Cain, in harmony with the natural riches of Nova Scotia: ". . . those Acadians are clever men with tools, and a man like Cascamond could turn their hands to building ships, just as he learned to build models in the prison. Here on this coast, with a forest behind and the ocean in front, with half the world at war, and ships wanted everywhere . . ." (pp. 419–20). Thus, where death has not intervened, as it did in the case of Roger Sudden, normality can be asserted, and human kind can begin again to make "their own joys and sorrows in this world" (p. 419) free from the intrusive stir of history.

In *The Governor's Lady* a somewhat different pattern exists. The novel is built around balanced portraits of Raddall's two protagonists, John and Fannie Wentworth. Both are real historical personages, and this undoubtedly limited Raddall in his freedom to create fictional situations, a particular problem in this instance since neither figure is convincingly linked with any deeply significant moment in the working out of history, in spite of Wentworth's being Governor first of New Hampshire and later of Nova Scotia. Much of *The Governor's Lady* is, in fact, concerned with Fannie Wentworth's attempts to use her sexual charms and social position to influence the world in favour of her ambitions for herself and her husband. Ultimately these ambitions are realized, at a price, but they are not really the stuff of historical fiction, and the book is a failure since it degenerates into something approaching costume romance with the historical context being little more than background.[49]

As mentioned earlier, Raddall has always received praise for his abilities to create a vivid and colourful sense of place and time, for his historical accuracy, much of it related to his meticulous research in original documents and "in the field," and for the dramatic excitement of his narratives. To this, however, should be added, in the light of what has just been described, an appreciation of his ability to work within the classic framework of the historical novel, the chief interest of which is the delineation of the interaction between the forces of history and the lives of individuals. Central to this is Raddall's skilful handling of intimate portraits of developing protagonists whose journeys from youth to maturity, innocence to experience, or, in the case of Cascamond, from a state of interior weakness to something more positive, are also representative of certain momentous historical transitions. Roger Sudden's growth matches that of the new settlement of Halifax and the subsequent development of English Canada; David Strang's rejection of the rebel cause is representative of the emerging independent identity of Nova Scotia; and Nathan Cain's and Michel Cascamond's choice of vocation hints at the great and prosperous era of shipbuilding and maritime enterprise that was to transform Nova Scotia in the nineteenth century.

The above brief discussion of Raddall's historical fiction has concentrated upon his six historical novels, but it should be recalled that before Raddall's success with *His Majesty's Yankees* his main concern as a writer had been with short stories. Many of these had been of a historical nature and had been published first in *Blackwood's*, then collected in *The Wedding Gift and Other Stories* (1947), a number of these then reappearing in *At the Tide's Turn*. Of the subject-matter of his historical short stories, Raddall has said:

In looking back farther and mulling over the colonial tales and documents, I strove to get on paper the story of the early Yankee

settlers and loyalists as it really was, as it was really lived. . . .
Many of the old colonial homes remained, with their attics full
of relics, letters and other documents, and there were old men
and women who preserved and treasured the tales handed down
from their forefathers. For example in the year 1924 I heard a
full account of the fight between the *Chesapeake* and *Shannon*
from the lips of an old gentleman who had heard it as a boy,
again and again, from his uncle and another old seaman of Port
Medway, both of whom had fought in the *Shannon*'s fore-top.[50]

More specifically the majority of the stories that Raddall brought
together in *The Wedding Gift* were set in Oldport, his fictional name
for Liverpool, and were designed sequentially to cover the Colonial
period from the founding of the town in 1759 to 1804, the year in
which the last daughter of Colonel Sumter Larrabee, the chief
character in many of the stories, is married.

From his major documentary source, the diary of Colonel Simeon
Perkins, a Liverpool man Raddall once described as the "Pepys of
Nova Scotia,"[51] Raddall derived considerable inspiration, but it was
only the starting point. In the short stories this document, which
Raddall made considerable use of in many of his other writings, is
ascribed to the fictional Colonel Larrabee. Several times the diary is
described and quoted, and it even figures in one story ("Memorial
to Miss Letty") as an instrument in some gentle blackmailing. In one
story ("The Outcasts"), Raddall seems to provide a portrait of his
own research methods and the ways in which material from the diary
provided a point of departure for the use of his fertile imagination
to flesh out the plainest of narratives into an evocative tale:

> The diary of Sumter Larrabee is the journal of a realist, written
> with an obsession for present facts and the deuce with past and
> future. Sumter seldom followed up an incident or looked back
> to compare anything but the weather or the date of last year's
> turnip planting. Sometimes you find several scattered entries
> with a common bearing, and there is the ghost of a story; but
> for the missing links you must pore over faded letters in Oldport
> attics, search the dusty files of dead newspapers, and nag old
> men for tales heard at the knees of their grandsires when they
> would rather smoke and talk politics and spit in the parlour
> fire.[52]

Raddall's use of the Perkins diary provides a strong and pervasive sense of historical reality, a quality that is a vital part of the attraction of his historical fiction. To this must be added Raddall's ability to capture in a single brief tale the essence of some crucial turning point in the progress of history. "At the Tide's Turn," which was later expanded to provide the theme and climactic episodes for *His Majesty's Yankees*, is just such a tale. It depicts the citizens of Oldport at the time of the American Revolution caught between conflicting loyalties. When persecution from American privateers becomes unbearable, they retaliate with gunfire, thereby placing themselves on the British side, and, so the story implies, setting an example for all the hitherto neutral Yankees of Nova Scotia. Had Nova Scotians responded differently, Canada as it is known today would not exist, since without the ice-free ports of Nova Scotia, Upper and Lower Canada would surely have become part of the United States in 1812. The destiny of nations, Raddall implies, is as much in the hands of the common people as in those of great political and military leaders. Equally effective is "Pax Britannica" in which Raddall portrays the first confrontation between the Indians and the new settlers. Here he touches upon a familiar theme of North American frontier mythology but succeeds in raising his tale above mere cliché to provide a telling insight into the collective wisdom that led to the laying aside of violence. What the story depicts is the historic recognition, at least in Nova Scotia, that mutual acceptance by Indians and settlers was the best course.

As in the novels, there is frequently a love story included. Never sentimental, the love-plots in the short stories are often surprisingly moving, for many of them depict young, and not so young, human beings living in a precarious environment in which the acquisition of a love partner can be all the more joyous because it comes unbidden. "Between the Lines," "The Trumpeter," and "The Wedding Gift" (the last two being among four non-Oldport stories in *The Wedding Gift*) all provide good examples of this feature, and, where in the novels Raddall's handling of sexual passions can be slightly heavy-handed or fraught with the clichés of heaving bosoms and firelight reflected in a lover's hair, in the short stories there is a lighter and surer touch, frequently accompanied by a measure of wit and humour, that makes them among his finest achievements.

When one turns from Raddall's historical fiction to his essays and books on history, one discovers that his subject-matter is largely complementary. The first nineteen chapters of *Halifax, Warden of the North* (1948), for example, employ much material already researched and used in *Roger Sudden, His Majesty's Yankees*, and *Pride's Fancy*, in which may be traced the history of the city from its founding until the Governorship of John Wentworth. Similarly a number of his historical essays are the result of research carried out earlier during the composition of his novels and stories. "Adventures of H.M.S. Blonde," for example, elaborates upon an episode recounted in "At the Tide's Turn," and "Nova Scotia's First Telegraph System" uses material already employed in the story "By Tellygraft" and in *Pride's Fancy*. This is not to say that the writing of history has been of secondary importance to Raddall. The truth is that to be self-supporting he had to stay with fiction. "My deep preference, now as before," he once said, "would be the writing of history. . . . But in the effort to support my family, put my children through college, and make some provision for old age, I must devote my time and thought to novels."[53]

Raddall's full-length histories consist of the early *The Markland Sagas* (1934), the central thesis of which is that Nova Scotia was the Markland referred to in the Icelandic sagas; *West Novas: A History of the West Nova Scotia Regiment* (1948), written at the request of the regiment in which he had briefly served during World War II; *Halifax, Warden of the North*, commissioned by his publisher as one of a series of books on American and Canadian ports; *The Path of Destiny* (1957), the third volume in a history of Canada edited by Thomas Costain; *Footsteps on Old Floors: True Tales of Mystery* (1968), an assorted collection of essays exploring a number of real-life mysteries which Raddall had researched; and *The Mersey Story* (1979), an account of the Bowater-Mersey Paper Company in Liverpool, commissioned by the company.

These works and the shorter articles are characterized, like Raddall's fiction, by a firm narrative line that holds the reader's attention whatever the subject. Not for nothing is Raddall the admirer of Trevelyan whose "The Muse of History" he quoted to Edith Rogers as representative of his own goals as a historian:

". . . history is in its unchangeable essence a tale. Round the story, as flesh and blood round the bone, should be gathered many things — character drawing, study of social and intellectual movements, speculations as to probable causes and effects, and whatever else the historian can bring to illustrate the past. But the art of history remains always the art of narrative. That is the bed rock." This is what I tried to do in my book on Halifax, what I should like to do with other aspects of Nova Scotian and Canadian history.[54]

Raddall's gift for narrative is accompanied by another gift, that of bringing to life in a few deft strokes the individuals that people his histories, and here again the techniques of fiction and history merge. Equally characteristic of Raddall's histories, though not necessarily attractive to every taste, is the near-colloquial style which he frequently employs (e.g., "The brothels of Water Street and Barrack Street . . . and more than two hundred dram-shops strove lustily to entertain the rank and file").[55] Its suitability for so-called "popular" history is undeniable, and two passages from *Halifax, Warden of the North* may best serve to illustrate Raddall's skill and success in creating history of this kind. First is a passage describing the arrival of the British in 1749 at the site of the future city:

It was that time of year in Nova Scotia when after the bleak east winds of April and May the sun breaks forth with almost tropical heat, when trees, shrubs, and grasses have a lush green only to be matched in Ireland, when the open spaces by the water are speckled white with wild strawberry blossoms, when huckleberry, blueberry and lambkill bushes are in bloom; when the forest floor is bright with lady's-slipper, bluet, sarsaparilla, starflower and false Solomon's-seal, when violets bloom along the brook sides and the swamps are a blue fire of iris, when small fruit has begun to form on the Indian pear branches and the leaves of young poplars make a silver flutter against the sombre background of the pines. More important to the settlers, it was a time when the cod had moved inshore from the Banks, when haddock and pollack were schooling in every sea creek and salmon were swarming up the streams.

It seemed to be a land of plenty if not quite one of milk and honey. . . .[56]

In this vivid passage, with its wry final sentence that balances any tendency towards over-romanticism, Raddall is actually making use of an intimate knowledge of both documentary sources (in this instance the report of the leader of the expedition to his superiors in London) and, in "Parkman" fashion, of his familiarity with the location being described.

Raddall's characteristic ability to create a sense of the tangible reality of what he describes, along with his intelligent perception of a broader significance even in minutiae, can be seen in his account of the dissipations rife in one area of the city in the nineteenth century and in the comment which follows, with its Dickensian awareness of the interrelations between rich and poor:

> All this, be it noted, was within a good bottle-throw of Argyle Street with its fine mansions and shady willows, within a shout of St. Peter's and St. Paul's. And all the seepage of that wallowing slum known as "the Hill" — enclosed by Brunswick, Albemarle (now called Market) and Grafton streets — came down with the rains into the ornate gardens and spotless cellar kitchens of Argyle and Barrington and the busy countinghouses of Granville and Hollis, to mingle at last with the fetid mud of Water Street. The town was not so much a whited sepulchre as a gilded chamber pot. (p. 151)

There now remains to be discussed Raddall's short fiction and three novels set in his own time. As already pointed out, Raddall's short stories form a major category in his writings. The majority, after appearing singly in *Blackwood's, Maclean's, Saturday Evening Post*, and many other often less well-known publications, were reprinted in his various collections of stories. Apart from the historical stories that were later collected in *The Wedding Gift* are those stories that deal with aspects of Nova Scotia life that seemed to Raddall at the time he wrote them to be rapidly disappearing. These stories are chiefly to be found in *The Pied Piper of Dipper Creek* (1939) and *Tambour and Other Stories* (1945). Of these stories Raddall once said:

> In my seafaring, and during my sojourn in the little sawmill village of Milton in the later 1920's, I was keenly aware that I was seeing things and people and a way of life that were passing rapidly, for the 1914–18 war and its tremendous effects were changing everything. . . . Although I was only in my 'teens and early twenties when these things were passing I felt a pang, for they seemed to me full of the romance of another time.[57]

Besides their attempt to capture aspects of a vanishing world, such stories often involved the retelling of some incident that Raddall himself had experienced, or of some anecdote that he had heard from another. Not surprisingly the stories draw upon his experiences at sea and in remote coastal stations as a radio operator, his connections with the wood and pulp industry, and his familiarity with the backwoods of Nova Scotia, with woodsmen, and with Indians.

The chief qualities of these stories are those of the yarn in which emphasis is upon plot and the working-out of some complexity of circumstances. Like the yarn, such stories are narrated in a colloquial style and casual tone appropriate to oral tradition. At the same time their implicit norm is naturalistic. They are told in a matter-of-fact way, and everyday life is their implied touchstone. At their best they possess the power to captivate readers and hold their attention until all complexities are resolved in some dramatic discovery or reversal that suddenly illuminates the perception of preceding events. Such a dénouement often provides some kind of moral. "The Taming of Mordecai Mimms" and "Lady Lands Leviathan" (both in *Pied Piper*) and "A Petticoat for Linda" and "MacIvor's Salvation" (both in *Tambour*) are all of this kind.

Frequently in stories like this Raddall uses a first-person narrator and the device, particularly in the *Tambour and Other Stories* stories, of a "frame." Typically, a first-person narrator will introduce another character who will tell a story with the original narrator as audience. The reader identifies with that "audience" and the sense of oral narrative is then reinforced. When the tale is complete, the "frame" returns. Often the storyteller is a much older person than the narrator, and his memory takes the tale a generation or more back into the past, thereby enabling Raddall to develop his portrait of a time that has gone. "Triangle in Steel" and "North from Vinland" in *Tambour* are both good examples of this.

Clearly such stories will not be to the taste of many twentieth-century critics whose plaudits tend to be reserved for those authors concerned, not with plot or moral, but with the subtle creation of a segment of time, of a mood, or of an emotion, or with the portrayal of the inner psychology of character. When judged, however, according to the criteria appropriate to a tradition that numbers, as Buchan suggested in his Preface to *The Pied Piper of Dipper Creek*, such exponents as Stevenson, Maupassant, Kipling, and Conrad, Raddall's stories have considerable merits.

Before turning to Raddall's three remaining novels, one should briefly mention *A Muster of Arms and Other Stories* (1954). The ten stories in this collection all deal in some way with World War II, as Raddall explained in the "Author's Note" to the volume:

> . . . the stories in this volume have to do with some random flickers that fell across my notice in the Canadian scene.
>
> Some were plain, some tragic, some merely funny or grotesque, but all seemed worth recording for their origin in that twice-experienced phenomenon of my time, the spectacle of men and women under the strain of war and the effect of it upon their lives.[58]

In spite of Raddall's desire to emulate the achievement of Philip Gibbs's *Now It Can Be Told* (1920) with its attempt "to get deeper into the truth of this war and of all war,"[59] Raddall's last collection of short stories is something of a failure. Though it employs the yarn-like effects, the humour, and the moral climaxes that had proved so congenial to his talents in *The Pied Piper of Dipper Creek* and *Tambour*, the extra emotional intensity deriving from the wartime background tends to degenerate into maudlin sentiment and much of the humour is somewhat facile. Only a few stories — "Mistress of CKU," "Resurrection," and "A Muster of Arms" — seem able to rise above the unexceptional quality of the remainder.

Following the completion of *Halifax, Warden of the North* in 1948, Raddall felt free to attempt an ambitious project of three novels set in his own time. Partly he wished to throw off the designation of "historical fiction writer" that his publishers had given him, but partly no doubt he desired, as in a number of earlier stories, to make use of his own direct experiences. Within a decade Raddall completed his project with *The Nymph and the Lamp* (1950), *Tidefall* (1953), and *The Wings of Night* (1956). The first of these is probably Raddall's most successful artistic achievement, but the other two are far less successful. Though at the time of their publication both *Tidefall* and *The Wings of Night* received high praise, Raddall returned in 1960 to historical fiction with *The Governor's Lady* and never again tried his hand at a work with a modern setting. Because of the special place of *The Nymph and the Lamp* in Raddall's fiction, discussion of it will be reserved for the conclusion of this essay, and *Tidefall* and *The Wings of Night* will be briefly mentioned first.

Tidefall depicts the dramatic career of Saxby Nowlan, something of a villain, who returns with an ill-gotten fortune to the small Nova Scotian fishing village of his birth. His dream is to be not only rich, but respected and envied by those less well-off and accepted as an equal by those he refers to as people of "Class."[60] He buys up an ailing local firm, marries a "woman of class" and, after a spectacular rise upon the high tide of success, has an equally spectacular fall. As in *Roger Sudden* and *Pride's Fancy*, the self-centred pursuit of material gain is set against less tangible but more humane values, here represented by Saxby's wife, Rena, and the lover she takes, Owen Pascoe, a radio operator and would-be novelist. Where Roger Sudden and Nathan Cain had ultimately opted for new values, Saxby remains intransigent and destroys himself in a dramatic shipwreck. In spite of the fact that for setting and characters Raddall is to some extent drawing upon his own experiences,[61] and in spite of working with variations upon a theme and structure already familiar, *Tidefall* is disappointing. The thematic and structural pattern just described is crudely handled and over-obvious and fails to involve the reader emotionally or intellectually. This is partly due to Raddall's treatment of character. Saxby is a melodramatic villain and barely believable. Though Raddall stresses his positive potential, in particular his courage and business abilities, Saxby never elicits any sympathy, and his tragedy hardly touches the reader. Rena offers no credible alternative. Her motives for marrying Saxby in the first place are unconvincing, and her lack of inner conflict regarding her affair with Pascoe suggests a certain shallowness. That Pascoe is a dreamer and intellectually lazy adds to the impression that the lovers are disengaged from reality in such a fashion as to stimulate in the reader little more concern than one feels for Saxby. It follows that one also cares little about the values they supposedly represent. Emotionally one remains unmoved.

The Wings of Night is somewhat more effective. Modelled on Raddall's observation of Milton between 1923 and 1930, the novel is given a post-World War II setting. It portrays the return of Neil Jamieson who attempts to revive the economy of the region which, he discovers, has been deliberately depressed by Senator Sam Quarender's buying up of most of the timber lands with the secret motive of selling them to a large paper mill company. In a hunting accident Neil kills the Senator's son, Steve. The Senator, now a broken man, sells off the lands. New industry can go ahead and future prosperity seems assured. Interwoven with this rather unpromising story is a romance element. Neil finds himself still attracted to his boyhood sweetheart, who has since become Steve's wife. She remains faithful to her husband, however, leaving Neil free to discover in time his love for a local school teacher.

The early part of the novel contains a vivid portrait of the economic decay of a once rich community, exemplified in the dilapidated state of the Jamieson house, now inhabited only by Neil's aged grandmother. Especially effective is the theme of imprisonment. Neil's parents and now his grandmother had all been prisoners of the house, while Neil had experienced his share of imprisonment in a German camp in the war. Their imprisonment is psychological, and a powerful symbolic climax to the novel is achieved at the end with the death of the grandmother and Neil's ritualistic burning of the house in which he leaves the identity tags he once wore in prison camp.

When Neil frees himself, he perceives his love for the school teacher, so that the pattern of quest and reward, familiar from *His Majesty's Yankees*, *Roger Sudden*, *Pride's Fancy*, and *The Nymph and the Lamp*, provides the structural foundation for the novel. However, where *The Wings of Night* appears chiefly to fail is in supplying any coherent meaning to the hero's final situation and choice. What is the meaning of the psychological impediment from which he is now apparently free? What does Neil's choice of woman represent? She appears to be associated with rural virtues, a closeness to nature, inner warmth, and dignity. This is all very well, but what, one asks, does the departure for Montreal at the end of the novel of Neil and his new love mean? Since the community is no longer "imprisoned" and now has, thanks largely to Neil's efforts, a prosperous future, what does their flight signify? Though less melodramatic and more coherent in its plot-structure and characterization than *Tidefall*, *The Wings of Night* is thematically confusing. Furthermore it lacks the kind of effective socio-historical context that provided Raddall's best historical fiction and *The Nymph and the Lamp* with a level of meaning additional to that provided by the individual stories of its characters. The ingredients for this are present, but the depiction of the death of the old and the painful birth of the new within the small rural community is never successfully developed and identified with the larger North American context to provide the reader with an equivalent for what is to be found, for example, in *The Nymph and the Lamp*.

The plot of *The Nymph and the Lamp* is set in the early 1920s and concerns a radio operator (Matthew Carney) on Marina (the fictional name for Sable Island), the woman (Isabel Jardine) he "marries" while on shore leave, her attempts to adjust to island life, her affair with another radio operator (Greg Skane), her decision to leave Carney, and her eventual rejection of Skane and return to Carney who, she has discovered, is going blind. The triangular love complication provides a familiar plot structure, but Raddall's treatment of it is far from ordinary.

In earlier historical novels Raddall had portrayed three of his four male heroes as undergoing a long and sometimes painful process of self-discovery that culminated in a final choice between opposing sets of values. Roger Sudden and Nathan Cain in particular seemed to be conscious at moments of being engaged in some form of quest that was fulfilled, so their stories imply, when each was united in love with a woman. *The Nymph and the Lamp* takes up this same pattern and offers Raddall's most complex treatment of it: in this instance his female protagonist is given equal if not greater emphasis than that bestowed upon the male hero.

Carney's quest initially involves a return to Nova Scotia in 1920 after ten years work on Marina. What brings him back is not any desire to sample the sophisticated benefits of civilization but the wish to revisit his birthplace in Newfoundland, and to seek out his mother. This, he has promised himself, would be "the supreme experience of his life."[62] Carney's quest is revealed as misguided, for his mother is dead and none of his family is to be found. His subsequent wanderings on the Canadian mainland reveal to him that Marina is the only place that has any meaning for him (pp. 28–30). While waiting in Halifax for a boat back, he meets Isabel, a woman brought up in rural Nova Scotia and now disillusioned regarding her current city life: "I can't accept the way things are, not so calmly anyhow. You said you'd found a meaning in Marina. I can't find a meaning in anything" (p. 32). Implicit in Isabel's malaise is her lack of sexual fulfilment, something powerfully evoked in Raddall's description of her solitary and virginal existence in a shabby Halifax boarding house (pp. 37–44). For his part, Carney has long been without interest in women, and significantly it is Isabel who initiates their first night together.

On their way to Marina, Isabel's puritan conscience, supposedly discarded in Halifax, assails her (p. 103), and once on the island she denies Carney her bed, believing now that she belongs neither to the world of Halifax and her past, nor to that of the island and a future with Carney. She finds temporary release with Skane, but fears, doubt, and guilt then pursue her; and when injured in a shooting accident and taken to the mainland, she hides her whereabouts from both Carney and Skane and returns to her rural roots in the Annapolis Valley where she is confronted by the immense changes that have followed World War II: "What was going on in her valley was happening all over the United States and Canada. It was as if some mighty hand had seized the land and given it a shake, so that all the human contents changed places, trades, amusements and ambitions" (p. 281).

In contrast to his earlier powerful portrait of the harsh and desolate landscape of Marina, Raddall now superbly evokes the natural riches of a golden land of orchards, blossoms, and fruit with which Isabel becomes symbolically associated. At harvest time Skane arrives to claim her. She has become the object of a quest of his own and has been symbolically perceived by him as the living embodiment of Rossetti's painting of a young woman in green with flowers in her lap and an apple in one hand, the goddess of fruit and gardens. With the revelation that Carney is going blind, Isabel is faced with a moment of choice typical of the Raddall hero. She rejects Skane, the embodiment of egocentricity and sensuality, and decides to return to Marina to be "a lamp for Carney" (p. 352), thereby perceiving the true end of her quest as love and self-sacrifice. She also rejects the worlds of her birthplace, of Halifax, "the scrabble for cash," and "the statesmanship that was only politics, the peace that led only towards more bloody war, the whole brave new world of '21 that was only old evil with a mad new face" (pp. 365, 366).

In place of what Isabel rejects is the sea ("the sharp clean reek of salt and kelp, rich in its own way, distilled from thousands of square miles of untainted ocean for the ventilation of the world" [p. 365]) and, at the centre of this symbolic world, Carney, variously described in the book as a kind of god, a Viking, and above all man of the sea (p. 357). Such symbolism links with a central mythic pattern hinted at by the title of the book. As Isabel's boat crosses to Marina, the sea significantly calm and serene in contrast to the storm of her first crossing, the captain reminisces about the Norse sea goddess Ran who provided every drowned sailor with a nymph "shaped in the image of the woman he'd most desired on earth" (p. 372), provided he had a piece of gold in payment. Arriving off Marina, Isabel becomes that nymph of the sea when she leaps into the water and runs to Carney, who is at that moment described as "like one of those Norse kings, right out of the *Heimskringla!* You sought for the winged helmet and the long war ax and saw nothing but the bit of gold [Isabel's wedding ring], Ran's tribute, slung by the cord upon his breast" (p. 375).

The effectiveness of Raddall's delineation of the quest motif and its underlying mythic pattern is not primarily due to the psychological subtlety of his character portrayals. Here as elsewhere his strengths lie in other directions, but that is not to deny the strength of some of his portraits, Isabel being perhaps the finest example in all his writings. What Raddall creates in *The Nymph and the Lamp*, something towards which he had been moving in *Roger Sudden* most noticeably with Roger's search for the Golden Woman, is a largely symbolic drama played out among the god-like, Viking sea-king Carney; the nature goddess, sea-nymph, Eve-like Isabel, embodiment of desire (twice [pp. 81, 150] Carney is compared to Adam); and the hater of sea and women, Skane. Accompanying this is the manner in which Marina, Halifax, and Kingsbridge (Isabel's birthplace in the Annapolis Valley) become mythic domains expressive of certain modes of life and their accompanying values, and the passing of the seasons (Winter on Marina, Summer in Kingsbridge) provides indicators of the stages in Isabel's quest that culminates in her final emergence from the sea on the shores of Carney's island.

Such characteristics suggest the world of the romance with its theme of love and concern with the fulfilment of desire, its remoteness of setting, its simplified characters, its suggestion of allegorical significance, its happy ending, and its underlying ideal code of conduct to which hero and heroine subscribe and which directs one to the heart of the book's meaning. Criticisms that are directed towards lack of psychological or social realism are really beside the point, as are those that complain that Raddall's historical romances are "escapist" or mere adventure stories. In fact, of course, with regard to the historical novels Raddall's historical accuracy, his use of the common rather than the exceptional person as hero, his constant ability to create a sense of felt experience and tangible reality, and his refusal to idealize his characters through such techniques as the use of an elderly, slightly sardonic narrator in *His Majesty's Yankees* and *Pride's Fancy*, all serve to place these works in the grey area between romance and realism. To miss the subtle blend of the two ingredients in all of Raddall's novels and the often delicate tensions that result from their mix, such as the bitter-sweet irony felt by the reader of *The Nymph and the Lamp* who can see that the reunited Carney and Isabel choose a way of life on Marina that within a few years is doomed by technological advances to disappear, is to miss what is perhaps Raddall's greatest achievement. Only when the dominant contemporary critical response to historical fiction and romance undergoes a change will Raddall's work receive full consideration and appropriate evaluation. For the moment, while perceptions of the canons of Canadian literature still remain largely shaped by such influential books as Pacey's *Creative Writing in Canada*, one must expect that Raddall's achievement will pass largely unnoticed among the literary intelligentsia. However, for those who are tempted to read and judge for themselves, there is the consolation that Raddall's considerable popular readership results in most of his books still being in print and readily available.

NOTES

The author is indebted to Thomas H. Raddall and to the staff of the Dalhousie University Archives for assistance with a number of bibliographical problems and for permission to quote from unpublished material by Thomas Raddall.

[1] Thomas H.Raddall, "Winter's Tale," *Blackwood's*, Jan. 1936, pp. 1–17.

[2] Thomas H. Raddall, *In My Time: A Memoir* (Toronto: McClelland and Stewart, 1976), p. 42. All further references to this work (*IMT*) appear in the text.

[3] Thomas H. Raddall, "The Singing Frenchman," *Halifax Sunday Leader*, 11 Dec. 1921, p. 3.

[4] "Three Wise Men" appeared in *Maclean's*, 1 April 1928, pp. 6–7, 56, 58, 61. Between September 1933 and December 1937, fifteen of Raddall's stories appeared in *Blackwood's Magazine*. From a third party, Raddall had heard that his stories in *Blackwood's* had been much admired by Kipling (author's interview with Raddall, 10 Aug. 1980). Buchan, too, also got to know Raddall in this way, and his admiration was expressed in the strongest terms in the preface he wrote for *The Pied Piper of Dipper Creek and Other Tales* in 1939. Kenneth Roberts, a leading American author of historical fiction, was the person who suggested to Raddall that he write an historical novel set in Nova Scotia,

expanding upon the material of "At the Tide's Turn" (Letter from Roberts to Raddall, 4 April 1941 [Raddall Papers, Dalhousie Univ. Library, Mss. 2. 202. S. 915–19]).

[5] Officially, Raddall's first book-length publication was *Saga of the Rover* (Halifax: Royal Print & Litho, 1931), an historical novel published in a limited edition by the paper company which then employed Raddall. He later revised the novel for adolescent readers and published it as *The Rover: The Story of a Canadian Privateer* (1958; rpt. Toronto: Macmillan, 1966).

[6] Thomas H. Raddall, "A Boy's Reading and a Man's Writing," *Canadian Library Association, Conference Proceedings* (Halifax: Canadian Library Association, 1964), p. 48.

[7] Thomas H. Raddall, "Sword and Pen in Kent, 1903–1913," *Dalhousie Review*, 32 (1952), 152.

[8] John Robert Sorfleet, "Thomas Raddall: I Was Always a Rebel Underneath," *Journal of Canadian Fiction*, 2, No. 4 (Fall 1973), 50.

[9] Thomas H. Raddall Papers, Dalhousie Univ. Library, Mss. 2. 202. K. 22. A., p. 7. See also his letter to Edith Rogers, 21 March 1954, Mss. 2. 202. S. 923–28.

[10] Thomas H. Raddall, Letter to Kenneth S. White, 18 July 1944, Raddall Papers, Mss. 2. 202. S. 1. See also Sorfleet, p. 62.

[11] See, for example, Thomas H. Raddall, "Tale of Life," *Globe and Mail*, 29 June 1946, p. 10. For the oral source of this tale, see Raddall Papers, Mss. 2. 202. V. 3. A.

[12] John Buchan, Pref., *The Pied Piper of Dipper Creek and Other Tales*, by Thomas H. Raddall (Edinburgh: Blackwood, 1939), p. v.

[13] Fred Cogswell, Introd., *Pride's Fancy*, by Thomas H. Raddall, New Canadian Library, No. 98 (Toronto: McClelland and Stewart, 1974), p. iv.

[14] See Desmond Pacey, Introd., *A Book of Canadian Stories*, ed. Desmond Pacey (Toronto: Ryerson, 1947), pp. xxiii–xxvii; and Gordon Roper, Rupert Schieder, and S. Ross Beharriell, "The Kinds of Fiction 1880–1920," in *Literary History of Canada: Canadian Literature in English*, 2nd ed., gen. ed. and introd. Carl F. Klinck (Toronto: Univ. of Toronto Press, 1976), I, 301–02.

[15] See Sorfleet, p. 63.

[16] For Raddall's correspondence with Costain, see Dal. Mss. 2. 202. S. 357–462. In *In My Time*, however, Raddall rather downplays Costain's role and stresses his own independence (p. 218).

[17] Thomas H. Raddall, Address to the Canadian Authors Association, Halifax, 5 July 1949, Raddall Papers, Mss. 2. 202. J. 12. A. See also his "Haliburton: A Lasting Impression," in *Beginnings: The Canadian Novel, Vol. 2*, ed. John Moss (Toronto: NC, 1980), pp. 37–39; and Alice K. Hale, "An Interview with Thomas Raddall," in her *An Introduction to Teaching Canadian Literature*

(Halifax: Atlantic Institute of Education, 1975), p. 31.

[18] Sorfleet, p. 49.

[19] Robert Cockburn, " 'Nova Scotia is my Dwellen Plas': The Life and Work of Thomas Raddall," rev. of *In My Time: A Memoir, Acadiensis*, 7, No. 2 (Spring 1978), 136.

[20] Edith Rogers, "The Life and Works of Dr. Thomas H. Raddall," M.A. Thesis Acadia 1954.

[21] See, for example, the reviews of *His Majesty's Yankees* by Margaret Wallace in *The New York Times Book Review*, 15 Nov. 1942, pp. 12, 48; by William Arthur Deacon in *The Globe and Mail* [Toronto], 2 Jan. 1943, p. 14; and by Wilhelmina Gordon in *Echoes: The Official Publication of the Imperial Order Daughters of the Empire*, No. 170 (Spring 1943), p. 39. See also the reviews of *Roger Sudden* by Burns Martin in *Dalhousie Review*, 24 (Jan. 1945), 489; and Thelma Purtell in *The New York Times Book Review*, 18 March 1945, p. 25; and of *Pride's Fancy* by Robert N. Schwartz in *The New York Times Book Review*, 3 Nov. 1946, p. 16.

[22] Pacey, *A Book of Canadian Stories*, p. 155.

[23] Arthur L. Phelps, "Thomas Raddall," *Canadian Writers* (Toronto: McClelland and Stewart, 1951), p. 60.

[24] Carleton F. Bowes, rev. of *The Nymph and the Lamp, Public Affairs*, 13, No. 1 (Autumn 1950), 88, 90.

[25] A.B.S., rev. of *The Nymph and the Lamp, The San Francisco Chronicle*, Christian Book Issue, 26 Nov. 1950, p. 6.

[26] Claude Bissell, rev. of *The Nymph and the Lamp*, in "Letters in Canada 1950: Fiction," *University of Toronto Quarterly*, 20 (1950–51), 262.

[27] Bissell, rev. of *The Nymph and the Lamp*, pp. 264, 263.

[28] John Cournos, "Power of Kindness," rev. of *The Nymph and the Lamp, The New York Times Book Review*, 10 Dec. 1950, p. 24.

[29] See also Desmond Pacey, rev. of *Tidefall, The Canadian Forum*, Jan. 1954, p. 237; *Chicago Sunday Tribune Magazine of Books*, 20 Sept. 1953, p. 5; and Stuart Keate, "Refreshing Sea-Change," rev. of *Tidefall, The New York Times Book Review*, 22 Nov. 1953, p. 44.

[30] C.L. Bennet, rev. of *Tidefall, Dalhousie Review*, 34 (1954), 95.

[31] Cockburn, p. 137.

[32] See, for example, Claude Bissell, rev. of *Tidefall*, in "Letters in Canada 1953: Fiction," *University of Toronto Quarterly*, 23 (1954), 270; and his rev. of *The Wings of Night*, in "Letters in Canada 1956: Fiction," *University of Toronto Quarterly*, 26 (1957), 314–15. See also G.M. Craig, rev. of *The Path of Destiny, Canadian Historical Review*, 39 (1958), 154–55; and Robert Harlow, "Varieties of Waste," rev. of *The Governor's Lady, Canadian Literature*, No. 6 (Autumn 1960), pp. 75–76.

[33] Allan Bevan, Introd. *At the Tide's Turn and Other Stories*, by Thomas H. Raddall, New Canadian Library, No. 9 (Toronto: McClelland and Stewart, 1959), pp. iii–ix.

[34] George Woodcock, "Venture on the Verge," rev. of *At the Tide's Turn and Other Stories*, by Thomas H. Raddall, *Canadian Literature*, No. 5 (Summer 1960), p. 74.

[35] Desmond Pacey, *Creative Writing in Canada: A Short History of English-Canadian Literature* (Toronto: Ryerson, 1952), p. 165.

[36] Desmond Pacey, rev. of *At the Tide's Turn and Other Stories*, *Queen's Quarterly*, 68 (1961), 180.

[37] Desmond Pacey, *Creative Writing in Canada: A Short History of English-Canadian Literature*, rev. ed. (Toronto: Ryerson, 1961), p. 196. For a similar critical position see "Unfaithful Loyalist," rev. of *The Governor's Lady*, *Saturday Night*, 24 Dec. 1960, p. 34; and F.W. Watt, rev. of *The Governor's Lady*, in "Letters in Canada 1960: Fiction," *University of Toronto Quarterly*, 30 (1961), 411–12.

[38] Alan R. Young, *Thomas H. Raddall*, Twayne's World Authors Series, No. 710: Canadian Literature (Boston: Twayne, 1983).

[39] George Woodcock, "Raddall: The Making of the Story-teller," rev. of *In My Time: A Memoir*, *Saturday Night*, Nov. 1976, p. 69.

[40] Malcolm Ross, rev. of *In My Time: A Memoir*, *Dalhousie Review*, 57 (1977), 187. See also Cogswell's comments on Raddall's ability to make us respond to our lost past (p. x). In his rev. of *The Wings of Night*, Claude Bissell suggests that Raddall "is at his best with the 'deserted village' theme; like his famous Nova Scotia predecessor, Thomas Haliburton, he loves a melancholy pastoral" (p. 315). In his "Thomas Raddall: The Art of Historical Fiction," *Dalhousie Review*, 49 (1969–70), Donald Cameron commends Raddall's ability to dramatize "the continuity between our present and our past" and to show us "the forces that shaped us" (p. 547).

[41] Donald Cameron, "Letter from Halifax," *Canadian Literature*, No. 40 (Spring 1969), p. 58; and "Thomas Raddall: The Art of Historical Fiction," p. 540. Cf. Introd., "Thomas H. Raddall," in *The Evolution of Canadian Literature in English: 1914–1945*, ed. George Parker and Mary Jane Edwards (Toronto: Holt, Rinehart and Winston, 1973), p. 103.

[42] J.R. Leitold, "The Spirit of Place: The Historical Fiction of Thomas Raddall," M.A. Thesis. Dalhousie 1972; David Stanley West, "Romance and Realism in the Contemporary Novels of Thomas H. Raddall," M.A. Thesis Univ. of New Brunswick 1977; John Moss, *Patterns of Isolation in English-Canadian Fiction* (Toronto: McClelland and Stewart, 1974), pp. 129–48; Phelps, pp. 60–69; Andrew Thompson Seaman, "Fiction in Atlantic Canada," *Canadian*

Literature, Nos. 68–69 (Spring–Summer 1976), pp. 26–39.

43 Georg Lukács, *The Historical Novel*, trans. Hannah Mitchell and Stanley Mitchell (London: Merlin, 1962), pp. 30–63. All further references to this work appear in the text.

44 *Saga of the Rover*, pp. 91–92.

45 Thomas H. Raddall, *His Majesty's Yankees* (Garden City, N.Y.: Doubleday, 1942), p. 21. All further references to this work appear in the text.

46 Thomas H. Raddall, *Roger Sudden* (Toronto: McClelland and Stewart, 1944), p. 340.

47 Thomas H. Raddall, *Pride's Fancy* (Garden City, N.Y.: Doubleday, 1946), p. 135. All further references to this work appear in the text.

48 Thomas H. Raddall, *Hangman's Beach* (Garden City, N.Y.: Doubleday, 1966), p. 383. All further references to this work appear in the text.

49 Raddall's portrait of Fannie Wentworth as a shallow, manipulative woman, chiefly of interest for her physical beauty and sexual exploits, is in part based on local Halifax tradition. His chief documentary sources were Fannie's letters to the Fitzwilliams and Rockinghams in the archives of the Leeds City Library, the Sheffield City Library, and the Northamptonshire Record Office; and *Dyott's Diary, 1781–1845: A Selection from the Journal of William Dyott, Sometime General in the British Army and Aide-de-camp to His Majesty King George*, ed. R.W. Jeffrey, 2 vols. (London, 1907). The accuracy of Raddall's portrait is confirmed by Philip Young in *Revolutionary Ladies* (New York: Knopf, 1977), pp. 102, 115–16, 119, 206.

50 Thomas H. Raddall, Letter to Edith Rogers, 5 June 1954, Raddall Papers, Mss. 2. 202. S. 923–28.

51 See, Raddall's *The Rover*, p. 6.

52 Thomas H. Raddall, "The Outcasts," in *The Wedding Gift and Other Stories* (Toronto: McClelland and Stewart, 1947), p. 123.

53 Thomas H. Raddall, Letters to Edith Rogers, 21 March 1954, Raddall Papers, Mss. 2. 202. S. 923–28.

54 Letter to Edith Rogers, 21 March 1954.

55 Thomas H. Raddall, *The Path of Destiny: Canada from the British Conquest to Home Rule: 1763–1850* (Toronto: Doubleday, 1957), p. 313.

56 Thomas H. Raddall, *Halifax, Warden of the North*, rev. ed. (Toronto: McClelland and Stewart, 1971), p. 23. All further references to this work appear in the text.

57 Thomas H. Raddall, Letter to Edith Rogers, 5 June 1954.

58 Thomas H. Raddall, "Author's Note," *A Muster of Arms and Other Stories* (Toronto: McClelland and Stewart, 1954), n. pag.

59 Philip Gibbs, Preface, *Now It Can Be Told* (New York: Harper, 1920),

n. pag. Raddall cited Gibbs's memoir when he discussed his desire to write a short story collection "in the spirit of Philip Gibbs' book" in a letter to Edith Rogers (Raddall Papers, Mss. 2. 202. S. 923–28).

[60] Thomas H. Raddall, *Tidefall* (Toronto: McClelland and Stewart, 1953), p. 40.

[61] Thomas H. Raddall, Letter to Alan R. Young, 4 Feb. 1981.

[62] Thomas H. Raddall, *The Nymph and the Lamp* (Toronto: McClelland and Stewart, 1950), p. 21. All further references to this work appear in the text.

SELECTED BIBLIOGRAPHY

Primary Sources

Novels

Raddall, Thomas H. *Saga of the Rover*. Halifax: Royal Print & Litho, 1931.

———. *His Majesty's Yankees*. Garden City, N.Y.: Doubleday, 1942.

———. *Roger Sudden*. Toronto: McClelland and Stewart, 1944.

———. *Pride's Fancy*. Garden City, N.Y.: Doubleday, 1946.

———. *The Nymph and the Lamp*. Toronto: McClelland and Stewart, 1950.

———. *Son of the Hawk*. Philadelphia: Winston, 1950.

———. *Tidefall*. Toronto: McClelland and Stewart, 1953.

———. *The Wings of Night*. Garden City, N.Y.: Doubleday, 1956.

———. *The Rover: The Story of a Canadian Privateer*. 1958; rpt. Toronto: Macmillan, 1966.

———. *The Governor's Lady*. Garden City, N.Y.: Doubleday, 1960.

———. *Hangman's Beach*. Garden City, N.Y.: Doubleday, 1966.

Short Stories

Raddall, Thomas H. "The Singing Frenchman." *Halifax Sunday Leader*, 11 Dec. 1921, p. 3.

———. "Winter's Tale." *Blackwood's*, Jan. 1936, pp. 1–17.

———. *The Pied Piper of Dipper Creek and Other Tales*. Pref. John Buchan. Edinburgh: Blackwood, 1939.

———. *Tambour and Other Stories*. Toronto: McClelland and Stewart, 1945.

———. *The Wedding Gift and Other Stories*. Toronto: McClelland and Stewart, 1947.

———. *A Muster of Arms and Other Stories*. Toronto: McClelland and Stewart, 1954.

————. *At the Tide's Turn and Other Stories*. Introd. Allan Bevan. New Canadian Library, No. 9. Toronto: McClelland and Stewart, 1959.

————. *The Dreamers*. Atlantic Classics Series. Introd. John Bell. Porters Lake, N.S.: Pottersfield, 1986.

————. *Courage in the Storm*. Illus. by Are Gjesdal. Porters Lake, N.S.: Pottersfield, 1987. [This is a short story for children.]

Historical Studies, Articles, and Memoirs

Raddall, Thomas H. *The Markland Sagas*. Montreal: Gazette Printing, 1934.

————. "Tale of Life." *The Globe and Mail*, 29 June 1946, p. 10.

————. *West Novas: A History of the West Nova Scotia Regiment*. Montreal: Provincial Publishing, 1948.

————. "Sword and Pen in Kent, 1903–1913." *Dalhousie Review*, 32 (1952), 145–52.

————. *The Path of Destiny: Canada from the British Conquest to Home Rule: 1763–1850*. Toronto: Doubleday, 1957.

————. "A Boy's Reading and a Man's Writing." In *Canadian Library Association, Conference Proceedings*. Halifax: Canadian Library Association, 1964, pp. 47–52.

————. *Footsteps on Old Floors: True Tales of Mystery*. Garden City, N.Y.: Doubleday, 1968.

————. *Halifax, Warden of the North*. Rev. ed. Toronto: McClelland and Stewart, 1971.

————. *In My Time: A Memoir*. Toronto: McClelland and Stewart, 1976.

————. *The Mersey Story*. Liverpool, N.S.: Bowater-Mersey Paper, 1979.

————. "Haliburton: A Lasting Impression." In *Beginnings: The Canadian Novel, Vol. 2*. Ed. John Moss. Toronto: NC, 1980, pp. 37–39.

Secondary Sources

Barkhouse, Joyce. *A Name for Himself: A Biography of Thomas Head Raddall*. Contemporary Canadian Biographies Series. Toronto: Irwin, 1986.

Bennett, C.L. Rev. of *Tidefall*, by Thomas H. Raddall. *Dalhousie Review*, 34 (1954), 95.

Bevan, Allan. Introd. *At the Tide's Turn and Other Stories*. By Thomas H.

Raddall. New Canadian Library, No. 9. Toronto: McClelland and Stewart, 1959, pp. iii–ix.

Bissell, Claude. Rev. of *The Nymph and the Lamp*, by Thomas H. Raddall. In "Letters in Canada 1950: Fiction." *University of Toronto Quarterly*, 20 (1950–51), 262–64.

———. Rev. of *Tidefall*, by Thomas H. Raddall. In "Letters in Canada 1953: Fiction." *University of Toronto Quarterly*, 26 (1954), 270.

———. Rev. of *The Wings of Night*, by Thomas H. Raddall. In "Letters in Canada 1956: Fiction." *University of Toronto Quarterly*, 26 (1957), 314–15.

Bowes, Carleton F. Rev. of *The Nymph and the Lamp*, by Thomas H. Raddall. *Public Affairs*, 13, No. 1 (Autumn 1950), 88, 90.

Cameron, Donald. "Letter from Halifax." *Canadian Literature*, No. 40 (Spring 1969), pp. 55–60.

———. "Thomas Raddall: The Art of Historical Fiction." *Dalhousie Review*, 49 (1969–70), 540–48.

Cockburn, Robert. " 'Nova Scotia is my Dwelen Plas': The Life and Work of Thomas Raddall." Rev. of *In My Time: A Memoir*, by Thomas H. Raddall. *Acadiensis*, 7, No. 2 (Spring 1978), 135–41.

Cogswell, Fred. Introd. *Pride's Fancy*. By Thomas H. Raddall. New Canadian Library, No. 98. Toronto: McClelland and Stewart, 1974, pp. iii–x.

Cournos, John. "Power of Kindness." Rev. of *The Nymph and the Lamp*, by Thomas H. Raddall. *The New York Times Book Review*, 10 Dec. 1950, p. 24.

Craig, G.M. Rev. of *The Path of Destiny: Canada from the British Conquest to Home Rule, 1763–1850*, by Thomas H. Raddall. *Canadian Historical Review*, 39 (1958), 154–55.

Fowke, Edith. " 'Blind MacNair': A Canadian Short Story and Its Sources." In *Folklore Studies in Honour of Herbert Halpert: A Festschrift*. Ed. Kenneth S. Goldstein and Neil V. Rosenberg, with Richard E. Buehler, Sonia Paine, and Leslie Prosterman. Folklore and Language Publications Series, Bibliographical and Special Series, No. 7. St. John's, Nfld.: Memorial Univ. of Newfoundland, 1980, pp. 173–86.

Fuller, Edmund. Review of *Tidefall*. *Chicago Sunday Tribune Magazine of Books*, 20 Sept. 1953, p. 5.

Gibbs, Philip. *Now It Can Be Told*. New York: Harper, 1920.

Hale, Alice K. "An Interview with Thomas Raddall." In her *An Introduction to Teaching Canadian Literature*. Halifax: Atlantic Institute of Education, 1975, pp. 27–33.

Harlow, Robert. "Varieties of Waste." Rev. of *The Governor's Lady*, by Thomas H. Raddall. *Canadian Literature*, No. 6 (Autumn 1960), pp. 74–76.

Hawkins, Walter John. "The Life and Fiction of Thomas H. Raddall." M.A. Thesis New Brunswick 1972.

Keate, Stuart. "Refreshing Sea-Change." Rev. of *Tidefall*, by Thomas H. Raddall. *The New York Times Book Review*, 22 Nov. 1953, p. 44.

Keefer, Janice Kulyk. *Under Eastern Eyes: A Critical Reading of Maritime Fiction.* Toronto: Univ. of Toronto Press, 1987.

Leitold, J.R. "The Spirit of Place: The Historical Fiction of Thomas Raddall." M.A. Thesis Dalhousie 1972.

Lukács, Georg. *The Historical Novel.* Trans. Hannah Mitchell and Stanley Mitchell. London: Merlin Press, 1962.

Moss, John. *Patterns of Isolation in English-Canadian Fiction.* Toronto: McClelland and Stewart, 1974.

Pacey, Desmond, ed. *A Book of Canadian Stories.* Toronto: Ryerson, 1947.

————. Rev. of *Tidefall*, by Thomas H. Raddall. *The Canadian Forum*, Jan. 1954, p. 237.

————. Rev. of *At the Tide's Turn and Other Stories*, by Thomas H. Raddall. *Queen's Quarterly*, 68 (1961), 179–80.

————. *Creative Writing in Canada: A Short History of English-Canadian Literature.* Rev. ed. Toronto: Ryerson, 1961.

Parker, George, and Mary Jane Edwards, eds. *The Evolution of Canadian Literature in English: 1914–1945.* Toronto: Holt, Rinehart, and Winston, 1973.

Phelps, Arthur L. "Thomas Raddall." *Canadian Writers.* Toronto: McClelland and Stewart, 1951, pp. 60–69.

Rogers, Edith. "The Life and Works of Dr. Thomas H. Raddall." M.A. Thesis Acadia 1954.

Rogers, Robert Amos. "American Recognition of Canadian Authors Writing in English 1890–1960." Diss. Michigan 1964.

Roper, Gordon, Rupert Schieder, and S. Ross Beharriell. "The Kinds of Fiction, 1880–1920." In *Literary History of Canada: Canadian Literature in English.* Vol. 1. 2nd ed. Gen. ed. and introd. Carl F. Klinck. Toronto: Univ. of Toronto Press, 1976, pp. 298–326.

Ross, Malcolm. Rev. of *In My Time: A Memoir*, by Thomas H. Raddall. *Dalhousie Review*, 57 (1977), 187–88.

S., A.B. Rev. of *The Nymph and the Lamp*. Christian Book Issue, *San Francisco Chronicle*, 26 Nov. 1950, p. 6.

Seaman, Andrew Thompson. "Fiction in Atlantic Canada." *Canadian Literature*, Nos. 68–69 (Spring–Summer 1976), pp. 26–39.

Sorfleet, John Robert. "Thomas Raddall: I Was Always a Rebel Underneath." *Journal of Canadian Fiction*, 2, No. 4 (Fall 1973), 45–64.

"Unfaithful Loyalist." Rev. of *The Governor's Lady*, by Thomas H. Raddall. *Saturday Night*, 24 Dec. 1960, p. 34.

Watt, F.W. Rev. of *The Governor's Lady*, by Thomas H. Raddall. In "Letters in Canada 1960: Fiction." *University of Toronto Quarterly*, 30 (1961), 411–12.

West, David Stanley. "Romance and Realism in the Contemporary Novels of Thomas H. Raddall." M.A. Thesis New Brunswick 1977.

Woodcock, George. "Venture on the Verge." Rev. of *At the Tide's Turn and Other Stories*, by Thomas H. Raddall. *Canadian Literature*, No. 5 (Summer 1960), pp. 73–75.

———. "Raddall: The Making of the Story-Teller." Rev. of *In My Time: A Memoir*, by Thomas H. Raddall. *Saturday Night*, Nov. 1976, pp. 67, 69–70.

Young, Alan R. *Thomas Head Raddall: A Bibliography*. Kingston, Ont.: Loyal Colonies Press, 1982.

———. *Thomas H. Raddall*. Twayne's World Authors Series, No. 710: Canadian Literature. Boston: Twayne, 1983.

———. "The Genesis and Composition of Thomas H. Raddall's *His Majesty's Yankees*." *Essays on Canadian Writing*, No. 31 (Summer 1985), pp. 142–57.

———. "Thomas H. Raddall: An Annotated Bibliography." In *The Annotated Bibliography of Canada's Major Authors*. Vol. 7. Ed. Robert Lecker and Jack David. Toronto: ECW, 1987, pp. 403–77.

———. "Thomas Head Raddall." *Twentieth-Century Romance and Historical Writers* . . . 2nd ed. Edited by Lesley Henderson. Chicago: St. James, 1990, pp. 537–38.